Write for Life

Healing Body, Mind, and Spirit
Through Journal Writing

Sheppard B. Kominars

Sheppard B. Kominars, Ph.D.

Cleveland Clinic Press

Cleveland, Ohio

Write for Life
Healing Body, Mind, and Spirit Through Journal Writing

Contact:

Cleveland Clinic Press

9500 Euclid Avenue NA32

Cleveland, Ohio 44195

216-445-5547

delongk@ccf.org

www.clevelandclinicpress.org

This book is not intended to replace personal medical care and supervision. There is no substitute for the experience and information that your doctor can provide. Rather, it is our hope that this book will provide information about ways that self-expression through journal writing can enhance life experience.

Kominars, Sheppard B.

Write for Life: Healing Body, Mind, and Spirit Through Journal Writing / Sheppard Kominars.

p. cm.

Includes index.

ISBN-13: 978-1-59624-077-3 (alk. paper)

1. Diaries–Authorship–Therapeutic use. I. Title.

RC489.D5K66 2007   615.8'51–dc22

2007016751

Book design by Meredith Pangrace & Whitney Campbell

Dedication

"No legacy is so rich as honesty."

William Shakespeare, *All's Well That Ends Well*, Act III, Scene v, line 13

For my children:
Kathryn and Linda • Hugh and Andrea
Matthew and Reeda

For my grandchildren:
Kevin • John • Derek • Isaac • David • Rebekah

For:
Marvin and family
Tom and Jeanie
Ariel
Sam

And for:
The miraculous survivors I have had the great
good fortune to encounter in my life

Contents

Acknowledgments

The workshops I have presented over the past seven years would not have been possible without the recognition of their value by Carole Viele at UCSF, Anna Dowling at Kaiser Permanente, Holly Gautier at Stanford Concierge Support Services, Dr. Anita Chatigny at the Cancer Center of the Desert, Dean Lockwood at the Mizell Senior Center, Nancy McGinnis at San Mateo Senior Center, Joe Sinico at Dignity, John Killeen at The Heritage, and Lisa Schott at Kenyon College Alumni.

Sandra Huet and Daigaku David Rumme were of special help to me in their workshop presentations on dreams and Zen. Cassette tapes created by Kachinas Kutenai on American Indian spirituality were invaluable. Barbara Kaufman's painting workshops continue to be central to my appreciation of the link between art and recovery. Bernadette Festa's expertise in matters relating to nutrition, Ellen Dorsey's nursing perspective, and Louise Lieber's insight into creativity are deeply appreciated.

Recommendations and ideas offered by readers helped significantly to improve the accessibility of the text and I am grateful to them for their time and effort: Corey Weinstein, M.D.; Kenneth Schmidt, Rector at All Saints Church; Allen Burke; Alan Marshall; Gretchen Gold; Glenn Skillen; Diane Warner; and my friend of forty-seven years, Frank McCourt. A special thanks to Ruth Cash Smith for advice on the book proposal and also to Michael Fish and David Azzolina for their help over the years.

Jean Schild read the manuscript with infinite care and insight; this book is much the better for her help and the depth of her understanding. Marvin D. Appelbaum's attention to the text and its accessibility and continuity was of the greatest help and support over the years needed to create it. Leslie Patrick's suggestions were invaluable. I am greatly indebted to each of them in helping me develop this work for publication.

Kathryn DeLong at Cleveland Clinic Press is an advocate such as any writer prays for, and Julianne Stein has been of major assistance through the final stage of manuscript preparation.

My thanks go as well to the individuals and organizations listed on page 252, who kindly allowed me to quote passages of copyrighted material in several chapters of this book. Their inclusion greatly enhanced my message.

And to all the workshop participants all over the world who offered their unique expertise in finding their way along the journeys proposed to them, thank you.

Foreword
by Frank McCourt

In my high school teaching days, I told my English classes, "When in doubt, tell a story. 'Once upon a time' was good enough for the Brothers Grimm, Hans Christian Andersen, Charles Perrault, and James Joyce, and it's good enough for you and me." I would also quote Jesus, "Be as little children," even though my students were mostly Jewish.

I was telling my classes these things because they were resisting a simple assignment: Keep an account of your life. That's all. One hundred and fifty words a day. Would it kill you?

Yes, they said. It would kill them, and that was because nothing happened in their lives, nothing worth writing about. They envied me for having had a miserable childhood and plenty to write about, and all they had was going to school every day and taking various tests and exams for college and putting up with parents hounding them about one thing or another.

That often irritated me and I told them so. "I'm trying to get you to open your eyes and ears, and all you do is whine, whine, whine."

That's where I lost them and that's where I wanted to tell them I was sorry. I wanted to tell them that even though I was in my 40s I was backward in my ways, a slow learner who had a long way to go. Yes, yes, they did whine, but there was a genuine substratum of despair in their complaints. There was a genuine questioning as to what the hell it was all about. They were looking for meaning in their lives but feeling trapped.

"All right," I said. "All right. Get it on paper. Let it all hang out – if that's something you can do on paper. And remember what D.H. Lawrence said, 'Write it, and write it hot.'"

Of course, I was talking to myself. Much of teaching, especially when it's English, is talking to yourself. I was whining inwardly, desperate as any teenager, till the teacher part of me said, "Write it."

I could tell the story of a relationship with my journals that went back to my middle 20s. While I think of it I might go and burn those journals, because even though they are a record of certain activities and experiences, they are nothing but one long lament over the futility of it all, etc., etc.

But then I recall reading extracts from the journals of Tolstoy, a litany of despair and disgust with his own gambling and boozing and fornicating self, and if he could be such a fool then there was hope for me.

In my 20s I knew nothing about the kind of healing Sheppard Kominars writes about in his warm, wise, and wonderful book, *Write for Life*. The only healing I knew about was what the church had told me: confession. You sin, you confess, you're forgiven. There was some relief in alcohol and sex, but that was ephemeral, and there was always a hangover, physical, emotional, spiritual.

The subtitle of Dr. Kominars' book is *Healing Body, Mind, and Spirit Through Journal Writing*, a compendium of experience, learning, and practical advice for anyone embarking on a journal or anyone who has been at it for years.

Why, oh why, didn't someone walk up to me when I was 25 and stumbling, and hand me a book like this? Would I have been smart enough to take it to a quiet place, not merely to read it like an ordinary book, but to savor it and learn from it, slowly, slowly.

That's how you have to read *Write for Life*. There's no hurry. Reading this book is a way of being good to yourself and you can't take it all in one greedy gulp. It took a while to get to where you are. It took a while to be what you are.

I have had a lover's quarrel with my journal. In bad times I have scribbled in it as if my life depended on it. (Maybe it did.) At other times I feel as if I have an obligation to write in it, as if I were a college student with a term paper hanging over his head.

And all the time, dear journal, you wanted to be my friend. You wanted to be the safe repository of my ecstasies and my miseries, my hymns and lamentations.

If former students of mine were to read this I would say to them, "Please forgive my short temper back then. When I asked you to keep an account of your days, I should have talked about those days. They were – and are – unique as fingerprints, and you'll never have them again. Those days were like jewels: Sunday, sapphire; Monday, emerald; Tuesday diamond; and so on. All days are jewels, aren't they?"

Frank McCourt
March, 2006

The Big Question:
Why Write a Journal?

Write for Life will help you cope with life crises such as aging, health and family problems, divorce, and professional setbacks. At the same time, it will bring you more joy in living. This is a book about recovering from a life-threatening emergency by learning to heal the body, mind, and spirit.

For over fifty years, I've been keeping journals; for the past seven, I've given workshops at cancer centers, senior centers, and conferences around the country about how writing can improve your life. This book will help you start journaling. I'll begin with my own story, then tell you why others have embraced this process, which is filled with surprises and excitement. Without ever leaving the comfort of your armchair or stepping off the front porch, you'll begin a new adventure with your life as you embark a voyage of self-discovery.

What will happen once you get started on your journey? You'll find this out for yourself as you go. If you're reluctant to begin this adventure, that's okay. You'll understand more once you read about why others are writing journals.

My journaling experience began in 1955, when I faced a health crisis.

1955: Wit's end

Chronic migraine headaches were giving me so much pain that I was willing to try anything that might offer relief. My brother's best friend, Dr. G., suggested that I begin keeping a journal and writing in it on a regular basis. This was something I'd never considered. Keeping a diary seemed like something only for famous people, such as Samuel Pepys, Madame d'Arblay, James Boswell, Elizabeth Barrett Browning, Anaïs Nin, Albert Camus, C.S. Lewis, May Sarton, Henry David Thoreau. In my imagination, I saw adolescent girls writing "Dear Diary" in their notebooks. *That's just not me*, I thought. *I can't do that!*

No, Dr. G. explained, my journal wouldn't be for publication; it was just for me to record what was happening in my life and how I felt about it. I was to write without any self-criticism, and I shouldn't try to sound like anyone who'd ever written a journal before. Just be myself. "Let the words come, that's all," he told me.

Writing about myself was the last thing I wanted to do. I wanted to escape from my torment, not detail it on a daily basis. What a prescription! "Please begin this week," said Dr. G. "You don't know how it will work unless you try it. I'll see you again only after you've been writing for two weeks." My session with Dr. G. ended and I was out the door.

I felt another migraine brewing as I turned my attention to the ultimatum I'd been given. I went home and dug out an old notebook with some blank pages in it. That day, I wrote my first entry. Writing about the events of my life was bad enough, but looking over what I'd written was even worse. How could I allow myself to say stuff like that? What was I thinking?

That was Day One.

Day Two was a blur, and by evening I was too tired to write. Day Three started off like the previous day, with a battery of excuses. I sensed another migraine sneaking up on me. It took a few days to come and a few days to leave, so I lost almost a week, during which I could do little more than grit my teeth in my darkened room and wait for the migraine machine to stop.

In desperation, I dug out the notebook from beneath the papers where I'd buried it. Turning the pages from the last entry I made, I began scribbling furiously about how angry I was that this was happening to me and how helpless I felt to do anything about it. Words and sentences tumbled out incoherently as my anger spewed over the pages. There seemed no end to my rage. When evening came, I was shocked to realize that I'd written in the journal for the entire afternoon. Where had the time gone? How had I so lost myself that everything else vanished? I was completely baffled.

Don't read what you've written. Just write. I remembered what Dr. G. had said. I closed the notebook, washed my face. Over the next three days, I went through all the blurred stages of the headache that had overwhelmed me. When it finally spent itself, I found myself back again at square one. I remembered thinking that this time, perhaps, I had a few weeks before the next migraine hit, and now I had to do something that would make a difference. Dr. G. had not promised that the migraines would end, just that they might not be as severe. And he'd said that I'd find out whether writing worked by doing it – consistently – for several months.

I took a brief glimpse at the pages I had written. I hardly recognized myself. What drivel! And what if someone in my family discovered this notebook and read what I'd written? If arguments and hurt feelings resulted from my journal, that would be a disaster. Yet something inside me wanted to find out whether Dr. G. knew what he was talking about. Curiosity got the better of me, and I began to write more.

I set up a daily schedule and a specific time during which I would "practice" writing as one might practice piano. Early morning before breakfast seemed good. I set a limit of three pages for each sitting and sometimes wrote less, but often I wrote more. And, of course, there were days when I just sat and stared at the blank page. Yet I noticed that journal writing seemed to help me launch the day from a better place in myself. Once I'd gotten some things off my chest, everything went more smoothly. That was a definite benefit.

The migraines didn't immediately disappear, but over the next months, I noticed a subtle shift in my attitude toward the headaches. There was a chink of separation between me and the migraine. *I* was not a migraine; I was merely having a migraine. And whatever the cause or causes, I wasn't swallowed up by them. To my surprise, writing in my journal each day became easier. Gradually, both the intensity and the frequency of the headaches diminished. I accepted that result, even though I didn't understand how it came about. But I continued writing, day after day, year after year, for the next fifty years. In some mysterious way, journal writing helped me find my way not only through health issues but through obstacles as well, such as the death of my brother and parents, an auto accident, divorce, and recovery from addictive/compulsive behavior.

In the year 2000, in the support group at the hospital where I was treated for cancer, I spoke about the writing I'd been doing in my journal since my diagnosis. Carolyn, the facilitator, told me about the research into writing as a healing modality that James Pennebaker had described in his book

Opening Up. Some of that information is offered in this book, in Part Two. I was amazed but not surprised when I read that what I'd been doing for decades had a compelling scientific basis.

Because journal writing has made such a profound difference in my life, I decided to let others know about this process. Since then, helping others has been one of my primary goals. Over the past seven years, I've held journal-writing workshops and seminars for thousands of people from all over the country. They've shared their own reasons for beginning and continuing to write. I hope that reading about them may encourage you to get started yourself. Here's what they've said, followed by what I believe.

Benefits: Body

1. "When I write in my journal, I feel more at peace with myself. My problems no longer dominate my life."
   Writing helps to release tensions associated with stress.
2. "I'm very hard on myself, and writing about what I need to do to make my life easier has become something I look forward to. It's a big change."
   Being self-caring has an inspiring effect on our outlook on life.
3. "I can't talk to my husband about my arthritis pain because it would worry him. And the doctor doesn't seem interested in hearing about it. But writing about it in my journal is a relief valve that I can use at any time."
   When chronic-pain sufferers no longer feel isolated, they experience less suffering.

Benefits: Emotions

1. "I don't like to argue with my wife because it only seems to make things worse. It feels good to express my feelings instead of stuffing them."
   The journal is a safe place to express feelings without fear of reprisal or recrimination.
2. "I've been very frightened of what will happen to me if this new treatment doesn't work. Since I began writing about it, however, I've been able to think about it in several different ways. This has been wonderful for me."
   Fear of the unknown is less frightening when we confront and write about it.

3. "Writing has become fun for me. I never realized I could enjoy myself so much writing down the adventures I've had in my life. Living them over again has given my day lots of sparkle."

Reading about what once gave us pleasure enables us to reexperience it.

Benefits: Mind

1. "Thinking about important issues I need to be concerned about often takes me in circles. When I write about them, they somehow sort themselves out."

Journal writing helps us connect with our search for answers to problems we don't understand.

2. "There's a lot going on in my head all the time. It's such a surprise to discover what's up there when I sit down to write in my journal. I'm always surprising myself."

Writing leads to insights because it enables us to see our actions and ideas in a larger perspective. Writing also brings to light thoughts we didn't realize we were thinking.

3. "It was only after I'd been writing about my medication for several months that I realized I needed to talk to someone about it. This week, I made an appointment with the doctor. When we discussed all of the things I'm taking, I discovered I could get rid of some of them and reduce the frequency of others. I've begun to feel much better, thanks to my journal."

Over time, journals help us to identify problems or recurring issues that may require help from others.

Benefits: Spirit

1. "After my wife died, I gradually stopped seeing all of our old friends. I came to the journal-writing class because I was lonely, and discovered a wonderful way to enjoy myself. Since I began writing I've been feeling much better about myself. I even called and talked with some old friends."

Health crises, divorce, and the death of a spouse can result in estrangement from those who have shared our love and friendship. Making a friend of the journal ensures that we have available a constant source of communication and comfort. With our journal, we're never alone.

2. "People are always asking me for advice. I've always wondered how I always have it for others, but am at a loss when it comes to my own problems. That is, until I started writing in my journal."
   Writing opens a pathway into the intuition – our wisdom center.

3. "Who'd have thought that by writing in my journal, I'd discover experiences in my past that actually made an important difference to others as well as to myself. This made me feel better about myself than I have in ages!"
   When we explore ourselves in greater depth, we reach a level of consciousness that helps us connect with something even deeper within ourselves.

Benefits: Body/mind/spirit/emotions

1. "Writing in my journal gave me the feeling that for the first time in my life I was important."
   Writing helps us to appreciate ourselves more and to value our accomplishments.

2. "I've been thinking about selling my house and going to live in a retirement community. Writing about this has brought many things to my attention that I would have never thought of unless I was writing them down."
   Using a journal offers us a safe way to reflect on transitions in our lives.

3. "Since I began writing, I've begun to think about new places I'd like to go, and I've started writing poetry again and going to the theater."
   Writing helps us explore the past, anticipate the future, and live more creatively.

Healing and self-expression

As you read these reasons for journal writing, an interesting question may arise. What makes journaling different from other forms of communication? Countless individuals have said they felt better when they talked over their worries and concerns with someone. Sometimes this communication took the form of letter-writing, which made it possible for people to share their feelings in ways they couldn't have spoken.

David McCullough, in his book *Truman*, included a letter the young Harry Truman wrote to his sweetheart, Bess, because he couldn't say the words to her face that he could write in his letter. (McCullough also mentioned unsent letters that Truman wrote to lighten the burden of what was troubling him.)

While old-fashioned letter-writing may have languished over the past few decades, e-mails and blogging have mushroomed beyond all expectation. Bloggers express feelings and ideas on the Internet to a multitude waiting for communication. The presentation of these views online offers immediate satisfaction to the writer, whose work trumpets, "Look at me! This is what I think!" And readers enjoy these peeks into the writer's mind.

More important is the fact that connecting with someone during crisis or joy offers real health benefits. Because communication plays a key role in well-being, the medical profession encourages the creation of support groups for patients and their families in hospitals and care centers across the country. Talking about problems instead of living in isolation accelerates the healing process.

Unfortunately, not everyone finds it possible to do this. Harry, who attended one of my sessions, couldn't bring himself to discuss a problem with a group of strangers. Instead, he called a friend in Texas twice a month to ease his stress. While picking up the phone is better than not sharing at all, talking about a problem is different from writing about it.

This difference has been extensively studied and researched. The act of writing moves problems into a different dimension of consciousness. You actually change the problem by framing it and moving it into an area of your experience more involved with problem-solving. A different assessment process is triggered. Writing about any problem with honesty and without concern for what others will think or do about it – when you're not thinking about making your writing public in a letter or blog that others will read – helps you tap into a storehouse of understanding within and begin to develop a healing solution. Through journal writing, you begin to construct a bridge that helps connect body, mind, and spirit.

Our need for answers

Children believe that everything will be different when they grow up. As adults, we're often startled to discover ourselves without a clue about how to find the answers to questions in our lives. When we lose a job, a spouse, a child, or a beloved pet; when we're diagnosed with a life-threatening disease or some other health predicament; when we must face our own aging – how do we make sense of these experiences? How do we get through the day? Where's help when we most need it?

The answer is literally at your fingertips. The pen or pencil you hold when you write your feelings into your journal is the key to unlocking the answers that are in your soul.

Developed in workshops with people who have survived many life crises, *Write for Life* is designed for those who have never thought of themselves as writers and have avoided writing during their lives. The reluctant writer as well as those who have been thinking about journal writing as an activity they might like to explore, will find exciting ideas and support for a personal journey into a new and healing way of life.

Newcomers to the journal-writing process and those who have kept journals in the past will find it easy to begin the process. All you need is a large tablet and something to write with. And while it's always helpful to have the support of people around you who are also writing journals, you can still journal on your own. I've been writing for five decades without a support group, and I continue to find the process valuable.

The only way to discover the benefit is by doing it – experiencing the change that's possible over time. Beginning the process can open the way to unexpected delights. Give it a try for ninety days, with the goal of gaining a new perspective on the past in order to live a richer and more satisfying life in the present and future.

I wish you well as you embark on this journal-writing expedition. A life-long program of self-discovery is here. Enjoy your journey.

The website www.writeforlifeccp.com has been created for readers who would like to read published reviews of this book as well as to offer entries of their own for future publications.

How to Use This Book

Part One: Initiating the Healing Process of Journal Writing

It's natural to have many questions when you're beginning something new. "Square One," the first chapter, anticipates some of these questions and offers five windows on healing that are explored in great detail in Part Two. *Write for Life* is not organized in a linear design, so feel free to open any of these windows at any time. Chapters Two and Three begin the writing process with ideas and suggestions for getting started and staying started. The task of discovering how writing works to begin healing takes time, so do this at whatever tempo is comfortable. The most important thing is that you try to be as consistent as possible with your writing efforts.

Material written by others as they moved into the unknown territory of expressing themselves will also appear in this book. Journal work of others can often offer support for our own efforts. Examples of journal writers' misgivings and confusion, along with the delight and accomplishment that are also part of life, find their way into these pages.

The process is step-by-step. "Getting Started" helps you to take the first step, and as the days of writing follow, you may encounter certain classic obstacles along the way. "Staying Started" helps you to move beyond these obstacles with useful suggestions.

Gaining a new perspective on the past enables us to live in a richer and more satisfying way in the present and the future. With that deep wish, you embark on these journal-writing expeditions, which you can pursue through the months and years ahead. A lifelong journal-writing program is here.

Part Two: Windows on Healing

Beginning to write in a journal is the first step toward healing. For most journal writers, what follows is curiosity about the way others have pursued this activity. Five chapters address this wish for more information. These chapters examine survivors and surviving, journal-writing excerpts from other journal writers, scientific research into journal writing and additional journal-writing techniques, healing, and expectations. Let them become a resource for your own writing process.

Part Three: Exploring New Directions into Healing

Each of these fifteen chapters is an itinerary and a passport to exploring different approaches to a new understanding about living life and enjoying it more. We'll be looking at experiences from the past and present as well as those we can anticipate for the future. You can change the order of these fifteen journeys at any time. They're options waiting for you to choose among them, and depending upon your personal interest and readiness, one journey may have greater appeal than another at a specific time. Choose the one that stimulates your writing process and begin.

Each of the journeys is organized with the same approach. "Getting Started" introduces the journey to be explored, "Staying Started" moves into additional considerations and new issues, and "New Directions" opens the way for you to further engage with and overcome obstacles and issues, and helps you to develop your understanding of this new territory. You'll get the most out of the experience of writing if you spend at least a week or more in each section before proceeding to the next. Take time to explore yourself.

Chapter 9, which discusses healing through self-caring, helps you to place your needs front and center in each journey and is an excellent place to begin. The choice of where to travel is always yours.

PART ONE

Initiating the Process
of Journal Writing

Chapter 1
Square One

I call the place where you begin these writing journeys "Square One," but it could also be called "Home Port." It's the place within yourself you're most familiar with. Whatever term you want to use, just remember this – the sooner you begin to write, the sooner you'll embark on your journey of self-discovery.

Being a survivor

Everyone understands what it means to be a survivor. The word survivor comes from the Latin *supervivere* – to live beyond. Perhaps you've faced a life-threatening disease, accident, or other condition that brought you face to face with your own mortality. Or you've lived through a crisis like divorce, bereavement, family separation, professional dissatisfaction, health concerns, or other issues that have the potential for changing lives. Hopefully, you've faced that crisis and now you live beyond it.

Perhaps you're facing a crisis now.

Just as with t'ai chi, yoga, meditation, massage, reflexology, or any other complementary therapy, journal writing is focused on healing and recovery. Through writing, you'll discover how to get more life from everything that you've experienced. In the process, you'll discover that what you've learned from being a survivor has enriched your life beyond anything you've ever imagined.

For centuries, survivors have used journals to understand and enhance their lives. I encourage you to read about some of these other journal writers if you're curious to explore their minds and motivations.

The mystery of healing

So much astonishing research has been done on the effects of journaling on the writer. You can get an even deeper understanding of how important journal writing is to healing when you consider the findings of Dr. James Pennebaker. He began his investigations in the late 1980s with the study of the effect of writing on traumatized rape victims, and his research suggests convincingly that expressive writing about emotional upheavals in our lives can improve our physical and mental health.

Many other researchers have investigated this subject and have made equally profound discoveries. To put it simply, writing enhances healing. Just knowing this can offer additional hope and motivation to reluctant writers.

The process of healing, with its many aspects and complexities, is more art than science. No one knows exactly why one person heals while another with the same condition doesn't. However, a mind-body-spirit connection essential to the process has been observed, and we'll explore that link throughout this book.

The reason for journal writing is to bring about healing. Understanding that the writing process can be as therapeutic as acupuncture, t'ai chi, yoga, meditation, or any other complementary therapy should encourage you to use your journal to bring balance and order into your life. Just as those who pursue these other techniques practice them for their healing effects, so too do journal writers enhance their health and well-being through putting pen to paper.

Personal expectations

One of the activities I begin my workshops with is getting people to express what they'd like to happen for them during our sessions. No matter what you do, where you go, or what you read, you anticipate what life has in store for you. It's always good to get in touch with your expectations, because recognizing what you want from yourself at the beginning clears some space inside you to receive what is offered, rather than focus on what you didn't get.

Ready to write? It's time to embark on your journey by turning the page to Chapter 2, "Getting Started," and to begin to experience the healing and joy that comes through writing about your life.

Chapter 2
Getting Started

Basics: The paper

Journal writing begins with choosing the journal itself – the actual paper on which you'll write. You need something with bound pages that's easy to keep with you (or on the shelf at home) for thoughts you want to save. Jotting notes to yourself on random pieces of paper that can easily get lost just won't work.

Stationers have many elegant offerings on their shelves. These books come in all sizes. Perhaps you've even received one as a present from a friend. Some have lines to write on, some contain completely blank pages. Many have dates already entered on each page or an inspiring sentiment in the margin. Perhaps you even bought one in preparation for *Write for Life* – just to be ready.

For the reluctant writer, these expensive bound volumes can be a daunting obstacle to overcome. The book is so pretty, so fine, so ... (fill in any adjective that occurs to you). As formidable as the empty page is to someone just starting out to write, an entire book of empty pages seems staggering. And since you haven't the slightest idea what you're going to write about, you may feel reluctant to open it. What a dilemma. Look at all those empty pages!

Some people in my writing groups who began with elegant journals have told me how difficult it was to write certain things in them. "The book is so pretty, I can't possibly include such ugly and depressing things in it," said one. And another: "I never feel easy about complaining or writing that anything is less than perfect in such a book." Be aware of your feelings about this. To write about everything imaginable in your journal, you need to feel comfortable.

So if the pricey blank journal sitting on the shelf has this effect on you, maybe you should choose something far less daunting, like a large legal pad, a steno pad, or a spiral-bound notebook that you can find in drugstores or office-supply outlets. Tablets like these don't have enough pages in them to worry you, and when you fill one, you can always buy another.

Journal writing is about the freedom to express yourself about *everything*. It's about not holding back or censoring yourself. If you handle your journal with kid gloves, you won't be able to get the most benefit out of it. In fact, gloves of any kind would make it hard to write – they get in the way.

Slip the tablet into a folder. Or buy a clipboard that will provide a firm surface instead of limiting yourself to writing at a desk or a table. Do whatever makes writing easy. Suggestion: Leave the first page or two blank to protect the entries against smudges and stains.

Basics: The pen

Now that you have the paper on which to write, what will you write with? Unless a physical handicap exists and writing by hand isn't possible, write with a pen and not with a word processor. Like many others, I'm much faster at a keyboard than I am with pen and paper. But the activity of journal writing isn't about speed; it's about connecting the body with the mind in regular practice that will improve, over time, much as pursuing any recreational activity will develop your ability. As your hand moves across the pages, you'll gradually develop the internal connection you need to enhance the quality of your life.

Also, writing in longhand will discourage something that's easy to do on the computer: editing. I can't write at the keyboard without editing, and I doubt that anyone else can either. On the monitor, when misspelled words and poorly punctuated sentences appear, you correct them immediately, right? And correcting these errors leads to further editing. This is exactly what you do *not* want to do. When you start editing, you stop writing. Don't let this happen; your goal is to write. When you edit, you're also practicing a form of self-criticism. Instead, give yourself permission to make as many mistakes as you want. This is the unspoken contract you make with yourself each time you write. *Nothing is a mistake.*

Many people have a brand-new, *special* pen to use for their journals. That's fine, as long as you can find that pen whenever you want it. Pens have a way of getting lost, and what will happen if you can't find it when you want it? Will you be unable to write? I hope not. Keep your special pen near your journal. Often, a special pen will give you a lift when you pick it up to write. Using different-colored inks may inspire you further. I have several cartridge pens, and I change the color when the ink is gone. It's always surprising to see my words in different colors, and this is at the center of the writing experience: surprising ourselves. You need the surprise, and you can have it any time you wish – with your journal.

Basics: The place

Where will you write? Choose a location that will provide the greatest comfort and support. If you enjoy writing at a special desk, one that has unique significance for you (perhaps it's where you always sat when you wrote as a child), then write there and discover what happens. Some people choose places they thought would work, only to discover difficulties. I know a woman who tried writing at her kitchen table, but that was where she always paid her bills. She had a hard time allowing herself to do a totally different kind of writing there. When she moved to a comfortable chair in her living room, the words began flowing from her pen. Please experiment with different places and find one that makes you feel safe and comforted as well as comfortable. Like many journal writers, I often write in bed at night.

Another choice is writing outdoors or on the patio, perhaps, which I did for years when I lived beside the ocean in Isla Verde, Puerto Rico. Other people like to write in a garden or park. You can even write in a favorite coffee shop if you enjoy having people around. (But don't let anyone intrude on your privacy.) I've written in every place imaginable in my fifty years of journaling: at airports and railroad stations; in planes, trains, and cars; at plays, concerts, and antique shows; in hospitals and at doctors' offices. Once you find a place where you like to write, explore several others as well, just so you don't feel limited.

Basics: The time

When will you write? This is another question that requires research. Some have found that unless they write first thing in the morning, they don't think about doing it for the rest of the day. Others have found that writing at the end of the day provides wonderful opportunities for additional reflection and a tidy rounding out of the day that has just flown by.

Write any time you can share your thoughts with yourself without being interrupted by anyone else's demands on your attention. Don't write when you're obliged to meet a deadline hanging over your head or while you're watching television. Television is about someone else. Journal writing is about *you*.

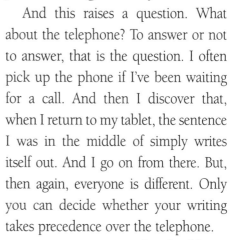

And this raises a question. What about the telephone? To answer or not to answer, that is the question. I often pick up the phone if I've been waiting for a call. And then I discover that, when I return to my tablet, the sentence I was in the middle of simply writes itself out. And I go on from there. But, then again, everyone is different. Only you can decide whether your writing takes precedence over the telephone.

How many times a day should you write? As many as you choose. Don't wait to be inspired. Make an appointment to write each day and remember to keep it. Set a specific time, even if that means setting an alarm to remind you. If you do this, you make writing as much a priority in your life as having a meal. It will then begin to be included among the activities and chores you maintain for your own comfort and well-being, and it will cease to be something rare or strange. Writing will become natural and easy. This is what you want journal writing to become in your life – something very natural and easy.

It's as well to stress for both the beginner and the seasoned journal writer that journaling is not an excuse for living. Writing *instead* of living is not the practice you're initiating. While writing can help you become more self-caring and responsible, it doesn't take the place of participation in life. This isn't about hiding behind your journal. Your purpose is to discover how to engage in life more completely and find deeper understanding.

If you've never written a journal before, start off with a time span you can easily handle, perhaps twenty minutes. When you first sit down to the tablet and pick up the pen, the noise of life may go through your head. There are appointments to make, errands to run, people to telephone. It usually takes about five minutes or so to run through your internal date book after you begin to write. But you can do it if you persevere. Give yourself twenty minutes to write and tell yourself you'll get back to taking care of your other responsibilities afterward. Now is the time for writing. Taking out the trash comes later.

Basics: How many pages?

Telling yourself you'll write a certain number of pages at each sitting is counterproductive to what you're trying to accomplish. You're also setting yourself up to punish yourself for not meeting some arbitrary goal. Some days just lend themselves better to reflection than others. What's most important is not the number of pages, but that you write consistently every day.

Encourage yourself to enter a space where you truly want to be, one that is rich, fulfilling, and precious. This is the place within yourself that needs your attention and care. You recognize it when you're in it, yet something may feel awkward. That may be one of the reasons you've avoided writing – you're unsure or even afraid of what might come out on the page. Or perhaps you fear something equally frightening, that there may be nothing at all inside that place.

This is simply not possible. You have a rich life and a wealth of experiences to draw on. Don't abuse yourself with self-doubt. From now on, you're going to become more comfortable with being in your body, mind, and spirit than ever before.

Many people have told me this isn't an easy start-up. One man I know puts his pen on the tablet and begins to write on the top lines of the page *lalalalalalalalalalalalalalalalalalalala*. After a few lines of this "jogging," as he calls it, he finds himself launched into his journal entry for the day. You'll find your own beginning, the one that works for you.

Basics: What to write about?

Beginning journal writers are often concerned that there might not be anything to write about on a certain day. Therefore, it's helpful to have some idea or subject that will serve as a catalyst. Here's a suggestion. Choose one of the following three questions, then start writing. No matter how much noise I have in my head, how fatigued I am from the day, or how much of a burden it is to commit myself to that twenty minutes, choosing one of these questions usually unlocks the door to my writing room.

- What surprised me the most today?
- What moved me the most today?
- What do I most want to remember about today?

Choosing one of these writing prompts should get your pen moving.

Questions that demand reflection have a surprising way of opening your eyes to what's happening to you now or what has happened to you in the past. The same is true about your feelings. You may be quite moved by something and not even be aware of it until you begin writing. Or you may not realize how blocked you are from feeling your emotions. Answering question two might unstop that block. As for what you most want to remember about the day, you may find that focusing on something you've just experienced will give you a deeper appreciation of yourself and your life. Another bonus is the souvenir in the form of a memory that you've preserved in your journal. Had you not written about that experience, your keepsake might easily have been lost.

Include dreams in your list of journal-writing possibilities. A dream from the night before may hold images you need to remember. Dreams offer key information about the way you live, as we'll see in Chapter 13.

What you're attempting to do is move the way you look at the world out of the ho-hum and into the "aha!" You're writing about people, experiences, and thoughts that may seem to have faded away, but you're really giving them prominence by connecting them with your past. And by connecting these seemingly unrelated moments, you'll discover a thread that, over time, stitches together the tapestry of your life. This cloth you're weaving is truly empowering. It provides a new way of looking at your life.

Here's another question you might like to address in your journal:

- Is there any "unfinished business" from the past that I can connect with a question I have chosen to write about?

As you begin to write about the event or person who surprised you today, try to recall whether there were previous events or people who surprised you in a similar (or slightly different) way. An emotional response today may be connected with a past experience in which you wish you'd acted with more understanding or less fear. Connecting the experience you most want to remember today with similar experiences in the past may be something to explore more fully.

Connecting with past experiences, whether uplifting or saddening, helps you to heal. So go as deeply as you can beneath the surface of the experience and express your feelings on the page. Writing in your journal will reveal the buried connections between body, mind, and spirit. The healing that comes through this discovery will move you beyond where you are right now.

Remember, honesty is the most important feature of your writing. If you're not writing about the truth of your experience, you're not writing a journal that can help you to heal.

Basics: You are the only audience

Be clear that you're writing for you and no one else. If you're writing for anyone except yourself, the journal will fail you. Writing to meet other people's expectations means that every line is waiting for approval or criticism, both of which are useless to the process you're beginning. If you're afraid of what someone will think about what you write, you'll find it impossible to be honest. And if you're hoping to delight others with cleverness and charm, you certainly won't be writing from that place within yourself that needs attention. You're not performing for any audience or authoring a book for publication; you're opening yourself to the healing that comes through being honest with yourself about your life experiences. You can't do this if you're afraid of what others (or you yourself) might say about your words.

Confidentiality is absolutely crucial to your effort. If you know anyone else will read your journal, you won't be able to write what needs to be written. You'll be too self-conscious, which will prevent you from discovering the truth you're searching for. The truth is there, but it's for you to discover, not for other people to point out.

Ensuring the confidentiality of your writing may not be a simple matter. Spouses, partners, close friends, or family members might be tempted to read your journal if they see it lying on a table or desk. This possibility needs to be addressed. Discuss your need for personal confidentiality with others. Another idea is to write on the cover page explicit instructions to anyone who might find it: THANK YOU FOR NOT READING ME! This is a good reminder for you as well as others. You may find that being honest with others about your needs opens the way to being honest with yourself.

A participant in one of my groups was reluctant about writing her feelings because, she said, the next day or week they would be different. She didn't want to commit herself to anything that would change. It's true that, unlike facts, feelings change. Change is part of the human condition. However, recording the way you feel today is extremely valuable because it enables you to reflect on how you once felt. It's a snapshot of you at the moment of writing, one of many such pictures in the album. And over time, you'll have a great many "photos" to cherish.

Basics: Datelines

In the margin, date every entry and include the city, location, and time of your writing. This provides a grounding for the entry. It's also useful when you look back over the pages in the months and years ahead. This grounding will help you connect with the "I" who was the writer at that particular moment. Without it, because of the many different kinds of changes you experience over time, you might lose touch with the image of the self who once embodied those feelings. The changes you endure with little or no awareness might shock you with how different you've become. This is a powerful source of self-revelation.

And whatever you see, avoid struggling with the logic of the connection you've made. The question "Why?" goes around and around on itself. It's a tangent that prevents further progress. Explore instead the amazing diversity of your life and experience.

I encourage journal writers in my groups to avoid reading what they've written for a while so that down the road, they'll be able to get a different perspective on themselves. And remember, your desire to edit and revise will be strong. Resist that temptation. Perfectionism is something you want to discourage. There's no right or wrong way to write in your journal, so accept what you do with approval and affirmation, and then move on.

Basics: Affirmations

Speaking of affirmation, most of us rarely receive the encouragement that we'd like when we fulfill our daily responsibilities. Affirmations provide vital energy to the healing process, and you don't need to wait for them to come from others. Offer them to yourself because they have valuable benefits. Honest praise does wonders for the heart and soul. Try some of these:

"It's a very good day; I've written in my journal!"

"Applause! I've opened the door of that difficulty I've been facing!"

"What a great entry. I've made an important connection in my life!"

"Thanks for caring about me enough to end my denial!"

"If that's what I want, I can go for it!"

Everyone needs to create affirmations to provide the understanding, self-caring, and self-acceptance necessary for healing to occur. Find your own words of praise – words that have special meaning for you. Include them at the end of each journal entry.

Also include designs, doodles, drawings, and other creative bursts that flow from your pen. Inviting both sides of the brain to participate in the exploration of experience is an intrinsic part of the process. I've looked back at journals from many years ago to discover in the doodles something about myself that I'd forgotten. Who I was then came alive for me, and I was grateful for the connection that had been forged between now and then.

You've experienced many influences and have found your way through many issues and areas of confusion. Everyone can connect the experience of living with the simple activity of setting pen to paper and allowing feelings to flow. It's almost magic, what can happen when you're willing to be open with yourself. And when you're honest with yourself, you cross the threshold for healing. You're writing to heal, and you're growing in health and understanding.

As a survivor, you understand that living *better* is going to be different. It requires giving yourself permission to explore the past, live in the present, and be excited about a future that will offer both joy and sadness. Some of the greatest delights you'll experience will come from connections you'll make in your journal. This has been my experience, and I don't doubt for a moment that it will be yours as well.

Putting the pen on the page

Now that you have the tablet, the pen, the location, and the wish to begin, what's next? Prepare yourself to write by making sure you're comfortable. If you're hungry or thirsty, it's a good idea to eat or drink something. If you've decided to answer phone calls, have a phone nearby. If you practice meditation or centering, complete it before beginning. Then, encourage the energy to flow by giving yourself permission to write whatever comes to mind. You're writing only for today and only for yourself. You can use any of the questions I suggested or begin with something that may be in your mind when you sit down to write.

Allow your hand to flow over the page in the way you'd start out on a walk, gradually and without hurry. The muscles in the hands, arms, and shoulders connect your body with your thoughts and open the way for your spirituality to flow easily into the words. Perhaps you may want to create a mantra that acknowledges your wish to heal through the words you write. Don't concern yourself with your handwriting or any other sound that comes through the window. As you write, include feelings about what you're writing. Let the activity of writing become something you can savor, like a fine meal.

Ready to write? Open your journal, write a date in the margin, then write one of the suggested questions or begin writing whatever you feel. You're beginning your journal today. For the next week, make a date with yourself to write each day.

When you've finished writing, put the tablet away. Just for today, don't read what you've written. Leave that for another day. Remember to make an appointment to write again tomorrow, and reward yourself in some way to acknowledge your accomplishment at having begun your journal. Getting started is perhaps the most difficult task of all.

Put the tablet away in a safe place. It's your private personal record. Over time it will become a treasure house in which you'll explore aspects of yourself. It will open the door to a deeper understanding of many things that you may not even realize you know about yourself. Treat your journal as you would anything that's precious to you, because it will grow in value as you fill it.

Chapter 3
Staying Started

The power of inertia

After writing in your journal for a week or more, you may have made this discovery: Starting to write wasn't as difficult as trying to continue writing. Here are a few comments from some beginning journal writers.

- "With all the other activities I have in my life, I don't need another."
- "It's too time-consuming; I don't have any room for it in my busy schedule."
- "I'm going to have to do this *every* day?"

Inertia is, perhaps, the single most powerful stumbling block to writing. It takes energy, courage, patience, and commitment to keep writing in your journal. It's no small thing to open doors, let down barriers, enter sealed rooms, and walk obscure avenues of memory that haven't been traveled in years – or perhaps *ever* been traveled.

When you write, you make yourself vulnerable to the page. In my experience, I've discovered that when I'm willing to risk, I gain in some way. I discover boundaries within myself that I can go beyond. I encounter ideas that challenge my creativity, my ingenuity, and what I take for granted. Pressing myself to go beyond the familiar keeps me moving on my journey. Going forward makes it impossible to yield to inertia. Put simply, writing on a daily basis makes me want to continue writing on a daily basis.

Here are some explanations people give for not writing. Do any of them sound familiar?

- "I'm in too much pain to write."
- "What good will it do? Nothing will change."
- "I could never expose myself in such a vulnerable way."
- "What will they (my parents, spouse, children, friends, boss, teacher, etc.) think of me if they know what I've written about them?"
- "Whatever I think is nobody else's business except my own, and I'm keeping it to myself."

- "I don't like making commitments, and writing a journal could become another commitment."
- "I'm too old."

What does inertia mean to you? Open your journal and write with as much detail as possible about how inertia operates in your life. Give yourself permission to surprise yourself with what you write. How you define inertia will illuminate what you need to know about ways to make a difference in your daily routine – whether it's about journal writing or something else.

Definitions of inertia

Here are some definitions of inertia that others have written.

- "I don't have anything special to write about."
- "I don't want to encourage myself to worry any further about my situation, and writing about it will make me do just that."
- "The details of some of the things I might write about are so boring that I don't want to get into them."
- "Nothing significant has happened yet. I want results now!"
- "My health has improved and I don't need to dump or complain about anything."
- "I've been writing for a few days; what's left to write?"
- "Writing is nebulous. I need to take action!"
- "I'd rather remain as invisible as possible in my life; it's easier."
- "I'm reluctant to feel the feelings."
- "I just don't want to do anything, and I know this is bad for me."
- "Anything I might think of doing or changing moves me to something different. This frightens me."
- "I don't want to begin feeling guilty about the things I've forgotten, which writing will remind me of."
- "I'm just too tired/too sleepy/no energy."
- "The telephone always comes first. I'm constantly interrupted."

Having drafted your own definition of inertia and considered what others have written, can you see how much everyone takes the nature of inertia for granted? Your definition may give you the first glimpse of the box you've built around yourself. Your mind imposes limitations for as long as you go along with this kind of propaganda. This is the story you tell yourself and come to believe. It keeps you from making the changes you need to make in order to live better.

Connecting with needs

With your own definition of inertia staring at you from the page, next think about what you want from your writing. When you need something, you do all you can to get it. Necessity isn't just the mother of invention; it's also the way to implement change in your life. Some of the needs identified by my workshop participants appear below. But before you read what they said, please create your own list of journal-writing needs.

Complete this sentence with ten different words or phrases:

"What I need from my journal-writing is:

(1)_____,

(2)_____,

(3)_____,

(...10)_____."

Keep this list handy. Here are some items that others have noted. Are any of them on the list you've just made?

> "Self-appreciation." "Honest communication." "To create an emotional breakthrough." "To leave behind some footprints of who I am." "To access my inner truths." "To create a more fulfilling life." "To develop a companion(ship)." "To develop trust in my inner voices." "To explore problems." "To find answers." "To receive some vision of enlightenment." "To dump pain." "To get more sense of accomplishment." "To get more energy." "To share more of who I am and experience the release of self-disclosure." "To put out my thoughts without receiving anyone else's advice or judgment." "To let off steam." "To have a place of sanctuary." "To make a friend of myself." "To offer myself an opportunity for organizing

my life with more order and discipline than I have now."
"To be less of a perfectionist." "To get out emotions instead
of dumping them on others." "To explore areas of myself
that are deep and don't usually show up." "To remember
good things/funny things that I enjoyed and to savor
them." "To write not because it's an obligation but because
it's a choice I'm making about how to spend my time."

It's essential for you to develop your own list of what you need from
journal writing. It will help you continue with your journal as your initial
enthusiasm subsides. Having this reminder at your fingertips means that
you'll always be ready with sound responses to the many obstacles that
stand in the way of your effort.

Now, complete this sentence with the first ten responses that come to
your mind:

"I would write every day in my journal if _____."
(Number from 1 to 10 down the margin of your journal and write your
answers.)

Let's look at what others have written.

- "... I had more time."
- "... I could find happiness."
- "... I had 100 percent faith it would get results."
- "... I weren't so tired."
- "... I had a contract with a publisher."
- "... I knew where to start."
- "... it would build muscle."
- "... it weren't so much about death."
- "... it would keep me from aging."
- "... I weren't so scared to write about what's on my mind."

Framing the obstacles

The more obstacles you identify, the better. There's always an imposing
army of them waiting, and you can't dismiss them or pretend they'll go
away just because you're feeling mellow today. Obstacles define the reality

of your world, and if you want to live in it with more satisfaction than before, you need to take them into account. Begin by acknowledging them, then consider ways to handle them. Let's begin with the obstacles that fall into this category: "I have no time for journal writing."

While there can't be more hours to fit into the day, there always seem to be more activities you can find time for if you make them a priority. You notice this immediately when a crisis appears in your life or a visitor comes who'll be in town for only a short time or the doctor says you must exercise for at least twenty minutes a day. These are just a few of the things that demand for space in life.

Keep this in mind. *You need to write for only about twenty to thirty minutes a day.* Much more time than this is spent daydreaming. Journal writing isn't wasting time. You're devoting time to your own health and well-being. You're making special time to pay attention to your life. Don't you deserve it? If you value your life, then you *do* deserve it.

Finding the *right* time for writing is often much more the point. Some people create extra time by setting an alarm clock twenty minutes earlier in the morning. Or they write on the bus on the way to work or bring a small notepad while taking a coffee break.

Something happens the moment you begin to think of writing as an activity you can do whenever you want, that the reasons for writing are important to your well-being, and that you'll experience the benefit of writing over time if you continue it. You find the time to write. Writing begins to energize you. You find the problems you've been worrying about are no longer stealing your energy. You may even feel less depressed.

The only way to discover whether journal writing works for you is by doing it on a consistent basis over time – the very thing you told yourself you didn't have. So, start using your journal to help you manage your time better.

Writing about feelings

Perhaps for the first time in your life, you'll be writing about your feelings – exploring them, acknowledging them. Be honest, and remember, no one else is going to see what you write. And because you're writing only for yourself, you're free to put into words anything and everything that comes to mind.

Earlier, I mentioned making yourself vulnerable to the page in order to get as much as possible from the experience. There may be some areas you regard as unworthy of attention or topics that you're unwilling to tackle. Sometimes, you don't even realize you're purposely avoiding writing about them.

In my work with men and women in recovery, I've discovered that the most persistent obstacles in the way of progress are often the hidden secrets – the "no-nos" that cannot be considered. The-one-thing-I-can't-talk-about. Well, secrets keep you stuck and inhibit healing. It's useful to make a list of these "no-nos" and look at them from time to time.

Write this list now in your journal.

Our "no-nos"

These have shown up on others' lists: "Failures." "Fear of failure." "Character defects." "Incomplete expectations." "Disappointments." "Painful incidents." "Things I cannot change." "Grudges." "Inability to forgive." "Humiliations." "My deepest dreams." "My darkest fears." "Other people's negative judgments of me." "My weaknesses." "My vulnerabilities."

Whatever is on your list will certainly, over time, become an obstacle to your writing, so be aware that these "no-nos" are waiting until you're ready to examine their impact on your life and your decision-making process. As you write about other things, you're also preparing yourself for your list of "no-nos." When you're ready to put down the baggage you no longer need, you'll address the items on your list.

Here's a good example. Of all our "no-nos," the subject of facing death – your own or another's – is perhaps one of the most problematic. Many people find it hard to acknowledge grave illness when they're in its presence. This concern can distort the way you respond to events around you, and what results can often be startling and painful. But writing about this in your journal will help you explore what you feel about mortality and help you identify any unresolved questions you're struggling to find answers to. Allow yourself to connect with your wisdom and intuition. Understanding is the first step toward healing.

Cary, an elderly participant in one writing group, told me that death was the only thing she worried about. It was also the one thing she found impossible to write about. I encouraged her to spend some time writing about all the wonderful things as well as the disappointments in her life, until she was ready to write about death. Another participant told me how painful it was to think about her mother's imminent death. I encouraged her to write about her life with her mother and then about issues involving her mother's nursing-home care that needed to be settled. One of the most significant comments of all, however, came from the son of a woman who'd been in my workshop during the last four months of her life. He told me that she'd said that writing about her own girlhood many years ago in China had made it possible for her to become reconciled with *her* mother, something she had wanted but not previously experienced. Because of this, she told him, she was dying a much happier woman.

When you write about what's truly meaningful to you and allow yourself to stumble into understanding as you journey through your journal, you'll be amazed at what can happen. Just don't start "shoulding" on yourself, as in "I should have done ..." That's a sure way to lose contact with your intuition. The judgments and self-criticism implied in that "should" have no place in your journal-writing time. Healing comes from accepting what has been and what is. The connections you make with the "unfinished business" of your past are for the purpose of understanding yourself from a new perspective. Through this change in perspective, you have the possibility of learning to embrace yourself and your life.

Trailblazing

Please appreciate that you're doing something very difficult. You're trying to hack a path through a wilderness where there hasn't been anything but confusion before. So you need to keep encouraging yourself. Whatever you write is the beginning of finding your way through the wilderness. Even when it might appear that you're not making progress, you really are. You're just moving a little at a time.

The task you've undertaken in your journal is an act of love for yourself. Think of yourself as a pilgrim who starts out on a difficult journey to a distant tabernacle located somewhere in the future. There are signposts along the way that you and others have prepared. You'll find them if you seek them out.

Many find this writing journey difficult to begin. One of the best ways I've found is to write in the form of a dialogue with someone you care deeply for, whether or not that person is alive, and write the responses as if they were lines in a play. Another method is to write your journal entry in the form of a letter. When you're writing a letter you'll never send, words tend to flow more easily. Many journal writers have used this technique to connect with themselves.

Our baggage

We're used to walking through life carrying a tremendous amount of baggage on our shoulders, and putting down these burdens for even five minutes can often be difficult. So many voices from the past are sounding off every waking minute (and sometimes, even when we're asleep and dreaming). Attempting anything new or different from what we've been doing can result in a chorus of naysayers that inhibits any effort. Thankfully, there's a useful technique to counter this – if we're willing to try it.

Develop a list of your inner critics and their criticism. Then, confront the "committee" inside your head by writing a positive statement to dispel each of the criticisms those inner voices have used on you. Some workshop participants have taped the affirmations they've written and then played them while driving.

At the heart of each affirmation is your knowledge and acceptance of yourself as you are and your willingness to give yourself encouragement and listen to it. While I underwent chemotherapy, I listened to *A Meditation to Ease Pain*, a guided-imagery tape recorded by Belleruth Naparstek (Health Journeys, 1995). Its affirmations offer a model you can follow in writing your own self-healing statements. Here are some affirmations that I wrote for myself:

- "The way I feel is the way I feel. Being angry, afraid, or sad is neither good nor bad. I know my emotional states will change. I accept myself as I am: a source of value in my life and the lives of others."
- "Living better means that I can stop being self-critical and start being self-caring today."
- "I can park my expectations of myself outside the door and use my energy and attention to live in this moment with everything I am right now."
- "By valuing myself as I am, I can nurture every part of me and allow myself to grow beyond my present self-limiting idea of myself."
- "Peace of mind is a gift I can give myself. No one else can give it or withold it from me as long as I remember that I am the giver."
- "No matter what has happened in the past, I can forgive myself today by loving my life and those who share it with me."

It's best to find your own words to encourage and support yourself for doing something entirely new and unfamiliar. Remember, intimidation and harassment don't work; patience and encouragement do.

Support for our efforts

It's helpful to be part of a small support group of other journal writers. There's encouragement in knowing that there are others, like yourself, who are interested in living better. Participation in a journal-writing group of two or three people is a great way to stay started. It becomes easier to find support as you write each day as more people who are also writing show up.

When you make the effort to write with others, you not only support them in their journal writing; you also begin to connect with them in a new way – one that may be a breakthrough in how you relate to people. Your journal writing includes you in an activity that opens a way for you to appreciate yourself and others from a new perspective.

For many, it has encouraged a new interest in exploring the writings of other men and women who have found the journal a source of delight and inspiration in their lives. A journal-writing group can also provide a sense of connection for people who live alone or who find themselves becoming isolated over time because of such personal circumstances as aging or illness.

Remember, while it's great to share a common interest, you should discuss the journal-writing process, not your journal entries. What helps you to write? What are the obstacles? What works? Warm yourselves around the hearth of the shared activity of writing.

Breach of trust

Problems arise when journals containing very personal details are read by someone who was never intended to read it, such as a spouse, sibling, or parent. The repercussions that ensue can be major. I've heard many of these horror tales, and I know how difficult it is to deal with the deep sense of violation, transgression, and trespass – not only with the offender, but also within yourself.

The cardinal rule of journal writing is that without the writer's permission, the confidentiality of what's written can *never* be breached. Picking up and reading a journal that happens to be on a table or in a drawer is a violation of trust in a relationship. Because you're writing *only* for yourself, you need to make it clear from the outset that no one else has permission to read anything you've written. Relationships thrive on setting sound and clear boundaries, and it's essential that you have the trust of spouse, partner, friends, and family members. They must understand how important it is to respect the privacy of your journal.

One of the best ways to handle this issue is to make your needs explicit from the outset. Most people understand this "contract" and honor it. For those who don't, there's a great deal more at stake than reading a journal without permission.

Using the journal entries themselves to repair the harm that's been done by others who have invaded your privacy will help you recover. This is, of course, after the trespass has been addressed. Silence will not be enough; without confrontation, the effects of the violation will persist. In writing about the trespass and its aftereffects, it's possible to explore crucial issues like trust, privacy, secrecy, subterfuge, intimacy, and other related themes. You may even discover some forgotten material to add to the journal. Use every opportunity that's presented to explore and reach new depths of understanding yourself and others.

New directions

"Staying started" is sustained by regularly giving yourself a menu of new possibilities for writing about your life. *Write for Life* presents a variety of new directions to continually stimulate journal writing for years to come. The chapters in this book have been designed to provide areas for exploration that will stimulate your imagination whenever you feel you've written all you can.

In several months, after you've pursued a number of different approaches, you may discover a hidden reservoir of events and feelings buried in your past that you wish to return to. By all means do so.

Look at the list in the table of contents for "Part Three: New Directions in Healing," and choose the categories that appeal to you most. Or, as we do in the workshops, launch your journal writing with Chapter 9, "Self-Caring." It's a useful place to begin.

As you'll see, many interconnections between the different journeys await your discovery. Your adventures begin now with the journal open before you.

PART TWO

Five Windows on Healing

Chapter 4
Survivors and Surviving

Revisiting places you've already been gives you the chance to see things you might have missed the first time. This is the first of five chapters that explore conditions and attitudes that may help you in your journal-writing adventures. This chapter, "Survivors and Surviving," is at the heart of my workshops because it helps participants connect with their lives in new ways. You began your journey in the previous three chapters. Now, here's an opportunity to expand your perspective and explore more of yourself in the writing process.

For many years, I've worked with men and women in recovery, and I've written two books about what I learned. People who have been through the daunting process of getting their lives together and eliminating dependency on compulsive behaviors or substances understand the life-shaping ordeal that makes the journey from addiction to self-mastery so powerful.

Between my cancer diagnosis and treatment, and the workshops I've led for men and women with their own experiences of operating rooms, CAT scans and MRIs, and in- and outpatient health-care delivery, I know firsthand the gratitude felt by most people who survive a health crisis. No one is left unchanged by the process, including family and friends made aware of their own vulnerability.

Here's a paragraph from an early journal of mine, written in January 1957:

> As I walked into my brother's hospital room, from the corner of my eye I could see tiny icicles covering the bare branches of the tree outside the window. Inside the room there was a different kind of chill. My brother, just 26, told me that the doctor had just left the room after telling him his tests revealed he had cancer. His words came at me across a sea of white linen: "How do you live when you know?" I thought for perhaps as long as thirty seconds, and

I answered with only one word: "Better." It was all I could think of then. And it is my answer today, still, for myself and for anyone who asks me what "living beyond" means. It means living better than the way I lived before I knew and understood I was not going to live forever.

No matter your age, it's a shock to come face to face with the fact that your remaining years are limited. A deep current of self-preservation runs through me as it does you, and two thoughts exist side by side in my head: "I'm going to live forever," and "Everyone else is going to die sometime."

Oh, yes, even now. I remember that my father and brother died of cancer, and my mother after her fifth heart attack. My parents were 70, though. Yet my brother was only 34, and I'm now older than my parents were when they died in 1966.

Nonetheless, in my mind, I hear the words "I'm fine!"

It's a peculiar quirk of the mind that, somehow or other, the older you become, the more "immortal" you believe yourself. When the names of friends or family or movie stars or the rich and famous appear on the obituary page of the newspaper, you may read the notice with regret, but rarely with alarm. And it's easy to appreciate why. You're still around to read the notices. And you have no intention of changing places with the dear departed – ever.

Of course, "I'm fine!" Thinking otherwise just isn't healthy. No matter what has happened to me today, yesterday, or the day before, "I'm fine!"

After all, who wants to hear about my problems, my confusion, my pain? And besides, it's no one else's business. I can handle it; no matter what, I'll manage. Anything less is weakness. Competence in the face of adversity is the rule. Endurance keeps you strong, and your friends and family are always able to rely on you for support and strength. It's other people who fall victim to problems relating to health, emotional distress, abuses, and accidents of every description. Not you.

Not you, that is, until something really big comes along, like a heart attack, cancer, AIDS, or stroke. Or the loss of your partner through death or divorce. Termination of your employment. A natural calamity like an earthquake, fire, or tornado. Or perhaps a catastrophic event: the attack on the World Trade Center or the tsunami in southeast Asia or the New Orleans flood. After that, everything changes.

The old rules change. You're a survivor now, like it or not. At some deep level within yourself you understand that you've lived through a crisis; your life has been altered. In a terribly meaningful way, you're no longer the person you were before the event occurred.

The order that you've always taken for granted has collapsed; you find yourself flung into chaos. The illusion that "it's just a bad dream!" melts into the air. No matter what you see, taste, touch, or think, everything reeks of loss. You no longer have what you thought was yours. You're diminished, less than you were the moment before, and you want desperately to leave that space in which you find yourself and be whole again. You feel yourself reduced to quaking, fragile bones in the middle of a wilderness you never knew was waiting for you.

"Can these bones live?" asks the prophet (Ezekiel 37:3). Poets (T.S. Eliot, "Ash-Wednesday, Part II") and philosophers (including Søren Kierkegaard, Jean-Paul Sartre, and Elie Wiesel) have written about the desperate, barren place that surrounds those who experience a crisis of being. If you've never read the work of these authors, reach for their books for what they might tell you about tragedy and isolation. You need their insight, because in your isolation, you abandon yourself in the same way you feel yourself to have been abandoned.

Victims

No wonder you feel like a victim. The life you've known has suddenly been stolen from you. Everything you expected – your health and well-being, the future in which you saw yourself growing old with your life partner and family – has vanished, and the loss reaches deeply into the understanding of who you are. You're suddenly a stranger to yourself. You're angry, resentful, and frightened. When you dare to look into the mirror, it's hard to recognize the face reflected there. The loss of self-recognition alone is enough to scare anyone into hiding.

Victims hide. They're at the mercy of the people, places, and things that remind them of the way their lives have changed. They punish themselves for surviving. It's an unbearable condition, and it lasts as long as they keep choosing it. Here's how the choice goes. As long as you see yourself as a victim, you're lost in chaos. Once you see yourself as a survivor, you can begin to live again. It may not be easy, but it's better than remaining in chaos. The longer you live in the chaos of denial, addictions, and other self-destructive activities, the more certain it is that the wilderness you inhabit at this moment will become your permanent residence.

"I'm fine!" is the automatic response of some survivors. For the individual struggling to move beyond damage and despair, "I'm fine" is a harmful lie. While it's not necessary to share the truth of your condition with anyone else, it *is* essential to acknowledge to yourself that you're *not* fine. To put it bluntly, for the survivor denial is a form of suicide.

Convincing survivors that it's necessary to open themselves to the need for self-acceptance takes time and effort. To live in recovery, to find one's way into a better mode of living, means giving up the denial that most people practice without blinking. But in this wilderness in which you find yourself, being dishonest with yourself can have fatal consequences.

It's another of life's paradoxes. To go beyond your situation, you must accept it for what it is right now. To take the journey, you must start from where you are. If you're going to heal, to become whole again, you'll have to embrace the battered and bleached bones you bring into the wilderness. You may be fine in time, but you're *not* fine now.

Remember what we said in Chapter 1? The word survivor comes from the Latin *supervivere* – to live beyond. Well, it's time to face your crisis and live beyond it.

The guilt response

The guilt you feel for having survived while others have not can imprison you and make you miserable. I've spoken with many survivors who have struggled in countless ways. I've spoken with HIV-positive people who find coping with the disease almost unbearable. But what startled me most was hearing the anger that one survivor directed toward other survivors.

I stayed in Caroline's guest house in Firenze, Italy, in 2003. Caroline spoke Italian fluently, without the slightest trace of her British accent. Her husband, an Italian attorney, had died of cancer in 2001. No longer in mourning, she impressed me as a very competent woman who managed a large household and three beautiful daughters. When I told her about my workshops to help cancer survivors with their recovery, she responded with vehemence: "What do they have to be unhappy about? They're still alive. They should be glad they're alive!" As far as she was concerned, survivors didn't need – or deserve – help.

It's unfortunate that when you believe you don't deserve help, the possibility of your getting it is gone.

When you wake up each morning and confront the fact that others in circumstances like yours have perished, it's difficult to be happy. Survivor guilt can be an insurmountable obstacle for many who have lost people dear to them. "How am I so different from Jim or Barbara or any of them?" you may think, or "How is it that I'm still around and they're gone?"

It's the question that everyone asks in the face of calamity. "Why me?"

This question leads inevitably to another: "Why *not* me?" Instead, ask yourself, "What am I going to do about it?"

Permit yourself to become self-caring instead of self-destroying. You have the ability to care, even in the face of terrifying adversity. The help and support of others is invaluable, but they aren't nearly so crucial as the help and support you can give yourself. When you're a victim, it's easy to wring your hands and "Poor me!" yourself to death. Allow yourself to step beyond this vision of yourself-as-victim. Become yourself-as-survivor and accept the responsibility for living better.

The survivor's way

Survivors don't cloak themselves in the posture and attitudes of victims. They look in the mirror without turning away. They can accept what has happened to them and the chaos that goes with it. Yes, it's painful, but survivors learn to feel the agony instead of denying it.

There's an authentic place within yourself that's waiting to initiate the process of recovery. Choose to live from there. It's where the journey out of the wilderness begins. As vulnerable as you find yourself, help can reach you and you can respond to it.

By accepting the choice to be a survivor, you can begin making your way into recovery. You didn't come into the wilderness without a past. You've made decisions on the basis of ideas, customs and traditions, education, career, relationships, and religion, and you've known successes and failures. You need to value who you are and appreciate what helped you become the person you are. Anything less than this erodes the ground beneath your feet.

To find a way out of the wilderness, you need to build upon that foundation. You're the creation that exists in this moment, you've survived the fire in life's kiln, and you value yourself *and* your life.

When you value something, you embrace it. The value you attach to your life as a survivor is fundamental to your recovery. It's the basis for accepting what you need to grow stronger.

The old rules

All the old rules have changed, and your attitude toward them needs to change. "Taking life for granted" is one of the most basic of the old rules, and it has to go. The truth of mortality is that when we're confronted with the end of living, what has been mundane becomes precious, and what has occupied so many hours of the year becomes trivial. It's as if you've crossed an imaginary line and see things more clearly than you've ever seen them before. This dramatic eye-opener is difficult to describe to anyone who hasn't experienced it.

A superb dramatization of this shift in perception can be found in Thornton Wilder's *Our Town*, a classic 20th-century play about the meaning of life. After her funeral, the spirit of young Emily Gibbs decides to return to her home in Grover's Corners, New Hampshire, to visit the living. Appalled at what she sees, she asks, "Do any human beings ever realize life while they live it? – every, every minute?" Another character in the play answers that perhaps saints and poets do; the rest are just blind.

In seeing the importance of each moment of life, Emily gets to the heart of the matter. She's overwhelmed by the discovery that everyone alive in Grover's Corners is afflicted with a form of blindness. They sleepwalk through life and miss its real gifts. By a painful irony, Emily learns this after her own life has ended and she's in her grave.

You don't have to be numbered among Wilder's saints and poets to appreciate the truth of Emily's revelation. For survivors, this is a fact of life in the wilderness. You awaken to the awareness that what you've been taking for granted is, in fact, very special. Life is a gift beyond comparison, and your gratitude for it is boundless. It's an amazing paradox. In order to truly appreciate life, you need almost to lose it.

In the wilderness, survivors begin to understand the need for engaging in activities they haven't pursued before. People who have never joined any-thing become members of support groups. They volunteer at hospitals and churches, and with charities that benefit the community. They offer help to others who are making their own journeys.

As you come to value your life, you begin to value others who no longer take their lives for granted there in the wilderness. You accept responsibility for yourself and for others.

In October 2000, near the end of my radiation and chemotherapy treat-ments, I thought about my experience of writing journals for forty-five years, my training as a counselor, and my cancer diagnosis, and how this could be useful to others. This is my journal entry:

> I have gotten a handle on the idea for writing workshops that will help others. The entire effort for me will be called "INVOCATION." All life is sacred ground, and the effort to step across the threshold of the ordinary with words that present me to the world, to the higher, to God, is what writing a journal is all about.

Katherine Mansfield, at the end of her life, wrote in her journal that she was terrified she'd not be able to show one of her stories to God! That IS what journal writing is all about – showing ourselves to God. And I believe this rings true for everyone who has ever faced a life-ending crisis. At the core of each of us is a belief that we have the profound potential to be as completely developed, evolved, as possible in this life we have been given. Many of us feel that we have come up far short of what we may have thought of as reaching even a modest degree of our potential.

Simone Weil, an existentialist philosopher, wrote a phrase in the 1950s that resonated deeply within my soul at that time and, in fact, never ceased resonating in my life as the years have added to each other. She wrote of the desperate condition in which a person is unable to reach out to God, a condition she called '*réfut a l'invocation.*' It was a place I knew well, for I had struggled and suffered in this place for what seemed like an endless interval after leaving the seminary in 1950. Then, somehow, through an act of grace for which I have been profoundly grateful through the remaining years, I was able to begin to invoke.

It is with the words themselves, puny, imprecise, often merely approximations of the innermost wish to express what is in the heart, that anyone crosses the threshold to a relationship with God, with others, with ourselves. And this invocation opens us to healing ourselves from whatever it is that is harmed, broken, or diseased. And as we learn to develop this connection, this bond – I and thou become one instead of separate and isolated, and we begin to see that we have been put here on earth to understand and participate in this relationship. The ground of being on which we have stood is sacred ground, and the quest that many of us pilgrims have gone in search of is right here, right now, right all-and-everything. It is the fabric of our daily lives.

Putting the pen to the page to write of this experience of what it means to live in our bodies, in our relationships, in the house and city and world where we breathe each breath, is the key to opening the door to life and a better way to live it.

The medical model has significant limitations as we have seen with other kinds of recovery programs. Taking a personal and active role in creating health is essential for the healing process. Writing is action of a very personal nature. It involves engaging the use of imagination, intuition, the unconscious, and the conscious. And it acknowledges the self that needs to be the recipient of healing.

I will call it *Write for Life*, and it will be a series of journal-writing experiences in which everyone who participates can explore how he lives daily, how he can participate more fully in the experience, and how he can discover what is necessary to heal himself with his own wisdom. It will enable everyone to share personal insights of every nature so that others, also, may benefit from what someone else has learned. Both the writing and the sharing will provide an opportunity for healing. And it may also be possible that insights and ideas from these sessions may prove useful in working with other support groups or with counselors.

The result has been several hundred workshops with participants who felt encouraged to begin their journeys into healing. From these workshops came the book you're holding in your hands. The journal that you're writing now is your journey into the discovery of new insights about yourself.

Elie Wiesel has written profoundly about Holocaust survivors, of which he is one. His understanding of the psyche of survivors reveals truths about the conditions of being that lie at the heart of darkness. Survivors of any tragedy or disaster can embrace Wiesel's ideas and explore them in journal entries, for they offer the key to healing and recovery. He says:

A survivor's testimony is more important than anything that can be written about survivors. It's important for them, important for the world. And for me, that is the most rewarding thing – to free, to open up the survivors. They live clandestinely. What made their being most unique was something they hid. That is most tragic – to suffer and then to suffer for having suffered.

When you begin writing in your journal, the time for hiding your suffering is ended. When you allow yourself to write in your journal today, tomorrow, and the day after that, you begin the healing that every survivor needs.

Chapter 5
Journal Excerpts

The odysseys of other journal writers

Men, women, and children from many different countries and cultures have used journals to record their thoughts. Their motivations for writing may reflect your decision to keep a journal. What's special in the following excerpts is that these writers were confronting significant obstacles over which they had little if any control. The lifeline their journals gave them was what prompted them to write.

One of the best-known journal writers of the 20th century was **Anne Frank** (1929-1944). *The Diary of a Young Girl* is known the world over. When the Nazis occupied Amsterdam in the early 1940s, Anne, her family, and four other people went into hiding to escape being sent to a concentration camp. For two years, they lived in a few small rooms hidden in an office building. While Anne's journal is filled with the terror of possible discovery, at the same time it's the story of a young girl aching to experience a normal school life with friends. She turned to her diary to make her life endurable.

To take the place of the friend she desperately wanted, Anne invented one, writing: "Saturday, 20 June, 1942. I don't want to set down a series of bald facts in a diary like most people do, but I want this diary itself to be my friend, and I shall call my friend Kitty."

The invention of an alter ego made it easier for her to begin a dialogue that over the years flowed as a conversation between different voices within herself. This conversational device has been used by many other journal writers.

In their 1975 book *Revelations – Diaries of Women*, editors Mary Jane Moffat and Charlotte Painter offer a trove of excerpts of journaled works, categorized under the headings of "Love," "Work," and "Power." Entries from these journals offer a tantalizing array of insights into their writers' lives. Here are a few details to whet the appetite.

Marjorie Fleming (1803-1811) was another very young journal writer. Only 7 years old when her cousin and tutor, Isabella Keith, gave her the task of keeping a diary, she wrote about how excited she was to go for a walk with a young gentleman, calling herself "his loveress" and hoping that she'd never forget him. In her journal, this passionate child confronts her feelings and emotions with amazing intensity. A meningitis attack killed Marjorie before her 10th year. Only in her imagination and through the words she set down in her journal did she experience a fleeting taste of young love, and those same words ring with authenticity today.

A repressive culture was the obstacle crushing an anonymous Japanese woman who lived from 1866 until 1900. She left a brief journal, translated by **Lafcadio Hearn**. At age 29, she entered an arranged marriage with a poor man. Though for her this was preferable to remaining single, she still had to resolve her repressed feelings about being a woman expected to perform her duties without complaint. Her terrible sadness grew as she struggled to please her husband without success; each year, she bore him another infant; each year, the child died. She feared that her husband's aversion for her would grow, that the deaths of her children were punishment for some deed of her own. The anxiety she felt made her anxious about the man she had married.

The death of her third newborn was the final event that even her writing could not help her reconcile. She died two weeks later.

This anonymous Japanese woman was married to an ordinary man. Marriage to an extraordinary man can be much tougher. Consider **Anna Dostoyevski** (1846-1918) and **Sophie Tolstoy** (1844-1919), who were married to two of the most significant Russian writers of the 19th century. Each woman wrote about her difficult home life.

Anna had been Dostoevski's stenographer and was in awe of his genius. He was a 46-year-old widower; she was in her 20s. After a trying love affair with another woman, he proposed to Anna, who accepted immediately. The newlyweds left Russia soon after to avoid the hounding of his creditors and began a gypsylike trek through the cities and casinos of Europe. In shorthand, Anna recorded the miseries she endured along the way. She knew that no one could read what she'd written and therefore felt free to express her despair over her husband's gambling addiction and his inability to feel love for her. Across the years, her words echo the pain of being in a relationship with an addict and the hopelessness of living with such an overwhelming problem day in and day out.

Like Anna, Sophie Tolstoy was much younger than her husband. It's possible that his sexual compulsion was the basis of her despair. In spite of the fact that she bore him thirteen children, his lust created a barrier between them. This and the political ideas he gradually developed drove her further from him. She turned to journal writing when she felt depressed and frightened. And she started reading his diaries, looking for clues to his state of mind, until he found out and hid them from her, deepening her despair.

Ruth Benedict (1887-1948), formerly Ruth Fulton, was an anthropologist before marrying Stanley Benedict. In her journal she recorded her motivation for writing, the need to help herself rebalance after a traumatic year. Over the years, she wrote her way out of her depression and ultimately came to believe in the value of her life.

Kathe Kollwitz (1867-1945) was a graphic artist and sculptor whose life was greatly affected by the death of her young son in World War I. In looking over her old diaries, she discovered that she had written only when life was disrupted and difficult. Yet in retrospect she saw that the period in which she wrote was one that she remembered as the best in her life. Her diaries originally provided a safe place to express her feelings. Later they offered a perspective on her history that might otherwise have been lost.

Alice James (1848-1892), sister of Henry and William James, suffered from periods of deep depression. (At the age of 30, she even asked her father for permission to commit suicide.) After arriving in London in 1884 to visit Henry, she had a nervous breakdown. For the rest of her life she lived with Katherine Peabody Loring, her friend and nurse. In 1889, she began writing a journal as an outlet for her wit and energy. A diagnosis of breast cancer gave a specific focus to her writing. She found relief in the expression of "this geyser of emotions, sensations, speculations and reflections which ferments perpetually within my poor old carcass for its sins."

Confrontation with the medical profession is a recurring theme among journal writers. Published in 2000, *Sweet Blood and Fury*, by **Mary Frances**

Connors, began as a journal in 1968. "I wrote to untangle my jumbled thoughts with the hope of understanding my persistent anger, depression and feelings of separateness," she notes in her book. A diagnosis of diabetes had devastated her. Writing in her journal gave her the support to witness to her pain and suffering, and the courage to persevere.

Virginia Woolf (1882-1941) wrote twenty-six volumes of journals, but the 1953 publication edited by her husband, Leonard Woolf, includes only selections that deal directly with her writing. If you'd like to learn more about her battle with manic depression, you'll have to research the journals themselves, which aren't easily available. The mental illness with which she struggled is a significant dimension of these journals. While there are many entries about the despair she felt on reading her manuscripts, it was the despair she felt about her life and the terror of madness that ultimately led her to suicide.

Fleeing New Zealand and the constraints imposed by her rigid father, **Katherine Mansfield** made her way to England, where homesickness and regret over the separation from her family weighed on her heavily. In her journals, she wrote about her memories of people and places in New Zealand with a vividness that revealed how much she missed what she had left behind.

In addition to the suffering she experienced when her husband, John Middleton Murry, abandoned her, she also struggled bravely against tuberculosis, writing compellingly about both experiences in her journal. On December 19, 1920, grieving the loss of her marriage, she wrote: "Life is a mystery. The fearful pain will fade. I must turn to work. I must put my agony into something, change it. 'Sorrow shall be changed into joy.' It is to lose oneself more utterly, to love more deeply, to feel oneself part of life – not separate."

Many men as well as women have used journals to explore themselves and life. Novelist, playwright, and essayist **Andre Gide** was one of the most prolific journal writers who ever lived. He revealed in a journal entry dated December 31, 1891, his view of writing as an act of self-confrontation. "When one has begun to write, the hardest thing is to be sincere ... The fear of not being sincere has been tormenting me for several months and preventing me from writing. Oh, to be utterly and perfectly sincere."

Gide confronted his sincerity and honesty every time he picked up his pen. Neither his private life nor his internal life was off-limits. For many writers, the journal is their opportunity to be honest with themselves – the greatest test of all.

In 1895, army officer **Alfred Dreyfus** was sent to Devil's Island under a sentence of treason. Dreyfus was a Jew hounded by French anti-Semites, who used bogus circumstantial evidence to condemn him as a traitor. He knew he was innocent, yet could do nothing to prove it. His diary reveals a man overwhelmed by the slander that destroyed his honor and reputation.

> I am so utterly weary, so broken down in body and soul, that today I stop my diary, not being able to foresee how long my strength will hold out or what day my brain will succumb under the weight of so great a burden.
> [A Book of One's Own, *Thomas Mallon, Tichnor & Fields, New York, 1984*, p. 253]

Another prisoner, **Alfred Kantor**, created a journal of drawings to commemorate the three and a half years he lived in the Terezin, Auschwitz, and Schwarzheide Nazi concentration camps. The narrative that accompanies his sketches pales beside the horror of the scenes he depicted in his drawings. This startling book has been reprinted several times, which is some indication of how many others have drawn strength from his effort to survive. Even though he knew there was no chance of getting his sketchbooks out of Auschwitz, he was determined to keep a continuous record. "And, once drawn, these scenes could never be erased from my mind."

The front note of Kantor's book is a brief passage from *"J'Accuse!"* by **Émile Zola**, a defender of Dreyfus, which appeared in the French newspaper *L'Aurore*, January 13, 1898: "Since they have dared, I too shall dare. I shall tell the truth because I pledged myself to tell it … My duty is to speak; I have no wish to be an accomplice." Speaking out against injustice and oppression is a great motivation for journal writing. The cleansing effect of such writing can be intense.

Albert Speer kept extensive diaries during the many years of his incarceration for war crimes after the Nuremberg trials. He could admit the moral guilt of his actions, but the legal guilt was something he struggled with. He asks himself whether he could have survived twenty years in prison "if I had not been permitted to write a single line?" Writing helped him to endure.

One of the most extensive journals published was written by **Arthur Crew Inman** (1895-1963). He survived nervous breakdowns, neurasthenia, paralysis, depression, influenza, sprains, encounters with doctors, and a lifetime as a semi-invalid, writing 10 million words in his diary all the while, until the demolition of the buildings around his sanctuary in Boston compromised his security completely and he finally shot himself. His journals had been his reason for living. "Rather perish than sleep, dream again," he wrote on October 25, 1963.

In 1982, **Randy Shilts** began reporting on AIDS in the *San Francisco Chronicle*. With the aid of Michael Denneny of St. Martin's Press, he turned these entries into the classic *And the Band Played On*. It was written to gather all the pieces of the AIDS epidemic together, "so that it will never happen again, to any people, anywhere." The prologue states:

> The bitter truth was that AIDS did not just happen to America – it was allowed to happen by an array of institutions, all of which failed to perform their appropriate tasks to safeguard the public health. This failure of the system leaves a legacy of unnecessary suffering that will haunt the Western world for decades to come.

The revelation of the shame and degradation endured by gays and lesbians was continued in Shilts' *Conduct Unbecoming*. By then, the journal was no longer a private document but a published demand for changes in the behavior of American society. The purpose of his books was to raise a hue and cry, and his candor opened many people's eyes.

An intimate journal won the Pulitzer Prize, the National Book Critics Circle Award, the *Los Angeles Times* Book Prize, and the Abby Award. Published in 1996, *Angela's Ashes*, by **Frank McCourt**, made literary history, addressing with its humor and lyrical language the brutal poverty he endured as a child as well as his experience of his father's alcoholism and his mother's codependency.

Frank had been writing journals about his life in Ireland for years. They helped him put into perspective the deprivation and hardship he faced. Journal writing also sustained him through many years in a contentious marriage and gave him invaluable insights he could apply to his efforts as an English teacher helping to kindle the creativity of his New York City high school students, who challenged him constantly. His writing gave him a different understanding of himself and raised the question, "If it has made me more alive, will it do the same for others?" Taking his journals from their comfortable place in a drawer, Frank let them become the inspiration for *Angela's Ashes*, *'Tis*, and *Teacher Man*, books that won for him the kind of attention that exceeded his wildest dreams.

This chapter identifies only a handful of writers who confronted obstacles over which they had no control. There have been many more. Writing a journal is one way to help you begin examining unresolved issues and problems in your life that need attention. Reading this brief survey of journal excerpts is another way to begin to explore feelings and emotions you've known in your own life. There are survivors everywhere, and knowing that they turned to their journals for healing may offer reassurance and a sense of companionship for your journey.

Chapter 6
Scientific Research and Writing Techniques

Scientists researching the effects of journal writing are discovering that self-expression promotes healing in the body, mind, and spirit. How does writing create healing? Let's look at some of these researchers' findings.

Pennebaker's "letting go"

James W. Pennebaker, who recognized the link between psychological events and recurring health problems, presented his innovative findings in *Opening Up: The Healing Power of Expressing Emotions*. In the book's first chapter, "Confession and Inhibition," he presents a framework he calls a "holding back-letting go continuum."

This framework recognizes the physiological effort that is required to inhibit thought, feelings, or behavior. When we attempt to hold back or ignore our reactions to meaningful events, we experience bodily stress, which unleashes short- and long-term biological changes. These changes, in turn, increase our chances of becoming physically or psychologically ill. Also, when we refuse to address an experience by acknowledging and talking about it, we fail to deal with it "in an integrative way," a process that depends on language. What we refuse to address directly is forced out in dreams, obsessive thoughts, or other types of disrupted mental processes.

Pennebaker points out that we can overcome these effects by confronting our experiences rather than avoiding or denying them. When we deal with our reactions to events by examining and talking about them, we gradually reduce our stress levels, because we're processing the experiences in a way that promotes understanding and assimilation.

Pennebaker studied the effect of writing on rape victims, people with eating disorders, and those with traumas caused by the accidental death of a spouse or job loss, among others. He discovered that the mental and physical health of such groups as schoolchildren, nursing-home residents, arthritis sufferers, medical-school students, maximum-security prisoners, new mothers, and rape victims improved when they wrote about their emotional upheavals.

People who wrote about traumatic experiences felt a distinct benefit when they expressed their deepest thoughts and feelings, compared with those who wrote only about their superficial concerns. Those who wrote more honestly actually displayed "heightened immune function, compared with those who wrote about superficial topics," Pennebaker noted.

In his studies of brain-wave activity during the writing process, he found that when people wrote about their emotional traumas, the brain-wave activity on the left and right sides of the head was correlated much more closely than during periods of thought about trivial topics. In other words, when individuals confronted difficult topics and then wrote about them, their brains began finding ways of helping them manage those problems.

Consider the implications of this: Writing releases us from the prison of our thoughts. We all have unwanted thoughts that surface soon after we experience a trauma or when we're reminded of a trauma that once occurred. But instead of confronting this trauma and allowing our minds to begin forming a coping strategy, we suppress the thoughts, the issue stays unresolved, and we become depressed. "Making an unacceptable thought acceptable is the first step to healthy thinking," says Pennebaker.

In *Opening Up*, he cites Freud's discussion of the maneuvers practiced by the human mind in the face of profound anxiety. To Freud, denial, suppression, obsessions, and other such defense mechanisms were similar in nature to "low-level thinking strategies." Distinguishing between "mindless" versus "mindful" thinking processes, he said, "When people are mindless, they are rigid in their thinking and cannot appreciate novel approaches to problems. When mindful, people are active problem solvers, looking at the world from a variety of perspectives … In a very real sense, mindlessness makes us stupid. Mindfulness makes us smarter."

In addition, the memory and value of the event have been preserved. "In the computer world," says Pennebaker, "this is analogous to downloading – where information previously residing in the chips of the computer or on the Internet is transferred to diskettes or printed on paper so it can be saved elsewhere." Similarly, downloading traumas into the journal offers the first step to recovery.

Writing in a journal, however, will not take the place of medical treatment, even though it may assist the recovery process. It can be considered "preventive maintenance," and its value, says Pennebaker, "lies in reducing the work of inhibition and in organizing our complicated mental and emotional lives. Writing helps keep our psychological compass oriented. Although it is not a panacea, writing can be an inexpensive, simple, and sometimes painful way to help maintain our health."

From Pennebaker's breakthrough discoveries, many other researchers have gone on to study the effects of self-expressive writing on health and well-being.

Ongoing scientific research

Publication of this exciting research can be found in two books that are easily accessible: *Emotion, Disclosure, and Health*, edited by James W. Pennebaker, and *The Writing Cure: How Expressive Writing Promotes Health and Emotional Well-Being*, edited by Stephen Lepore and Joshua Smyth. (See "Resources," pages 255 and 256-257.)

Here are some of the findings that appear in these books:

- Writing about traumatic experiences leads to improved immune function, fewer visits to physicians for illness, and better performance in school and at work.

- Writing about traumas results in reduction of blood pressure, muscle tension, and skin-conductance during or immediately after the disclosure. A significant link is forged between written disclosure and health that is not formed when one is merely talking about worries. (This holds true even in comparison with as many as twelve therapy sessions.)

- People who experience stressful life events and patients suffering from hypertension, chronic pain, asthma, rheumatoid arthritis, and cancer experience a decrease in physical symptoms when they practice expressive writing.

- Healthy and chronic-pain patients who become aware of their deepest emotional secrets or pains open the door to measurable positive changes and healing.
- Social relationships are enhanced. The freedom to reveal traumatic events without concern for the effect on someone else is extremely beneficial to the individual and has a beneficial effect on relations with others.
- Writing about a stressful problem evokes positive emotions and increases skill-building behaviors. Happiness triggers social abilities, which strengthen social ties.
- Women who were relatively optimistic found writing about a positive future lowered their distress level and made them pay more attention to their medication.
- Writing produced the fastest transition from one emotional state to another; for example, people who were anxious or suffering became relaxed after a writing session.
- Expressive writing has a direct influence on improving memory. Stressful life events hinder thought processes, and expressive writing can restore them.
- Finding something good in negative life experiences helps individuals disengage from past traumas and aids in personal growth.
- Writing about their life goals made people feel happier. They also got sick less often.

As you pick up your pen to write, consider Pennebaker's insights into the value of using writing for self-healing. He suggests that the process makes you think about your life – something many people scarcely do. You can honestly take stock of your past and consider your future without feeling accountable to someone else, since only you will see your words. It's an opportunity to discern the predominant themes framing your personal experience, to decide what's important to you and what you want out of life, and to think about the person you've become. (More on this can be found in *The Writing Cure*, by Lepore and Smyth; see "Resources," page 255.)

In 2004, Pennebaker published *Writing to Heal: A Guided Journal for Recovering from Trauma and Emotional Upheaval*. He offers many useful suggestions for dealing with traumatic events and helping you move on from them into a fuller, more integrated life. I encourage you to use your own journal to explore as much freedom of expression as possible. Reach out to explore both the traumas and the triumphs of your life, and gain access to all areas of body, mind, and spirit.

Other journal-writing approaches: Julia Cameron

The Artist's Way: A Spiritual Path to Higher Creativity, published in 1992 by Julia Cameron, is a guide for artists and writers who want to explore themselves and their creative side. In her systematic approach, Cameron encourages readers to write three pages every day and use the experiences of their lives to support their artistic endeavors, whether by writing, painting, dancing, photography, ceramics, or other means. Many have used this nurturing book to enter a new dimension of creativity and the spiritual life.

These are some excerpts of entries from my own journal that I wrote about the experience of using *The Artist's Way*.

> September 12, 1996.
> She [Cameron] insists on three pages of writing each morning, and I remember that it is quite a while since I put in three days, one after another in entries. And, when I did, lots of stuff that was in the way got cleared out and I was more able to get on with the projects – writing and other-wise – that needed to be done, or that I wanted to do.
>
> Somehow, clearing out all the stuff that clogs up the works is a very healthy and creative-juices-encouraging method. I found this was true back in 1976 when I was desperately struggling with the effects of the drugs and alcohol follow-ing an auto accident. So, once again picking up the good practice, I will embark on a regular program of writing here anything and everything that flows through my brain.

September 13

The effect of these pages seems to change the priority of things that might otherwise seem of greater significance than they are ... I have not taken nearly enough time or care with my writing – my stories, or my recovery book [*Accepting Ourselves & Others*]. If this is, indeed, of value to me, then I must use my energy on it. The artist's way is through his art. An artist "arts." To this end, these pages. This is what it takes to get back on track and living through writing and not just the scenario of the ever-changing daily events of business and politics.

September 18

A brief check-in re morning pages: since beginning last Thursday, I've written every day. Yesterday was the first day I simply allowed my hand to write without any preparation from me. I have not done my "Artist Date" [a date you make with yourself to go to a museum, see a play, walk in nature, etc.] this week; arrange it! Other issues in my increased creativity are the beginning of revisions, already a revised first draft of Chapter 1 of *Undeceived* [a novel I was writing at the time], and a great deal more energy to direct into creative projects.

Cameron emphasizes the need of the child in all artists to be nurtured. I have been very clearly aware of the fact, for most of my life, that artists who are well received are terribly productive. They give more back. With a small circle of support, it is possible to thrive on this kind of nurture that primes the pump of creative projects. The "sacred circle" we are forming can do this. [Cameron recommends getting a small group of people to form this "sacred circle" in order to go through the entire series of exercises in the book.]

September 26
As much as is possible for me to do it, I want to encourage young artists, old artists, and those who are afraid to be artists to explore their creativity and evolve beyond the moment on the circle they now see themselves. To free the consciousness(es) of everyone to be the creative witnesses to life that it is possible for them to be.

Sept. 17
The way forward is through the infinite reaches of your heart. It is always an opportunity to explore, both yourself as well as the world around you. What you discover is always of value for your personal evolution, and if it supports and encourages this, it will also support and encourage others who come in contact with you.

Fear is the great inhibitor. When I find myself afraid, for whatever reason, I must ask myself not only, "Of what?" but also, "Of whom?" I am waiting for myself around each curve of the spiral as it ascends/descends. The tangents I take, as long as I return to the circle, are merely pauses, beats along the journey. I have a long way to travel, and I need not concern myself at this time about the duration of my effort. What I need to be about is the journey itself.

Yes, I am resisting the challenge of writing; yet it is time to appreciate the significance of this area in my life as I consider how to use my energy at this time. Do not resist. Write!!!

Within everyone may be a sleeping or unborn artist, Cameron believes, and anyone who identifies with this buried artist must be willing to undertake the spiritual journey, which is filled with inspiration.

Natalie Goldberg

Natalie Goldberg's two books, *Writing Down the Bones: Freeing the Writer Within* and *Wild Mind*, explore the practice of writing and the kinds of efforts anyone who wants to be a writer can undertake in order to learn the craft of writing. Writers need to write, Goldberg says, and her book is filled with challenging exercises that help writers mine their experiences and turn them into words on paper.

Ira Progoff

For more than a quarter of a century, Ira Progoff has been developing work-shops and seminars on journal writing. *At a Journal Workshop* is, to quote Joseph Campbell's cover quote, "one of the greatest inventions of our time." Having spoken with people who have attended Dr. Progoff's workshops, I know that they are life-changing experiences.

Each of the 422 pages of *At a Journal Workshop* is filled with encourage-ment, prescriptions, and advice about journal writing. Though I found his approach a bit daunting, I know others enjoy the Progoff method. His focus is personal growth and renewal, and the elaborate program he presents is designed to help writers reap positive results.

Kay Leigh Hagan and others

A more intimate book is *Internal Affairs: A Journalkeeping Workbook for Self-Intimacy*, by Kay Leigh Hagan, a journal-keeper of twenty years, who has also led workshops for eight years. The workbook format she provides for the reader makes it possible to write one's own book. Her interest in oracles, such as the Tarot and I Ching, injects an interesting dimension into the practice of journal writing.

JourneyNotes: Writing for Recovery and Spiritual Growth, by Richard Solly and Roseann Lloyd, was published in 1989 and is no longer in print, though used copies can be ordered at www.amazon.com. Even with its focus on individuals in Twelve-Step recovery programs, anyone can use her valuable ideas and suggestions for the process of journal writing.

Twelve-step-program journals

Many books have been written for participants in twelve-step programs to encourage journal writing as a way to move beyond addictive/compulsive behavior into healing and recovery. They are very useful for getting at the hidden causes of life-threatening conditions. Hazelden publishes many of these guides.

This third "Window on Healing" has discussed scientific research into the psychological and physiological benefits of journal writing, and has looked at some different approaches. Feel free to compare and contrast other approaches to journal writing with the Write for Life program offered in this book. My greatest hope is that every *Write for Life* reader will find it possible to begin today to experience the healing process of journal writing.

Chapter 7
Healing the Survivor

Elinor

Elinor was one of the first people I met when I joined a cancer support group right after I heard my diagnosis. When she told her story in the group, I was struck with how matter-of-factly she spoke and the feistiness in her voice. She'd just been told by her oncologist that she didn't have long to live. This pronouncement in no way interfered with the daily full-to-bursting schedule she maintained. She wasn't going to allow anything — even a fatal diagnosis — to stand in the way of enjoying life.

Elinor had an amazing number of interests, many of them with a spiritual focus. In addition to the theater, to which she was devoted, she participated in a folksinging group and went camping with them. She invited me to meetings of the Jane Austen Society, which I joined and now attend regularly. She went to dinner every evening with her friends. She told me that she'd written journals for years, but at some point she'd stopped. When I spoke of the Write for Life program, she said that she missed writing, so she joined my group in 2001.

Two of my most vivid memories of her concerned not the group but other public events. Our support group had a Christmas celebration at a large restaurant run by people in recovery. Elinor had come out of the hospital a few days before this and had been unable to eat. Nevertheless, she made plans to come to our event. Carole, the facilitator of the group, drove her. During the meal, Elinor began to have severe pains and before dinner was over, she rested her head on the table. It occurred to me that not attending the celebration would have given her *more* pain than what she experienced in front of us.

The following week, she was back in the group as if nothing had happened. The doctors, she said, had just told her she now had only three more months to live. Over the next weeks, she missed a group meeting now and then because of another event on her calendar or a doctor's appointment, but by the time spring arrived, she was ready to attend a staged reading of the play I'd written. During the course of the reading, Elinor was in so much pain sitting on the uncomfortable seat that she had to lie down on the floor. But the play went on. During intermission, Julie, another woman in the group, drove Elinor home.

Following this, there was a string of other predictions about how long Elinor had to live, none forecasting more than three months. With incredible determination, she refused to allow anything to stand in the way of whatever she wanted. Her frequent stays in the hospital were brief, and each time she emerged she seemed more energetic than ever. Everyone in the group marveled at her recuperative powers.

In the spring of 2002 she died, but not before becoming an icon of courage and resiliency for all of us. She is with me today as I write about the life-enhancing connection between body, mind, and spirit. Her body, as far as the doctors' predictions were concerned, was a lost cause, but that was merely information that applied to one aspect of her existence. She believed that she was

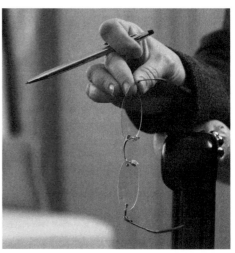

more than just her body, and she never hesitated to prove it to herself and others every day.

Elinor survived, year after year, as many others do also. In 1993, the Institute of Noetic Sciences published a survey titled *Spontaneous Remission: An Annotated Bibliography*. It covers many cases of people who survived for years after being told they had not long to live. Each time I hear someone tell me of a terminal prediction like that, I'm reminded of Mark Twain's cable from Europe to the Associated Press: "The reports of my death are greatly exaggerated."

Physicians of every ilk often stand in amazement at the seemingly miraculous changes that occur in their patients, for which they have no explanation. The body alone doesn't hold all the answers. Healing, we're learning, depends upon the connection between the body and the mind, the body and the spirit, and the mind and the spirit. This is why healing is both a science and an art.

New – or old – ideas

The vital mind-body-spirit interconnection has gained greater acceptance, partly due to increased interest in the medical practices of the Asian and Indian cultures, which embrace the mind-body-spirit connection. Just as Søren Kierkegaard wrote about the need for a "leap of faith" in matters of religious belief, others are taking that leap in their need to heal the body.

The Directory of Complementary Therapies (2002), edited by Viv Croot, contains several chapters on different kinds of alternative therapies that involve touch, yoga, art, the mind, manipulation, and eastern therapies. Fifty years ago, a health-oriented compendium wouldn't have offered information like this. Obviously, there's been a revolution in the world of treatment.

Unfortunately, *The Directory of Complementary Therapies* doesn't include journal writing in its "arts therapies" section. In light of the tremendous significance of self-expression on health and recovery, this omission is surprising. When people tell me all the things they're doing to heal, I'm amazed to hear that they never considered journal writing as part of their treatment. If they have the time to use these alternative therapies, they also have the time to write about it.

What it takes to heal

A simple illustration will help you understand what the healing process requires. Take, for example, a paper cut on the tip of the finger. What a tiny injury – yet how painful it is when it occurs. It happens when I'm not expecting it at all. Still, if I don't pay attention to it, there could be even more pain or even infection, so I apply antiseptic or a bandage to the site in order to speed its recovery. With attention and care, the cut heals without even leaving a mark, and I forget entirely about it – until the next paper cut.

A great deal has been written about paying attention in this book. For now, the paper cut serves as a metaphor for an injury that has been healed.

But there have been other physical, emotional, and spiritual experiences that you've undergone throughout your life that have injured you in ways that, in some instances, have left permanent scars or affected certain aspects of your being. As James Pennebaker's research with rape victims showed, writing initiates a deeper healing process. As painful as it was at first to confront the anguish of their feelings, those who had written about them were better able over time to go on with their lives than those who had not.

Getting on with your life is, for some, a matter of suppressing the source of the distress. But denial works for only so long, and when it stops working, you're faced with the need to change.

Attitude toward healing

You take for granted the way you *think* about healing. It's only when the way you've chosen isn't working, you're faced with an operation for which you're totally unprepared, or you learn of attractive alternatives others have chosen that you realize you can step outside the box you've been living in and benefit from a new way of thinking. I'm not advocating the use of any particular complementary therapy. I'm suggesting that the way you *think* about healing has everything to do with the process itself.

Benign neglect is a very common attitude. If you ignore the pain or problem, it will go away, right? You've been schooled from your earliest years to hide anything that might appear as weakness. (Consider the many related expressions. Tough it out. Chill out. Keep a stiff upper lip. Stonewall. Dummy up. Stay cool.) This works for some people – until they realize with dismay that what might have been a simple procedure is now a hospitalization with long-term consequences or worse. Their neglect may even prove fatal.

In spite of our cultural tendency to make a virtue of denial, it's impossible to watch any television show that doesn't show ad after ad for pain medication. The drug companies know that many people have some sort of pain or condition they believe they should medicate. Perhaps they don't talk about it with others, but they do medicate themselves – often in secret, because they're horrified at the thought of identifying themselves as alcoholics or drug addicts. (It's a familiar story. "When saintly Aunt Mary passed away, the empty bottles of cough medicine down in the basement were too numerous to count. She took the secret of her habit to the grave.")

I learned of homeopathy in 1960, as a professor at Long Island University in New York. A friend there observed me constantly swallowing pills to control my ulcer and told me about Dr. James Stephenson, a homeopathic physician. I decided to visit him.

When we met, I asked how he'd become a homeopath, since I'd never met one. He told me that as a prisoner of war during World War II, he suffered an acute attack of appendicitis. Surgical facilities at the prison camp were inadequate, and no drugs were available to prevent infection or pain. The Germans offered him this blunt choice: Use homeopathy or die.

Needless to say, he made the right decision, and upon his return to the United States he enrolled in the Weill Medical College of Cornell University as a student of homeopathy. His life-or-death experience resonated with me and I became his patient. His approach to treating my ulcer put an immediate and permanent end to the condition. I found other homeopaths when I moved to other cities and have continued to enjoy the benefits of this specialized treatment over the decades.

Encountering Dr. Stephenson was an accident. Many people aren't as fortunate as I was to be introduced to the right system of healing at the right time. It's your responsibility to discover as much as possible about the cause of your illness and the treatments available. Fortunately, the Internet has put a wealth of information at your fingertips. This resource has changed the lives of many who, previously, might have remained in the dark.

Hopelessness

An attitude of hope is crucial to the healing process. Without it, nothing is possible. If you believe you're hopeless, you *are* hopeless. And that's the biggest roadblock on the road to recovery.

Think of the first step of any twelve-step program: "We admit we were powerless over [fill in the blank] – that our lives have become unmanageable." Only after the acknowledgment of powerlessness can the following steps be taken. Paradoxically, once you acknowledge yourself as powerless, you become powerful enough to ask for help.

When you're hopeless, you aren't able to recognize help because you believe there is no help. You feel like a victim, someone nobody wants to help. Healing begins with acceptance, and hope creates the possibility of healing. The moment hope enters, the possibilities of healing rally themselves on all sides. This change in dynamic is the root cause of the recovery that countless "terminal" patients have experienced. (The diagnosis "terminal" is itself deadly, and many people have condemned its use. It encourages hopelessness, and hopelessness is not an attitude to live by.)

Readiness

Elinor, the cancer patient we met at the beginning of this chapter, was receptive to help from every source she could find. And in turn, she offered help to everyone she met. She never felt under a sentence of death and loss; her days were filled with life and healing. Even when she died, her appointment book was full. She was ready to live, and readiness is what healing requires.

Many cultures and religions use a symbolic act called "laying on of hands" to bring healing to an individual suffering from physical or emotional pain, and this intervention has encouraged healing in many who have received it. Being ready for and open to the possibility of healing is the attitude that's necessary for healing to work.

Four years after I sustained an injury from a freak accident, my friend Fernando took me high into the mountains of Puerto Rico to visit an ancient *santera* – a woman healer with a great reputation. At the time, I didn't know what was in store for me, but the constant ache in my legs and back was making me desperate for relief. The woman greeted me in Spanish and spoke at length with my friend. Then she told him to seat me before a little altar in the corner of her room. She lit several candles and laid her hand on the base of my spine where I'd been injured. She recited several sentences in Spanish and then dismissed us, saying that she was very tired and needed to rest. We left and returned to Isla Verde where, for the next few days, I felt an unusual kind of warmth exactly at the place she had touched. As the pain became less intense, I accepted the possibility that my agony could diminish. I crossed the threshold of hope; somehow her effort stimulated in me a belief in the healing process.

I wrote about this experience in my journal and began to understand what was buried within me. She reminded me that I was more than my pain. Pain and despair had shut me off from enjoying my life. Wanting to end the hopelessness I felt about my condition opened me to my inner self, my intuition. Writing in my journal, I began to pay more attention to all the connections essential to healing: the body, emotions, mind, and spirit.

Paying attention

When you exercise, you pay attention to the way your body moves. When you pick up a brush to paint, you're aware of your creativity. When you love someone, you pay attention to your emotional reactions to them. When you sleep, you receive powerful symbolic information through dreams, which you can explore when you awaken. (Chapter 13 offers some tools for working with this rich source of intuition.)

Emily Gibbs' lines in Thornton Wilder's *Our Town* remind us to wake up and stop losing out on life. She tells us to start *paying attention* to life. All too often it's only when a shock occurs, such as a frightening diagnosis or the death of a loved one, that we remember this.

Back in 2000, writing daily in my journal was definitely responsible for my conscious attention to the persistent symptoms I was experiencing. Paying attention made it possible for me to connect those symptoms with the memory of my brother's and father's cancer.

Sometimes you know things without knowing that you know them. It usually takes some event to ring that little bell in your head. When you let yourself make these connections in your journal writing, you tap into your intuition and begin to live a better, more complete life.

Healing and wholeness

"They that be whole need not a physician" (Matthew 9:12). The notion of wholeness exists today as a kind of ideal state that we journey toward. But who among us is whole? It's not the critic but the journal writer in me who asks this question. The more I write and the more the years pass, the more I appreciate the truth Yeats offered in his poem "The Second Coming": "Things fall apart; the center cannot hold."

A fundamental connection exists between the words "heal," "whole," and "holy." In fact, the words have sprung from the same root. To heal is to make whole, or "hale" (sound or healthy). The Anglo-Saxon root of the word "holy" means "whole" or "sound." Holy beings heal others who are ill, and being healed makes us "whole" again.

There's also an interesting link in the German usage. *Erholung*, the word for taking a vacation, comes from the idea of making yourself whole again through the experience of being away from your customary environment. By taking a holiday, you make yourself whole again.

If you recognize your need to be restored to health, it's likely that you'll actively seek solutions. With an attitude of benign neglect, however, you won't. Yet the most stalwart of benign neglecters has been known to change his attitude after receiving a diagnosis of life-threatening proportions. It's fortunate that you can change the way you think and act at any time.

Healing is not an instant "abracadabra" charm. The process demands patience, yet patience is difficult to sustain in the face of severe pain. You visit the doctor so that he or she will "fix" the condition that's causing the problem. Most ads, whether on television and radio or in newspapers and magazines, are centered on quick "fixes." Not many people are prepared to be patient and wait for results. Funny, how you're identified in doctors' reception rooms as "the patient." It is the rare patient who is patient.

In some instances, you have every reason to lose patience with health practitioners if, month after month, they fail to listen to your reports of persistent symptoms and conditions. In this interaction, you begin to feel powerless. You may be reluctant to confront the physician whom you believe to have failed you. And you may fear that seeking a "second opinion" will be regarded as disobedience. Under these circumstances, healing is problematic. But the wise patient begins to ask questions. The answers can provide a catalyst for a change, which is critical in the healing process.

Implicit in the idea of paying attention is the idea that prevention doesn't always depend on someone else, such as a physician. The power is within you, the patient. Many people use vitamins, improved nutrition, meditation, yoga practice, and prayer to maintain health and healing, recognizing that the body, mind, and spirit need attention every day.

The effect of journal writing

When you write in your journal, you begin the process of taking a more active role in maintaining your health. Writing is action, very personal action. And you're writing about ideas that nourish you. When you pay attention to these impressions, it can help you understand that not all the mental "food" you've consumed has been beneficial for you. You've binged on too many negative thoughts.

This is where your journal is so useful – it helps you see the nature of the "food" you've been living on during your life. And when you write about the stuff that you've heaped on your mental platters, you begin to understand your deepest need for healing. Unless you appreciate this, you'll never concern yourself with changing your life for the better.

Fragmented as you may feel, you have the ability to effect a reconciliation with yourself and make some order out of the confusion you struggle with. By reclaiming your spiritual self, you open the door to receiving help from yourself as well as others who have gone through the same struggle. As you write, you'll find joy in exploring the difficulties you've overcome through the writing process. And we begin the effort to pay attention to ourselves by acknowledging that everyone has difficulty writing.

Simone Weil, in her book *Waiting for God*, wrote an essay on prayer as an act of love. Prayer, she says, is paying attention to God. Loving our neighbor is an act of paying attention to our neighbor. And loving yourself is the miraculous act of paying attention to yourself.

As you continue to write, you grow in the conviction that within you is a deep understanding of what you need in order to heal yourself. You don't know this when you begin, but you will, through patience and consistency, find your way to it. Because you're paying attention to your own complexity, healing images that you recognize and can create for yourself will appear before you. This is a rare opportunity to reprogram your customary way of thinking and responding to life. As you engage your own intuition and imagination, healing will begin.

It's very difficult to encourage participants to believe that within themselves – and not "out there" in the mind of someone else – is the help they need, the answers they're looking for, and the healing they seek. The basic building blocks for creating a better life may be buried within you, but they are within you. Writing in your journal helps you find them.

What you're doing for yourself is a symbolic act of self-healing, or "laying on of hands." When you write in your journal, you're laying your hands on the material of your life. You're not just waiting for inspiration; you're taking an active role in healing yourself. Healing comes through writing, but you discover this only through doing it. As an experiment in healing, will this journey be worth the effort? If you value your life, it will.

Chapter 8
Expectations

Write for Life workshops begin with an invitation to participants to share their expectations, what they hope to get out of journal writing. This is practice is fundamental, because what you receive from the journal-writing process is directly related to what you wish for. Wherever you are in your journal-writing process, when you read this chapter, you'll find that the vistas of your own expectations will open wider than when you began.

How can you discover a way to get more out of life? By drawing on your innermost expectations when you sit down to share yourself with your journal. Now is a good time to consider what you'd like to create as you continue writing in the months and years ahead.

In the beginning

In one of my workshops, someone asked, "How do you begin to write? How do you continue writing?"

You've already had a lifetime of writing experiences – some of them wonderful, some of them dreadful. I've been told of grammar school, high school, and college English composition courses that turned people off writing for the rest of their lives. For some, the judgments and criticism resulting from these school exercises were so painful that writing anything more than a shopping list today provokes distress. Howard, a participant in a group in Palm Springs, told me that he's had difficulty writing ever since his high school teacher accused him of plagiarizing his essay because it was "too good."

There are incompetent teachers like Howard's as well as those like my youngest son Matthew's first-grade teacher, who assured me that he "would never burn up the world." I told her how little I valued her assessment of a 6-year-old, not to mention her attitude. (I got Matthew into a different school fast.) Unfortunately, too many people have been influenced by teachers with their own wounded psyches and little understanding of the harm they do. Through the healing experience of journal writing, it will be possible to annul the harm done by others as well as yourself.

Many adults have barely survived unsound and destructive educational practices. You may also have memories of being ordered to write thank-you letters to relatives who sent something you didn't want yet had to be acknowledged. To this day, the taste of your own dishonesty may linger on your palate.

Obstacles of all kinds interfere with the writing process. There's a no-man's-land of embarrassing incidents that may be buried in your unconscious. This book has been designed to make it possible for you to stop carrying the burden of criticism and failures. In writing about these events, you'll get beyond them. Much energy and vitality has been lost in your life because you've been suppressing thoughts about some of these obstacles. Give yourself permission to examine them. Slowly, over the weeks and months of writing in your journal, you'll discover that it's possible to leave all this old baggage behind and travel on your way without the weight of any suffering you've endured.

Who's waving?

You're writing now. That you are writing is what's most important. The emphasis is on the content, of which you're the expert. From the perspective of today, you begin to write about your experience with the intention of discovering new and different ways to reach a primary goal: getting *more* out of life. This introduces a second expectation. In spite of your wish to do it, you may find it hard to fit journal writing into your life. "Where, oh, where is the magic wand I can wave to find time to write a journal?" you ask.

So wave your magic wand – and behold! You've made time for writing by staggering work hours, going to the gym at a different time, or changing the evening you play cards. Revise your personal schedule. You'll make magic in your life whenever you decide to value yourself. Miraculously, you find the time because you love the experience of connection and joy that it offers.

Whether you're just starting out or facing the end of life, journal writing helps you understand that everything that has happened to you is valuable. No matter what disasters or triumphs you've endured, you need to celebrate them. Survivors have a story to tell. Will you turn your back on yours? Pretend it never happened? Erase the blackboard and leave it blank? Live in denial as if you do not deserve the gift you've been given? That's not what you deserve.

Each story is a blessing, not a curse. You're alive in these stories, just as they're alive in you. And you must not fail them, for they go on far beyond you into the distant future and provide the strength and support that you and others need for the rest of the journey.

"A pair of ragged claws" and writer's block

Write from a place within yourself that values your stories as something you've lived and learned from, rather than from the perspective of T.S. Eliot's creation J. Alfred Prufrock, who says, "I should have been a pair of ragged claws/Scuttling across the floors of silent seas." Beginning today, you can begin to *care* about what has already happened – not as a source of worry, but as a basis for loving your life in a new way. What you care about, you value.

Workshop participants always want to learn how to overcome resistance to writing. A blank page in the notebook prompts the same terror as an empty canvas on the easel, except that instead of a brush in your hand and colors on the palette, you have a pen in your hand and words in your head. But the moment you sit down to write, you meet resistance. The blank page dares you to lift a finger against it. In the workshop, someone hoping for an easy way out asked, "How can I have writer's block when I'm not even a writer?"

I'm reminded of Newton's First Law of Motion – commonly called the law of inertia – which basically states, "A body that is not in motion tends to remain in that state, and one that is in motion tends to remain in motion." Remind yourself that you've already learned to live with inertia and that the role it plays in your writing need not scuttle your efforts. If you'll allow yourself to consider your effort in a positive, creative way, you'll embrace it instead of allowing it to become an obstacle. Throughout this book, you'll find many suggestions about how to use resistance as a tool to help, not hinder, the writing process.

What's important?

Workshop participants also want to learn how to discover the "important" things to write about and how to avoid everything else. Perhaps you'll make the same discovery Diane did when she finally got the opportunity to read the journals her grandmother left her. "I was expecting all sorts of wonderful stuff," she said. "Instead, I found the entries really quite boring." Upon her grandmother's death, Diane had inherited the diaries along with her grandmother's express desire that she read them. The journal entries detailed the day-to-day routine of her grandmother's life. This was what her grandmother *needed* to write about. It's the most basic aspect of journal writing: Write what you need to write. There's nothing too insignificant or too important to write. Everything that flows from your pen is what *you* need to express, and it finds its way into your journal because you need it to be there.

Having sat through twelve-step meetings where men and women, year after year, tell their stories in exactly the same way they told them the year before and the year before that, I realized that some people not only live their stories, they're also stuck in them. By writing in a journal over time and then reading the entries months later, they would discover how their present lives are shadows of events and feelings they've already survived. For them, what *happened* to them in the past is far more influential than what *happens* to them *now*. Recognizing this provides the kind of shock that encourages them to step out of the past and into the present. It also provides the kind of insight needed to halt their addiction to suffering.

You'll get more out of journal writing if you don't read what you've written for at least several weeks, if not months, after you've written it. Several months later, if your journal is still locked onto the same events and feelings, consider seeking professional counseling. These entries will be of tremendous benefit in identifying the kind of help that's needed and perhaps will be a prediction of success as well. The reason it's a good idea not to read what you've written for a while is that the moment you reread the lines, you begin to edit them. This isn't the activity at the heart of your journal writing. Editing is criticism; it is not the way to discover yourself. Not reading the entries for a while helps you to write more today, tomorrow, and on down the road.

In considering the question of what's important to write about and what's not, remember that what may seem unimportant today may be significant several months from now. Everything you write about today is important for you today. Write about it – and include your feelings. Be as emotional as you can. Don't just jot down items as if you're keeping a list of daily appointments. When you write about your true feelings, you're launching an effort to live beyond your story.

Improving perspective

Some journal writers create an obstacle for themselves by thinking that their journals are some kind of passport into a literary Hall of Fame. This is a significant obstacle because it shifts the focus from the process of writing to the result. Over time, the material you enter on the page might be developed into a memoir, an autobiography, or even a novel. But that's another enterprise and not the one that engages you now. Indeed, many famous authors have kept journals, and they wrote them for publication. But their audience was different from yours, and whatever benefit they received is another matter. Unless you write for yourself, you'll miss the opportunity that journal writing has in store.

"I'd like to know how journal writing can help me to deal with change," said a workshop participant. Through writing about events, relationships, and feelings, you uncover insights that are buried in your consciousness. You've learned to endure hardships and you've celebrated accomplishments. You've also forgotten about many of the little victories and losses that seemed so momentous when you encountered them. In this process, you've changed and your goals have changed. Sometimes you can even remember what was responsible for the change.

Martha, a participant who came to two seminars, was unable to write in her journal because, she said, "Tomorrow I may change my mind and not feel the same as I do right now. I just don't want to commit myself on paper." For many people, what's written down assumes far more significance than what's spoken. If it appears in print, it must be true. Martha, you see, was deeply worried about her daughter's survival from a bone-marrow transplant. She was afraid that if she allowed herself to record her fears on the page, they would be realized and her daughter would die.

Writing about the fear of death in a journal will not magically affect someone. Your "magic" waits in your ability to make your life better. Giving words to her pain would have been of great benefit to Martha and would have helped her deal with feelings about her daughter's precarious condition.

You benefit through the process of accessing your own wisdom and intuition through your writing. You know what it's like to be in the midst

of a problem you've been struggling with without even understanding how you fell into such a quagmire. You're troubled and you've found nothing to diminish the intensity of the forces confronting you. Suddenly a friend telephones or arrives on your doorstep with a problem of her own. From a place within that is accessible and familiar, you begin to make suggestions about what she might consider doing or the kind of assistance she should consider seeking. From your own experience and wisdom, you're able to offer some insight, some perspective, that your friend needs.

You have within you great strength as well as an insight that comes into play the moment it is called upon or requested by those you care about.

If you don't have it yourself, you usually know where to look for it to help others. When it comes to your own issues and problems, you have this same ability, even though it may seem beyond you. What you know and understand is often buried within, and exploring experiences from your past through the process of writing in your journal opens the way to discovering what you may not remember you already understand. You make connections with similar experiences and write about what you did in the past to resolve them. Sometimes you discover that what you chose before did not work, and this opens the door to your exploring different alternatives – ones that have a better possibility of success. Frequently, it's in these failures and not the successes that you learn more of what you need to live better. Writing in your journal puts you in touch with this if you're patient and consistent with your efforts. You've been able to reach this moment, now, only because of what has gone before.

Returning to journal writing

Quite a few people have reported that they stopped journaling during different periods in their lives. Their goal in the workshops was to find the way back to writing on a daily basis. If you've stopped journaling and it wasn't because of an unpleasant experience (such as someone intruding on your privacy by reading what you've written), then the way in again is quite simple. Just do it.

Just as you might stop exercising, reading, or working in the garden, you can always begin again. No is one looking over your shoulder. There's no guilt for your having stopped in the past. Don't even think about it. Simply start writing today.

Dealing with change

The search for ways to deal with life's passages is another reason that people write. The aging process, like the recovery process, is a mystery. It's as if you need to write your own book to understand what's happening to your body and mind. You need to see your own problems and confusions on the page in order to appreciate that you're center stage and the bow coming up is yours – for you to applaud!

Aging is about change, and nobody likes change. Even when you know change is coming, you usually try to avoid thinking about it. But in spite of everything you might do to convince yourself otherwise, change is inevitable. People's biggest fear about change is that they will suffer some kind of loss that will affect how they handle their life.

Journal writing is the opposite of hiding your head in the sand. By identifying alternatives and exploring them in the safety of your notebook, you can also think of resources you might consult for advice. While writing a journal, you open the drawers of your life catalog and research your experience. Asking yourself "What *will* I do about this circumstance tomorrow?" lets you imagine events from a new perspective. New strategies are good for dealing with change and anticipating the feelings that arise from changes. Reflecting on those changes will open an avenue to access your own wisdom.

When you're willing to explore the cause of stress and anxiety, you begin to diminish its hold on you. Burying problems causes an increase in worry, and prolonged worry triggers psychological and physical problems. You don't get rid of the problems, you "infect" yourself with them. The result is disease and dis-ease, neither of which assists your efforts to live better.

Talking with others on the telephone about problems does not provide the benefits of journaling. Most of the time, you're not even listening to what you're saying. And there are so many things you say that you don't even realize you've said. It's essential that you hear yourself. Having tried, I know what a difficult task it is to listen to each word I say as I say it. Make the experiment. Repeating problems or worries to several people is not nearly as beneficial as writing about them in your journal. You attend to what you write, and this attention makes a difference in your ability to manage your life.

Some people become expert at avoiding what's unpleasant. This requires denial, which is at the root of all addictive/compulsive behavior. Avoiding the realization of change has a much worse effect on your system than acknowledging your fear and giving yourself permission to handle it. After all, it takes energy to suppress something. Journal writing helps you deal with changes such as aging by giving you a safe forum in which to express yourself. Being honest is a necessary step to living better. And you'll also feel less stressed about seeking help to resolve your fears.

When you believe that journal writing has only minor significance in your daily routine, you achieve limited results. But when you view the activity as serious and life-affirming, there's a change of attention and intention. Once you discover how significantly writing benefits your life, you look on it in a different way. Just as you feel better after physical exercise, you feel energized after writing – a mental exercise.

Having fun

Heloise wanted, through her journal writing, to develop in herself the ability to "see the funny side of everything." She wanted the ability to get the kind of perspective on her life that comes with distance. When you get lost in the experiences of events just as they're taking place, you're rarely able to have a sense of perspective. But when you write about the events, a new dimension enters the process. You're both the one who participates in the event and its observer. This can often help you develop greater affection and patience with yourself as well as laugh at the seriousness that absorbed you. You'll begin to see yourself in a new light.

What a wonderful way to avoid boredom! Workshop participants always enjoy discussing what it takes to have fun. Here's their list: "laughing," "discovering something new," "spontaneously reacting to something unexpected," "meeting new people," "letting go of expectations," "being with friends," "losing reserve," "indulging the senses."

The simple fact is that it's impossible to have fun without showing up in your life. If you're not present, you *can't* have fun. By showing up to write in your notebook, you can have as much fun as you want. You'll find out that when you write on a consistent basis, boredom goes right out the window as soon as you pick up your pen. Self-discovery is one of the most exciting adventures you can undertake, and you have all the tools you need at your fingertips.

Workshop participants' responses

Workshop participants named a number of things they hoped to learn through journaling.

- "To stimulate thoughts and make things concrete."
- "To deal with changes."

- "To make more connections with my life."
- "To be more present in my life."
- "To take advantage of the opportunity to live with feelings and thoughts."
- "To lift my head out of the sand and face my life more completely."
- "To write a memoir."
- "To find healing."
- "To get unblocked."
- "To be able to write more clearly about my medical problems."

And here's a list of expectations from another workshop group.

- "A lot of $ or/Pulitzer Prize. Or a well-paid advance."
- "I got away from journaling. It's been on my to-do list. I'd like to get better at recording."
- "I'm more interested in journal writing than creative writing. I wish I'd been writing for years. I've had wonderful experiences and regret not having written about them."
- "I do painting & pottery. I'm looking for more feedback/discipline from journal writing."
- "Support from the group."
- "Fun."
- "No pressures to do something well. The doing – putting something on paper – I want to overcome my fear of this."
- "Get rid of the idea of brain-drain. I want to enjoy doing my journal, so that it's not a chore."
- "Develop a new and useful skill."
- "Dream: no longer being a prisoner in my own house."

Your possibilities

Expectations are powerful. When you identify them and find ways to act on them, it helps you appreciate more in your life. Your expectations also offer a glimmer of something that functions deep below the surface of your consciousness – your hopes and dreams. You know the things you hold dear in your life. All your wishes surround them like a skyful of stars. There are many ways to reach this spiritual dimension within yourself. In *Write for*

Life, you'll find a sequence of journeys designed to help you discover your deepest wish.

Your journal, unlike anything else you may have used to gain self-awareness, is like a spiritual key that opens regions within you. The first step toward finding your wish is to pick up your pen. You live your wish in how you respond to life as well as what you expect from it.

Write in your journal about today's expectations. Make a calendar note for a month from now to write about your expectations again, and do so once every month for the rest of the year. At the end of the year, when you look back over the monthly entries, you'll discover what amazing ground you've covered. You'll see the way your wish evolves over time and feel the excitement as your healing process unfolds, leading you out of the past and into the present, toward a future that's being created in the pages of your journal.

PART THREE

Exploring New Directions
into Healing

Chapter 9
Self-Caring

Getting started

Time is always at a premium. We never have enough of it. When asked to take on additional responsibilities, people often become apprehensive about completing the tasks they already have, much less something new.

Anxiety about time may dog your heels as you leave your bed in the morning. Maybe you're used to this. You chug into your daily routine and before you know it, it's time to go to sleep again. Time has a way of slipping through your fingers, leaving you feeling as if you're getting only half of what you hope for.

A man I knew in Puerto Rico always urged people to "stop and smell the roses!" I hope he took his own advice, because he died from a sudden heart attack at the age of 43. Like many who give others advice, we rarely take it ourselves when it comes to being self-caring instead of self-critical. How much more generous we are with others when it comes to looking after matters related to health and well-being. Most of the time, we're at the end of the list instead of at the top.

Consider what it would mean to become self-caring. For some, this effort seems too self-centered. Many people are so conditioned to think in ways that are not self-caring that they have a difficult time changing these attitudes. As you begin this journey, see where you find yourself on your own list of people and the priority they enjoy in your life. Then see where you end up after you've been writing in your journal for a while.

Valuing ourselves

When you don't value yourself enough for what you do, what you have, what you feel, and the way you've lived your life, is there any wonder that you feel undervalued by others? Think back to your childhood. When teams were being chosen for neighborhood pickup games, were you the last to be selected? And what about nowadays? Do you work hard all day, only to come home to a sink filled with the rest of the family's dirty dishes?

To change this perception of yourself, you have to begin thinking about yourself as a source of value. Begin this by acknowledging your accomplishments. Write some affirmations in your journal that support the efforts you're making to sustain your life. Whatever you do over the course of the day, whether you only start it or actually finish it, can be a subject for affirmation. Asserting support for the way you deal with others is a great subject for affirmation. And you can write several affirmations about your approach to health care and the way you deal with problems.

These affirmations aren't going to make the problems disappear, but they'll help you feel better able to deal with them. Appreciating yourself for who you are, without any ifs, ands, or buts, is a vital first step toward beginning the process of self-caring.

When you begin seeing yourself affirming your life, many things you were taking for granted suddenly become valuable to you. The expression "Charity begins at home" is absolutely true. Your sense of value begins with you. A few days of writing about how difficult it is to do this helps to reveal aspects of yourself that have been buried under layers of criticism. Let yourself savor this over several entries, because it's powerful information to process.

Whenever you have trouble writing about something, you can either devote several entries to writing about the obstacles you're encountering or you can put it on the list of "no-nos" that you set up on a separate page in the journal. Don't let yourself get stuck. One of the journeys you'll take later is concerned with "no-nos" and "not yets." You'll get to them later.

Staying started

Body, mind, and spirit inventory

Begin by creating a body, mind, and spirit inventory, listing what is essential to your taking better care of yourself in each of these areas. Do this by leaving a complete page for each list, or make three columns on one page so that the categories can be developed side by side. You'll discover that some items may appear on two lists or even all three.

Before you read any of the lists that workshop participants developed below, create your own personal lists in your journal. Start by answering the question, "What do I need to do to become more self-loving, self-caring, and self-accepting today?"

In Body   **In Mind**   **In Spirit**

After developing your inventory, look at the following lists written by workshop participants. If you find some of the entries appropriate, add them to your own lists.

Body. "Good food and nutrition." "Diet and weight-watching." "Drink more fluids." "Exercise." "Regular attendance at swimming pool." "Regular medical checkups." "Adequate rest." "Pamper myself: long baths, lotion, massage, manicure, visits to the hairdresser." "Make an effort with appearance." "Clean out the closet." "Breathe deeply." "Work in the garden."

Mind. "Create a list of stimulating books and materials." "Attend workshops in new areas." "Seek input from others." "Debate issues; problem-solve." "Examine the past – read old journals." "Play games." "Go shopping." "Plan a trip." "Participate in support groups." "Identify ways to get a sense of accomplishment." "Encourage spontaneity." "Focus for fifteen minutes on worries, then leave them."

Spirit. "Help a stranger." "Prayer." "Meditation." "Visualization." "Paint." "Listen to music." "Explore yoga and other spiritual practices." "Travel." "Find a spiritual director." "Live with an attitude of self-caring." "End each day with a sense of closure." "Seek opportunities to create new relationships." "Read spiritual texts." "Get a pet." "Forgive the unforgiven." "More sex." "Pay attention to dreams." "Allow the 'Force' to be with me."

Participants also found it helpful to set up a separate column for **Emotional Self-Caring**. Here's what they listed.

Emotions. "Give myself permission to feel happy, sad, angry, lonely, ambivalent – whatever comes up in the course of the day." "Do not bury feelings or pretend they're unimportant." "Express emotions in journal writing and to others." "Spend time with people I enjoy." "Let others know I care about them." "Paint." "Write poetry."

After creating the lists, write during the week about each item's significance in your life. This will help you become clearer about the value of your own attributes, and you'll be less inclined to dismiss them as frivolous.

Next, write in your journal what it will take to implement these attributes in your life. Before reading what other participants have noted, look at your list and form a plan of action to create the reality you want.

Body. "See a nutritionist for ideas about a better diet." "Find and use the bike paths this week." "Use the qigong tapes each morning." "Take a ten- to twenty-minute walk every day." "Try not to be Wonder Woman." "Everything in moderation." "Appreciate my body and its value." "See the body-mind, body-spirit connection in everything I do." "Clear my house to get rid of the allergens." "Get a foot massage." "Acknowledge limits and relax." "Take time to meditate every day." "Give and get more hugs daily." "Walk on the beach this weekend." "Lose fifteen to twenty pounds."

Mind. "Join a Great Books group/attend lectures/take classes." "Rent classic films." "Pursue foreign-language study." "Take a mindfulness class." "Do some creative writing." "Exchange thoughts and ideas with others." "Develop better coping skills." "Control thought processes." "Learn something new on a regular basis." "Stop procrastinating about the things I want to do." "Make spiritual direction more of a priority."

Spirit. "Daily yoga." "Make time to meditate and pray." "Make time each day to do what I want." "Enjoy myself more (e.g., this class)." "Go to museums and gallery exhibits, and join the art museum." "Start piano lessons." "Eat raspberries." "Take my daughter to Michigan." "Take hot baths with bubbles." "Take naps." "Self-improvement through reading, learning new skills." "Self-evaluating and correcting mistakes." "Helping others."

Emotions. "Write a letter to a friend." "Return to Monday-night art classes." "Develop an action plan for the next twelve months." "Get rid of clutter." "Support my intuition." "Feel my feelings." "Help people who feel isolated." "Explore grief training." "Strengthen connections with friends and family." "Find volunteer work." "Make time for myself."

New directions

These lists are useful stimuli for making changes in the way you plan your day and use your time and talent to undertake new activities. Once your ideas are on paper, write about what happens. More ideas may present themselves as you initiate these activities. You may also notice that instead of having a vague idea that something's missing in your life, you can now appreciate what you have.

Bear in mind that it's important to write about the efforts that seemed like failures as well as your successes. Every dead end you reach is an opportunity for future exploration. When you show up for your journal, you begin to make it your traveling companion in the search for new approaches to self-caring. Unlike someone you talk with on the telephone, your journal offers continuity over time. This helps you discover where you've been, enabling you to appreciate the changes that have occurred within. It's difficult to see the changes in yourself that you make from one year to the next. Journal entries offer this insight.

As you explore, you always encounter obstacles. Often these obstacles can't be surmounted through your own actions, and you feel disappointment or regret. It won't be either the first time or the last time. It's especially useful to remember this and connect it with previous experiences. The question "How does this connect with my past?" will help you get in touch with yourself in a revealing way. What you haven't understood about past experiences, you can begin to consider from a different point of view. Often you were too close to events to see them with any clear perspective; as you look back from the vantage of today and connect them with what you know and feel now, you can support yourself in a way that was previously impossible. And if the problem you're assessing is more than you're able to manage on your own, you can also explore additional avenues for help and support.

When they make connections with "unfinished business," people often respond by dumping all the old baggage from the past onto their shoulders today. If it comes up for you, be sure to write about it in your journal. A powerful act of self-caring is to bring as many "I-should-have" thoughts into the open as possible, so that you get them out of your unconscious. These "shoulds" are the source of many of your worries, and now is the time to begin to drain them of the power they've exercised in your life.

In the vacuum left from this conscious effort to exorcise "shoulds," consider writing affirmations for what you've done in the past and will do in the future. Affirmations support your efforts to be self-caring. Including them in journal entries gives you a kind of strength to begin healing yourself.

Consider the types of support you wish you had from others. List them in your journal. Then explore whether *you* give yourself that kind of support. Do you look for opportunities to praise yourself? Think of the last time you told yourself, "You did that really well!" You learn that the glass is always half-empty when you don't give yourself this kind of support.

Journaling helps you appreciate the efforts you're making to find joy and deal with experiences of grief and conflict. You can begin to assess progress by reading what you wrote three months ago. It can be startling to see what you've written previously, and you'll be amazed at how differently you appear to yourself – and how little you realized the change.

Looking back over previous journal entries helps you feel much more appreciation for yourself than you experienced at the time of writing. When you take the time to make journal writing a priority in your life, it becomes one of the most self-caring activities you can do on a daily basis.

Chapter 10
Food and Nourishment

Getting started

Everyone in my workshops who has written about what it means to live better has identified good food and nutrition as things that improve the quality of their lives. The reason for this is easy to understand.

From the moment you took your first breath, you've been nourished by the oxygen that fills your lungs and sustains your life. You've also been nourished by solid and liquid food, and by impressions that entered your psyche through the mouth, ears, eyes, and skin as tastes, sounds, images, and sensations. These things have sustained you and fueled your emotional growth.

Many of life's greatest pleasures have come through experiences you've had eating and drinking. And some of your worst memories, especially from childhood, are connected with the food your parents made you eat because it was "good" for you. As an adult, you may be reminded of some of these moments when you travel to foreign countries and dine on the food of each region and culture. To use Hemingway's title, life has always been "a moveable feast," and you've partaken of it.

Memories and anticipations are a plentiful source of nourishment for your journal. What kind of attention do you pay when you choose what, where, and how you eat? Is there a richer topic to explore in your journal?

Who's interested in food?

Everyone. Everywhere you look, you can see an increased consciousness of all aspects of food development, production, and consumption. The Food Network on cable television is one indicator. Americans have become more knowledgeable about wine, and more and more acreage is devoted to it. More markets are selling organic produce. The news media reflect growing public awareness of the new hybrid plants developed by biomedical engineering. A rising interest in the "slow food" movement has resulted in numerous books and websites devoted to alternatives to "fast food." Over the past decade, there has been a burgeoning world consciousness about the development, preparation, and marketing of food.

Setting aside the dimensions of politics and the media, you can see the importance of the subject in your own daily life. You'd be unique if at some time during the day you didn't think, "What's for dinner?" People daydream about pleasurable ways to delight the palate. For some, eating in restaurants is a great pleasure – even if it does mean worrying about waistlines and cholesterol.

Anything receiving as much of our attention as food and nourishment also deserves exploration in our journals. Here are a few questions you might consider as you look at your past, present, and future relationships with food and the people who share it with you. Use these prompts as a springboard for writing. Give yourself permission to write about whatever you think and feel. Don't limit yourself in any way. Enjoy this exercise as you would a banquet prepared in your honor. Your journal awaits.

1. The list of my favorite foods includes _____.
    The list of my favorite beverages includes _____.
    (*After making the lists, write about some memories of these items.*)
2. The list of my least favorite foods includes _____.
    The list of my least favorite beverages includes _____.
    (*After making the lists, write about some memories of these items.*)
3. Are there foods I can think of that I haven't yet tasted?
    (*This list may also include some recipes as yet untried.*)
4. Is there any condition or diagnosis that requires me to begin thinking in some new ways about the food I eat? Are there any foods I need to avoid or limit
    (*Writing about this helps you focus on the issues under consideration instead of on some vague worry.*)
5. What are some ways to handle this concern? Have I begun to implement them, or am I still thinking about them? Have there been any results? How does this make me feel?

6. Looking back over my life, what are some of the most delicious meals I've eaten, and where did I eat them?
   (*Devote some journal entries to exploring this list in detail.*)
7. What are a few of the worst culinary experiences I have ever had?
   (*Make a list and write about them.*)

You may find the idea of writing about food easy or difficult. When you no longer take it for granted, you can begin to appreciate the process of nourishment from a new perspective.

Staying started

"How can you propose a subject that caters to our basest instincts?" asked one workshop participant when the subject of food and nutrition was raised. They're sources of delight and distress, so they're significant areas of your life and can help you understand and appreciate more about yourself.

Writing about limitations often brings up feelings of vulnerability. These are illuminating, because they reveal changes you've had to make – some of them significant. For example, after you've been through certain medical procedures, you may have had to restructure your diet in significant ways. Perhaps, as the result of a particular treatment, you're unable to easily digest raw vegetables or fruit. After chemotherapy, there can be a complete loss of the sense of taste or some ongoing taste impairment. As we get older we have fewer active taste buds. People with endocrine or cardiovascular diseases or conditions such as diabetes have additional restrictions.

Food and our identity

What you eat and don't eat helps make you who you are. Dieters discover that eliminating certain foods changes their attitudes. The effects can be surprising. Sometimes, cutting out "comfort food" – bread, pasta, potatoes, and carbohydrates in general – leaves you not only hungry but in a state of definite discomfort. Why is this so? Maybe it would be beneficial to seek comfort in other sources of nourishment.

Something else that can have a profound effect upon both your health and your perspective is alcohol. If you've indulged freely over the years, you may not recognize yourself without a glass of wine in your hand.

You are what you eat. And every day, our consciousness is being raised about food-related subjects that we've taken for granted.

With this in mind, here are some questions for journal entries this week.

1. Are there holiday feasts that occurred during childhood or at any other time in life that I will always remember with delight?
   (Consider the kinds of food and the amount served. Write about this and include as many details and feelings as possible.)
2. What meals have I most enjoyed preparing? What meals did I least enjoy preparing? What associations do I have with these events?
3. Explore some memories associated with dining that extend beyond food into another area of experience, such as travel, romance, illness, etc.
4. If you could have your choice of anyone to dine with, who would that person *(or those people)* be?
   (Create a guest list and write about the people on it. What would you talk about with them?)
5. Think back over the years to the restaurants you remember best – where they were, what they specialized in. What were the occasions and who were the people you enjoyed the most and the least on these occasions?

Take a look at the way you're thinking about food now. Has it changed since you began writing in your journal? Note your observations.

New directions

Consider what you eat and drink from the perspective of exploring a foreign country. Write about some of your discoveries and adventures. Sampling different regional foods and styles of cooking may have left you with some impressions that you can write about now, as you consider improving your health through nutrition. Do the size of the meals and the hours you ate them offer some ideas about changing the way you plan your day? Perhaps you'll make some additional discoveries as you write.

Along with the times, attitudes have changed. At one time it would have been almost unthinkable to walk into the supermarket and stare at shelf after shelf of plain bottled water. Evian water and Perrier, to name only two, have been common in Europe far longer than in the U.S. However, increased awareness of pollution has made many people conscious of different needs. What are your thoughts and feelings about the water you drink and the genetically modified food you eat? Have they changed? Have these affected any other attitudes you hold? Have they caused your buying habits or style of consumption to change? If so, what is different now from in the past? Do you anticipate making further changes in the future?

In 1998, California's concern over secondhand smoke resulted in the nation's first legislation prohibiting smoking in all restaurants and bars. Since then, similar initiatives elsewhere have caused other states to pass measures of their own. What are your feelings about smoking in public places? Have they affected your politics? Your social behavior? Your activities at home? Your journal is a good place to record your reactions.

FDA requirements for labeling packaged foods have revolutionized the food industry. The banning of trans fats is the most recent development in this area. The next time you're in the supermarket, check labels for what will best nourish you and support your health. For many, this approach to food is consciousness-raising.

For centuries there have been food systems based on balance, such as the Chinese principles of yin and yang, or individual types, such as the Indian Ayurveda. These are focused on maintaining harmony in order to preserve the health of body, mind, and spirit. This key concept is rewarding on many levels to those who explore it, whether they come to it with the intention of controlling their weight or from a desire to achieve greater well-being. If you introduce this idea of balance into your relationship with food, write about what happens to your appetite and food preferences. If you've decided to lose weight or gain weight, consider using your journal to write about your

feelings in overcoming obstacles as well as about the success (or lack of success) of your efforts. Your journal can provide unexpected support as you
face each day.

Food metaphors

Here are some food-related phrases that reveal how extensive the connection
is between eating and the way we think. "He doesn't know beans!" "You've
got to know which side your bread is buttered on!" "I'm so hungry I could
eat a horse!" "It's a piece of cake." "Pork-barrel legislation." "What a ham!"
"You've given me some real food for thought." "She's the apple of my eye!"
"You're a peach." Two terms of endearment that enjoyed wide usage not so
long ago are "cupcake" and "dumpling." And then there's "sweetie," "sugar,"
and the ever-popular "honey"!

Add some of your own to your journal. Then consider a few more ideas
about food that you might explore:

1. What are some of the most compelling concerns about food in my
   life today?
2. Are there associations with food that I didn't realize before?
3. What role does my self-image play in planning my daily menu?
4. Do I need to research questions of food or diet? Where should I look?
5. Have there been any surprises as I write these entries about food?
6. When I pay careful attention to myself as I eat, do I observe any
   difference in the taste of the food or my digestion?
7. Where can I find new and interesting ideas for introducing greater
   variety into the foods I eat?
8. Have I put off arranging a social opportunity? What sort of event might
   it be? Who would be involved? When could it take place?

It's a challenge to turn buying, preparing, and eating food into an
opportunity for better living. "What's for dinner?" can be an invitation for
mindfulness as you approach your goals for health and balance in body,
mind, and spirit. If you don't accept the challenge, though, who loses?

The spiritual dimension

Until this point, you've considered the significance of food from the vantage of its effect on your body. But don't leave this encompassing journal subject without considering the spiritual implications. For many, the presentation of food is an opportunity to offer thanks for everything received in life.

Food provides an opportunity to exchange hospitality as we share our bounty with others and receive theirs. And food has figured as a sacrament in primary religious practices. For Jews, the sanctity of the Sabbath is ushered in with the Kiddush, which blesses the fruit of the vine and the bread that comes from the earth. For Christians, Jesus, at the Last Supper, transformed these two offerings in the symbolic rite of the Eucharist, which is central to the celebration of the Mass. Both bread and wine are held up at the altar in the retelling of the sacrifice of Christ in this passage from *The Book of Common Prayer*:

> On the night he was handed over to suffering and death, our Lord Jesus Christ took bread; and when he had given thanks to you, he broke it, and gave it to his disciples, and said, "Take, eat: This is my Body, which is given for you. Do this for the remembrance of me."
>
> After supper, he took the cup of wine; and when he had given thanks, he gave it to them, and said, "Drink this, all of you: This is my Blood of the new Covenant, which is shed for you and for many for the forgiveness of sins. Whenever you drink it, do this for the remembrance of me."

The ritual of Communion, with its symbolic consumption of wafer and wine, and the Kiddush that opens the Sabbath meal both focus on the spiritual dimension of food and nourishment. Even the humblest meal shared with a friend or neighbor has about it an aura of the sacred, as the opening line of the Lord's Prayer acknowledges with "Give us this day our daily bread."

When you share food with others, you end your own isolation and become part of a community. No one need feel left out. Opportunities to volunteer in neighborhood food programs are a way to participate in your community and receive from this effort priceless experiences that you may find yourself writing about with gratitude in the months ahead.

There is a chronic epidemic of hunger in the world today. As you become more aware of its dimensions, it can have an transformative effect upon your attitude toward food and yourself as a member of the world community. When you begin to write about it, the food you eat becomes a source of nourishment that sustains your mind and spirit as well as your body. And by becoming more conscious of the role you can play in the struggle to end world hunger, you assume responsibility for healing others along with yourself.

Chapter 11
Travel

Getting started

Travel is one of the best ways for us to gain new impressions. It's likely that you have at some time used a road map or train or bus schedule, or held a brochure describing a place you wanted to visit. Sometimes your journey existed only in your imagination; other times, you've actually gone there. In your journal, you're writing about your life journeys, both literal and figurative, exploring some of the roads you've traveled and what you've learned about yourself from these experiences.

The traveler

Does travel excite you? Perhaps it's the idea of "romance" – stories about far-away places that spark the imagination. Some of the first novels ever written described the journey of a hero through an unfamiliar world. A few well-known explorations that have delighted readers over the last few centuries are *Don Quixote* by Miguel Cervantes, *Gulliver's Travels* by Jonathan Swift, and *Tom Jones* by Henry Fielding. But they're the imaginary journeys of imaginary characters. What about your own journeys and their importance to your evolution?

Don Quixote, Captain Lemuel Gulliver, and Tom Jones ended up making discoveries that affected their basic sense of identity. Each character was changed by the obstacles he encountered, and upon returning home, each was different from the man who set out on his journey. They didn't plan this transformation. It happened because they left the place they were comfortable with and encountered a new world. Reading about their adventures, you marvel at the Don's persistence; you root for Tom, hoping that he'll overcome his tribulations; and you're amused by Gulliver's confrontations with both giants and tiny people only six inches tall. You follow with growing interest the adventures of each fictional traveler as he makes his way to the destination or goal he's seeking.

Think about the journeys you've taken, the observations you've made, and the roles you've played. Start with the first trips you took as a child. In these, you may find that some of your most memorable experiences were with your parents. Perhaps your first trip was taken alone. Remember where you went and what you did there, and make a list of twenty or more of the travel adventures that took you away from your familiar environment. Separate these journeys into different periods (ten- or fifteen-year periods are convenient).

Write the year and the destination of each trip, along with the names of the people you remember from it, then add some details about the experience. Allow these, as much as possible, to recreate the richness of your first encounters with the world. Participants have shared their amazement at the extensive impressions still fresh in their minds today. Make room for surprises.

Staying started

A few journal writers found the creation of this list so interesting that they extended it all the way to the present, making a return visit to a neighborhood they once lived in, taking a trip to the "old country" from which their parents or grandparents emigrated, or attending a high school or college reunion. Some of the journeys listed were very short; for example, one included a 10-year-old's intention to run away from home.

Many forms of transportation were mentioned. The lists included travel by car, bus, plane, ship, sailboat, helicopter, dog sled, and on foot as well as journeys that could be taken only in imagination and dreams. Interest in exploring these journeys was very high, and many of the journalers planned to write about their memories in future entries.

For destinations, journeys included trips across the country, to different lands, and to visit unfamiliar people. Sometimes these experiences were exactly what the travelers hoped for; often they were not. You'll explore this later in greater detail. When any journey is considered, there are expectations. But because you don't or can't really know what to expect, all you can do is focus on the preparations.

Basic travel preparations

Even if you're going across town, you need to get ready for the trip. Securing your home before you leave is something you do automatically. You don't want your belongings stolen in your absence. So you lock the door behind you when you start out. (The nagging thought of an unlocked door or open window has caused many a traveler to turn back after starting out.) When you plan a long journey, you stop delivery of the newspaper and arrange for someone to pick up your mail.

More than a few travelers have discovered that unwittingly traveling with an expired credit card can have serious consequences. It's easy enough to confirm the expiration date before you set out. Sometimes it's better not to take it for granted.

A passport is a necessity if you're leaving the country. An updated address book with telephone numbers and e-mail addresses is indispensable. Inoculations against disease may be required. A careful review of your medical coverage is useful as well. Familiarity with the local language and currency is also prudent when you travel abroad, and making reservations that take your comfort into account will make the journey more enjoyable.

Packing the right clothes is a daunting task. Most travelers take too much with them and are burdened by their own baggage. And even seasoned travelers can forget to bring something as basic as a comfortable pair of walking shoes. "The lighter you travel, the easier the trip," said an expert whose advice I forgot before my last journey, to my profound regret.

Whether you're preparing for a long journey or a short trip, a few moments spent checking travel websites on the Internet make it possible to learn everything you need to ensure comfort and safety.

If you write in your journal now about preparations you've made for past trips, it will stimulate valuable memories about yourself and what your needs have been over the years, and it will help you understand how much you've changed over time. When you were small, a teddy bear or favorite toy might have been absolutely essential for a visit to Grandma; now that you're grown, perhaps it's sports equipment or a diet supplement that you find indispensable. Without these necessary items, you travel unprepared. This will become clearer as you write.

Traveling companions

Another key aspect of preparation is your choice of traveling companion(s). Do you want to travel with one person? A group? Many people prefer to

travel alone, preferring to risk feeling vulnerable rather than deal with others' wishes, which might be vastly different from their own. Perhaps you'd like to explore this issue in some journal entries. Create several journal entries about the experiences you've had traveling alone as well as with others.

Traveling with a friend can have unexpected consequences, as this excerpt reveals from my journal of 1999, when I traveled in New Zealand with someone I didn't know. "Traveling with someone is better than traveling alone," M. had insisted when we discussed visiting the South Island. Here's a brief excerpt, written six days into the journey, that clearly disproves such an idea.

> Feb. 19, 1999: Just outside Queenstown:
> We have driven from Dunedin to this lovely cottage in the country to stay with M.'s daughter and son-in-law and grandchildren. From the ridiculous to the sublime. There

is an enormous Swiss-style mountain in the distance out the window of my bedroom. And, at last, it is raining! We have driven through parched countryside since leaving Picton and while the eastern half of the island may not get even a drop of this, at least here the skies have opened and fat drops are falling all around.

I slept not at all last night at the Leviathan Hotel. The incident at the café with M. truly fired all my furnaces, and the room we had on the first floor over one of the busiest thoroughfares in the city never ceased reverberating from the cars, trucks, and buses that passed all night long. I did rest a little and my body took some refreshment from the sound mattress, but my brain would not shut off.

(As I write this, M. is singing in the other room "I don't get no satisfaction." He is not only deaf, he is also tone-deaf. He does this frequently. I know he considers himself a fabulous songwriter as well.)

When M. did not return to the café last night, I was driven to the Leviathan by Alistair. M. was not back in the room either, and he did not return until after 1:30 a.m. In no time at all, he was snoring away the night. After about an hour of this, I got up to put in earplugs, which were completely useless in blocking out either the snoring or the road noises. At 7:30, he stirred and I got up and shaved. Afterwards he said he'd meet me at Cobb's Restaurant where we had eaten the day before about 1 p.m. I had not eaten since then, except for ice cream on the Taieri train. Empty of stomach was I along with being sleep deprived.

The woman at the hotel desk gave me the wrong directions to get to Cobb's. (Later she said she thought I said "Park's" and I still found it.) When M. finally showed up, he sat down directly across from me as I continued eating. He was incredibly smug and obviously had something he wanted to say. I told him how angry I was by what he had said to me and the man I had an appointment with to talk about play writing. I said that I would not be treated that way and that his aggressive behavior was unacceptable. He avoided my eyes and then, with pauses, he said, "You know, I don't like you very much."

In retrospect, my visit to Katherine Mansfield's Wellington birthplace, the vast panoramas of New Zealand's South Island, and the wonderful people whose hospitality I enjoyed completely overbalanced the torture of traveling with M. The caveat "Traveler beware" is a valuable one. Writing about these risks in your journal will provide some revealing insights into yourself as a traveler on a journey into the unknown. The banquet of impressions presented will enrich body, mind, and spirit.

Expectations

As a survivor, you've faced many unknowns. Long journeys present unknowns in abundance. "Will I be happy?" "Will I meet people who can help me if I need it?" "Will I meet someone very special?" "Will I discover something about myself that I hadn't known?" "Will this trip change my life as I've known it?"

From her vantage of 90 years, Cary described in her journal an early experience that left an indelible lifelong impression. When she was young and newly married, her husband took her to Italy. In Rome, they went to the oldest part of the city, and the tiny twisting streets and the ancient buildings delighted her. Suddenly, she broke her heel on a cobblestone. She and her husband found a tiny shoemaker's shop where the heel could be repaired. While she waited, her husband went off to buy some fruit. In trying to find his way back to the shoemaker's shop, he took the wrong turn and lost his way. She found herself alone in the shop without money, without a map, and without knowing one word of Italian. Nor did she have any idea what had happened to her husband. It was unknown territory for her in every way. Reading the journal entry she wrote years later about the panic she had felt, she was overcome all over again by the strength of her emotions.

We've all survived the experience of getting lost. It's a basic part of your journey, for while you don't expect to get lost, it happens, and the memory of finding yourself can be powerful. Now is a good time to start a list of your most memorable journeys. Begin it with an entry about your most difficult journey and how you handled it.

Not all memorable journeys are difficult. A charming childhood memory of Cary's involved going to a distant city and staying in a hotel with her mother. The next morning, she asked her mother why they were stopping at the desk in the lobby. "To pay the bill," her mother answered. "For *sleeping*?" asked the amazed child.

Over the next few days, add details of other memorable journeys to your list, exploring them from the vantage of today. Did the impressions left by these events influence other journeys you've taken? Even perhaps your life's journey? What happened on your trip might account for the way you look at tomorrow. It might even have set one of the "compass points" of your life.

New directions

You set out on a journey to meet a person or to visit a place that you either want to see or are obliged, for whatever reason, to reach. Think of the way you read murder mysteries. Your goal is to discover the culprit and motive. In order to solve the puzzle, you follow your curiosity about people you don't know and places you haven't seen. Many people travel from a wish to satisfy this curiosity. And sometimes, after you set out on a journey, you discover that the significance of your motivation has changed entirely. Whether you're aware of your reason for embarking on a particular journey, one is waiting there for you to discover.

Every quest has a mission

In Homer's *Odyssey*, Ulysses' destination was Ithaca; he knew where he wanted to go, he just couldn't get there easily. In James Joyce's *Ulysses*, Leopold Bloom's adventures occur as he wanders about Dublin. Your quest may involve a hobby or special interest such as photography or sketching. Or you may wish to create a rewarding professional relationship or explore the possibilities of a romantic connection with someone you want to get to know better.

Some travelers stay on the move in order to avoid intimacy. They fill their time with packing, unpacking, and making travel arrangements. Constantly moving from one place to another is a phenomenon familiar to people with addictive behavior. It's known as "taking a geographic cure." When circumstances become too difficult in one city because of debts or compulsions, moving across country or to some new city becomes the solution to the problem. Escaping to another place may put off today's problems, but it doesn't take long for the same difficulties to arise all over again in the new location. Sooner or later, the geographic cure gives out, and eventually such travelers must embark on a more truthful journey.

No matter where you travel, you always bring yourself along. That's why it's revealing to look at the list of your most memorable journeys and connect each one with what you expected would happen as you were planning the trip. Was standing in the Coliseum in Rome as vivid as losing your wallet and traveler's checks to a smiling urchin? Was drinking Scandiano, the local wine, with Florentine friends nearly as memorable as the Ponte Vecchio? Was Niagara Falls, Piccadilly Square, the Pyramids, the Metropolitan Museum, or the *Book of Kells* the goal of your itinerary? What happened when you reached it? Or perhaps you set out to leave someone behind, only to discover how much you needed that person. Often on a journey, you start out for one place and end up somewhere else because of what you learn about yourself along the way.

It can be very instructive for you as a traveler to compare the external journey you're taking with the one you experience internally. What are you looking for? What have you found? What did you leave behind? You may wish to answer these questions in your journal now.

Having fun may be your only goal when you plan a particular trip. Can you remember arriving somewhere with this intent, only to discover that you're at the wrong place in *yourself*? The next time you travel, bring your journal along and note the contrasts between the actual journey and the one you experience through your intuition.

Travelers on healing journeys have pursued their quests through doctors' offices, examination rooms, and enormous hospital machines that resemble instruments of torture. They've sought to return to the life they lived before the onslaught of symptoms that shattered their health.

Their journeys took them a long way from home. As strange as it may seem, I've heard many who faced this type of ordeal speak of the gratitude they feel for what they've learned about themselves on their journeys. Subjects to explore in your journal include the discoveries you've made about yourself and your relationship with those who have traveled with you through these trials.

Journey's end

The familiar image of a weary American Indian drooping in his saddle, spear dangling from his hand, appears on prints, bookends, and other antique decorative pieces. Its title is "End of the Trail." A stark comparison can be made between this image from the beginning of the 20th century and a photo of the astronauts who made the first moon landing in 1969.

You, too, have faced certain dangers and you've reached many different destinations. At times, you may have felt weary enough to have reached the end of your own trail. At other times, you may have thrilled to the thought of adventures that lie ahead. In light of unfolding technological advances, you may even be planning your own trip to the moon!

Through travel, you enter different worlds, either literally or in your imagination as you read what others have written about their own journeys. As survivors, we've learned that we heal by making ourselves available to the quest.

As you make your way through *Write for Life*, you're exploring new ways to experience yourself through your journal. In "Pilgrimage," Chapter 23, you'll go more deeply into the meaning of what you've discovered on your journey. It's all part of your legacy, which we'll explore in detail in the next chapter, "Legacy Letters, Part One."

Chapter 12
Legacy Letters, Part One: Laying the Foundation

Getting started

By now, you may have acquired new insights about some areas within yourself that need healing and attention. Consider what has been happening to you as you've been writing in your journal. It's useful to "take your pulse" from time to time, and it's especially helpful when you come to the end of the year, a birthday, or any other significant milestone. Is your writing helping you become aware of the good things happening in your life? That's one useful index of self-caring. Take a page or two in your journal to create this gratitude inventory, as some have called it. And while you're at it, consider some of your obstacles as well.

Some workshop participants noted these items in their gratitude inventories: "Reduced stress." "Support for solving difficult issues." "Strengthened friendships." "A heightened appreciation for what's happening at this moment." "Things you didn't even realize." "Excitement in discovering details of forgotten events." "A deeper sense of daily completion." "A new source of entertainment that promises even more delight in the future."

For almost everyone who writes with some consistency, there's a growing sense of empowerment. Through the act of writing, you discover new ways to appreciate what you've done in the past and feel good about what you're doing right now. This lends great value to your sense of your legacy in life.

Your legacy

Many people have heard of legacy letters. Perhaps you've thought about writing one. The task can be rather daunting. Having worked with several groups on ideas for these letters, I've designed a two-step approach to help you with this task. The first step lays the foundation for writing the letters, and the second develops the letters themselves.

A legacy is more than tangibles such as property, real estate, and *objets d'art*. A legacy is synonymous with heritage and tradition; it's something handed down from ancestors, friends, teachers, and others who have made a significant impression in your life. Your legacy includes knowledge, ideas, and traditions you've inherited. You may even bear the name of an ancestor, saint, or other person your parents hoped you would grow up to emulate.

A legacy is also more than what happened in the past. It's right here,

right now: *myself as I am*. It's for *you* to appreciate. Explore yourself today from this perspective: "How do I wish to remember *myself*?" Then take some time to create as many different pictures of yourself as you can develop. Don't get stuck in only one image; allow descriptions to flow freely. Let your pen cover the page

with whatever comes. Over several days, explore different aspects of the person you are, such as the physical entity, the emotional responder, the intellectual reflecter, the spiritual aspirer. Create snapshots of yourself from many different angles and perspectives. Include in these sketches as many details as possible. Let nothing inhibit you. Wear many hats and be sure to have fun.

Staying started

Perhaps you encountered some surprises as you considered the question, "How do I wish to remember myself?" Make a note of these surprises in your journal, so that you can return to them and write more later. But for now, focus on your legacy. Consider it as more than the pull of your wishes. You're already creating a history that will live on. Writing it down is part of its foundation.

You've made decisions based on what you regarded as life-sustaining. Now stand in this moment and look into the future. Use your journal to write about what you've valued in the past and (because you've changed over time) some of the values you presently hold. Look at it as a "then and now" inventory.

Creating a framework

Few people sit down to acknowledge their accomplishments. Because of this, there's often a sense of unease that makes writing about their legacy difficult. Make it a high priority to take a few days to write about the values that frame your key decisions. Headings like "My First 25 Years," "My Second 25 Years," "Years 50 to 65," and "65 to Now," if appropriate, may prove helpful as you sort through and identify some of the values that have motivated you over the years.

Remember, you're writing this inventory for you, not for anyone else.

Workshop participants have identified such values as health, family, friends, education, job security, travel and adventure, taking care of parents, wealth, excitement, higher consciousness, getting published, "success at any price," being well loved, youth, sex, luxury, reputation, living well, and dying well.

Over the years, some values remain the same, others change. One group associated the following values with age 30: appearance and youth, independence, autonomy, friendships, "being able to explore," popularity, skill, and to be loved. Another group identified these with age 70: "Every decade seems better," health, sunshine, security and care, friendships, parties, humor, "hobbies and everything I never had time for," renewing contacts with people from the past, and "having the time of my life!"

Your values have had a major influence on your life choices. They've created your legacy. Being as honest as possible with yourself about the significance of your values will help you achieve deeper understanding. Remember, don't be critical about anything you set down. You're interested in understanding your legacy, not judging it. You did what worked for you at the time, and that awareness needs to sustain you as you write.

Values in context

It's not possible to write legacy letters until you can acknowledge your accomplishments and examine the choices you've made, the events that have changed you, and the things you've done or left undone. Creating an inventory and writing about it will broaden the first phase of this journey. Use the following framework as a guideline to creating the value context of your legacy:

Values

My First 25 Years: _____

My Second 25 Years: _____

Years 50 to 65: _____

65 to Now: _____

Next, using the values identified in each time period (or in a time framework that better fits your own life), make a list of the significant decisions you made during each of those periods.

With this framework, write about some of the choices you've made that reflect the values you identified in your inventory. These values were responsible for the kind of education you chose, the places you lived, the projects you completed or abandoned, your jobs, your partners, your friends, and your spiritual efforts. Your values underlay what you did and did not do. Give yourself permission to remember as much or as little as you choose. Your goal is to achieve an intimate image of yourself.

By acknowledging the changes in your values, you'll be able to experience a new sense of continuity, one that can provide a basis for writing the letters you're contemplating now. Until you create a foundation based on your own experience, it's very difficult to begin to write these letters. Daily life is sustained through the passage of minutes into hours, days, and years. Because of this, our existence appears to be fragmentary and lacking the continuous thread of meaning that is evident in a novel or a play. Biographers pick up the threads of their subjects' lives and connect them in some kind of order. As a journal writer, you're laying out some of these threads so that you can consider them and then use them to support your efforts to understand your legacy.

Participants often ask about using the material in their journal to write an autobiography. An autobiography is a literary endeavor embodying an implicit expectation of publication in some form. Journal writing is a healing activity aimed at encouraging health and well-being and personal empowerment. You write your journal for yourself, and the material you develop is for your own benefit.

In the same way, you'll be writing these legacy letters for yourself to help you heal yourself. Publication is not your priority. If you decide to write legacy letters to others, or if you want to send them the letters you've written, that's your decision. By putting yourself at the center of the process, you're offering yourself a gift that only you can give.

New directions

You've been laying the foundation for your legacy letters by paying attention to your past. Many people are eager to pass on to family members and others ideas and information they couldn't know without being told. Some are eager to tell children or grandchildren what their lives have been like. To start themselves off, participants have found it challenging to make a list of questions they wished they could have asked their grandparents.

Write some of the questions you wish you could have asked your ancestors or strangers you wish you had known. Following are four lists developed by workshop participants.

One participant wrote, "This is what I wish I knew about my grandparents":
1. A chronology of their lives.
2. Comments by them detailing their feelings about the events they experienced.
3. A description of their interests.
4. Descriptions of people in their lives and their feelings about them.
5. Descriptions of events that were important to them and their feelings at the time.

Sara, another participant, wrote this list:
1. How and where did you meet your spouse? Why do you think you were attracted to each other?

2   What did you study in school?

3. What are your favorite things to do now?

4. What did you like to do as a child?

5. What was your first job? Did you like it? What things did you do throughout your career?

6. What were your parents like?

7. Are you mostly happy with the choices you made? What would you do differently if you could?

8. As you were growing up, who did you look up to, and why?

9. Did your ideals change when you were an adult? If so, why?

10. Do you feel you continued to grow as an adult? If so, in what ways?

11. What are some of your favorite melodies?

12. When were the times you were happiest? What were you doing?

13. How do you feel about your children and grandchildren?

14. What's your favorite music? What's your favorite kind of art?

15. What were some of the hardest times you lived through? How did you get through them?

16. What struggles did you face growing up? As an adult? Were you ever assailed by doubt?

Here's Janel's list of questions for her grandparents:

1. Who had mental illness?

2. Why were my father and mother raised the way they were?

3. What was your greatest fear?

4. What was your greatest joy?

5. What were your greatest sorrows?

6. What do you regret about your child-raising experience?

7. What are you most proud of?

8. What are the greatest changes you've seen during your lifetime?

9. What wisdom have you gained? How have you sought to pass that on?

10. What were the happiest times in you life?

11. Will you please write the stories of your lives?

12. What was health care like, and what were your health issues?

13. Why did you name your children as you did?

14. What were the ten defining moments of your life?
15. What were the seven most significant choices you made in your life, and how did they influence the course of your life?

Diane made this list of questions for her grandparents:

1. Who influenced you the most?
2. Who dampened your enthusiasm?
3. Who spurred your creativity?
4. What educational opportunities did you have?
5. Was nature an ingredient of your childhood? Did you have a "hiding place"?
6. What happened if you did something "wrong" or "bad"?
7. What happened if you did something "right" or "good"?
8. How did you choose your marriage partner? Where were you married? Who came to your wedding? Who didn't come?
9. Did you have dreams that you realized? How did it happen? Who helped you?
10. When did you first glimpse your separateness, your sense of "I"?
11. Did you have a hobby? Why did you choose it?
12. What were some of the books that influenced you or touched you deeply? Describe the circumstances in which you read them.
13. Were you able to use your natural talents? What were those talents?
14. How did you make decisions?
15. Have you had long-term relationships? What kept the relationships going?
16. Describe the houses you lived in, the neighborhoods, and what you liked and didn't like about each one.
17. What kind of parent were you to your child/children?
18. How many people were in your extended family? Talk about them.
19. Did you have someone to confide in and in whom you could trust? What was that person like?

Feel free to add some of these to the list you're writing now in your journal. These questions for ancestors provide interesting details. Your own list identifies the kinds of things your children and grandchildren might want you to write about in your legacy letters to them in Chapter 16, "Legacy Letters, Part Two."

Answering the questions

For your next journal entries, use the questions you've written in your journal as if they had been asked of *you*. You may find yourself responding to only one of the questions for several days. As you write, more and more details will occur to you.

Over time, these entries will help you appreciate your legacy and begin to heal some places you never knew were bruised. Just allow the thoughts to come and write them down. Don't edit or censor them. Discover how many different aspects of the past emerge with their own vitality in your consciousness. Invite them in. Spend time with them.

You've been creating the foundation of your legacy from several different sources. The more willing you are to explore these areas, the greater your perspective will be in the future. With this information available to you, it will be much easier to write your letters when you decide that you're ready to write them. In the meantime, you can enjoy several different kinds of adventures that will offer new understanding and healing.

Chapter 13
Dreams

Getting started

"Who, me? I *never* dream!"

Many people who are unable to remember their dreams believe they don't dream at all. But that's incorrect. Whether we remember our dreams, we all have them. If we were deprived of the opportunity to dream, we'd be seriously harmed because dreams allow us to rebalance our energy. They also provide an opportunity for problem-solving, as the phrase "I need to sleep on that" indicates. When we sleep, our intuition is activated and our creativity is enhanced.

In this journey, you're going to explore ways to enrich your waking life by getting in touch with your dreams.

At a recent Write for Life dream workshop, participants shared some of their concerns about their dreams. "I find that I want to have more dreams and I would like to know how to remember them." "I know I experience great anxiety in some of my dreams, but I don't know what to do about it." "How can I encourage myself to have more dreams?" "There must be more than just Freudian interpretations of dreams, and I'd like to know about this." "I'm interested in the metaphysical dimensions – the astral level – of dreams." "There are times when I dream the same dream over and over again. Why does that happen? What am I being told, or what is it that I'm telling myself?"

Some participants were very specific about their dreams. "I remember only the nightmares, never the good ones." "After seeing a film recently, I started dreaming of nude men." "When I was younger, after a lot of stress and pressure, I used to dream of packing a big trunk." "I have four kinds of dreams: One is that I am working hard and everything goes my way; another is that I can't find something; a third, in which people disappear; or the worst – I'm driving over a cliff." "A very familiar dream for me is from childhood: being chased and barely escaping my pursuer." "I dream of magnificent, creative, constructive details, elaborate panorama, encrusted jewelry, and coats of arms. Toward the end of the dream there is usually a logical problem, such as difficulty finding the right subway." "Sometimes people who are no longer alive appear in my dream, and I always want to have more from them, but they disappear."

Make a list of some of the dreams you've had over the past year. It may revive additional memories of dreams. You may also write about dreams you'd like to have.

Making connections

There are many different kinds of dreams. The important thing is the connection between your life and what's happening in your dream. Dreams are prompted by life experience and are a valuable source of information. The best way to begin understanding your dream is to consider actual events day to day. You'll find your journal an excellent place to note what's happening in your life next to your dreams about it.

Your dreams are like messages from your inner self. You may have terror dreams or anxiety dreams, during which you're struggling with events that have caused you concern. You may have dreams that lift you up or make you aware of things you need to know about yourself. A recurring dream may mean that a problem you're facing is still with you. Bear in mind that all dreams are benign, even those that frighten you.

All mammals dream. Consider the fact that 20 percent of sleep time is spent dreaming. If you live ninety years, you spend about thirty years of that time sleeping and six years dreaming. In the course of each night, you have five or six different periods during which you dream. The last period before waking is the longest.

Freud characterized dreams as the royal road to knowledge of the unconscious mind. The Talmud says, "A dream is like a letter you haven't opened." If you give no importance to your dreams, there is less chance of receiving and remembering them. For some, trying to remember dreams is difficult. Here's a technique you may find useful.

1. Make an agreement with yourself that you value your dreams and want to receive them. If you condition yourself to looking forward to receiving dreams, they'll be easier to access.

2. Suggest to yourself, "I will remember my dreams tonight if they're important to me."

3. Keep pen and paper beside the bed.

4. Don't move on waking. Don't open your eyes or shift your body; shifting the body diverts attention from the dream.

5. Don't go back to the beginning of the dream. Starting at the beginning is an intellectual process. Instead, try to see the dream going backward as if you were rewinding a videotape, asking yourself what was the scene before the last one, and then the one before that and the one before that, until you get to the beginning. Then, after you've come to the beginning, play it all through from beginning to end. Let yourself recollect a frame at a time. Do this several times. After you've gone back frame by frame, play it through several times.

6. Next, on the notebook you've left beside your bed, write down the sounds, colors, and phrases from the dream. Try to give it a short title, like "Father at the wheel" or "My blue dress."

7. Be neutral. Don't try to figure out what the dream means. Write what you see and hear, not what you wish were there.

8. You may not be successful the first few times you try this. It will take some practice to be able to do this easily. The process becomes easier as you continue to do it.

There's a short form for writing the dream. Focus on key words, intense images and emotions, and sounds. Don't get bogged down in details. You may use this technique to get started. Then, move on to the long form.

For the long form, write the date and day of the week. Note whether the date was a special event like a birthday or an anniversary, or had any significance in your life. Give the dream a title. Don't try to put down too many details (it will bog you down). Get the broad outlines. In the margin, try to remember what you were thinking about when you went to sleep. The life context is far more important than trying to interpret the dream. If you can make this connection, you'll clarify the dream content.

Staying started

It's possible to invite dreams that you'd like to have. One way to accomplish this is a practice known as incubation. Before going to sleep, write about the events of the day and lay out any problems or concerns. Then begin to meditate, or pray to receive a dream response to these concerns. Responses are often not what you might expect, but they still contain answers.

Don't try to force images. And remember that no matter what you've dreamed, it is *not* the basis for taking any action. Let the ideas of the dream play in your consciousness instead of deceiving yourself that "my dream told me to do this!" Your dream is presenting you with information that's held at a deeper level of consciousness, but it may be doing so in a way that is symbolic and requires interpretation. Dreams are very useful in helping us identify causes of distress. Only after we understand  them can we determine an appropriate response.

Sometimes we don't understand immediately how to apply what we've learned. At other times we do. Consider the case of the woman who kept dreaming of driving off a cliff. She responded to her dream by not driving for several weeks, and then she began driving with far greater caution than she had in the past. Until she had the dream, she hadn't realized that she was in danger of having an accident.

Encouraging the dream

It's helpful to understand that bad dreams are good. They help us purge problems and conflicts. Of course, there is always a wanting-to-know and a *not*-wanting-to-know. Consider making a list of reasons for encouraging dreams, and then list concerns that get in the way of your doing this.

Looking these over may help you identify an action or point of view you need to change in order to remember your dreams.

Even when you decide to encourage your dreams, they may not come easily. Dream energy can be very easily dissipated. Dreams are fragile, and the slightest disturbance can cause them to slip away. Using an alarm clock to wake yourself up is too harsh an approach. The ringing alarm destroys the dream memory. Instead, program yourself to wake up before the alarm goes off. If you stay still, you won't divert the flow of body energy.

Another way to encourage dreams is to write in the notebook beside your bed, "I will remember any dream that is important for me" or "I want an answer to this question: _____." Priming the dream pump is a very effective device.

Intuition works in amazing ways. People who fear recurring nightmares should be aware that these dreams may contain some small aspect that will reveal how the dreamer can put an end to them. The goal of finding this buried clue would be a good reason to encourage such dreams.

Revealing examples

In dreams, symbols have great importance. For example, transportation symbols may show how you're progressing in life. Maybe you should examine the steps you've been taking. Don't forget to observe the condition of the vehicle you're in as well as whether you're the driver or a passenger. And what kind of road are you on – a superhighway, a rutted road, a road that leads nowhere?

Here's one participant's travel dream. He crossed the Atlantic on an ocean liner and arrived in Genoa, Italy. On arrival, he found himself surrounded by huge pink arches and towering edifices. It turned out that the arches in the dream were just like ones in framed lithographs that had hung in his childhood home. The dream indicated the calm strength and maturity the dreamer had achieved during his journey through life. The happiness he experienced was a revealing acknowledgment of his own personal growth.

In the dream of a Lebanese woman, she served her friend a rat for dinner. This friend had actually been her dinner guest the previous night and had left early, to the hostess' dismay. It turned out that the woman had driven her friend away by talking of unpleasant memories about Lebanon, one of which involved seeing rubbish heaps infested with rats.

Another participant's dream revealed a dilemma. In it, she was in France, wondering whether she should return to California after the death of her husband. She repeatedly dreamed of driving a Buick and being unable to find a parking space. Her American car was too big; the parking was too limited. Night after night, she searched for a parking space unsuccessfully.

In the dream, she needed to either get a smaller car or find a different city/place to park in. Going to California symbolized the new environment; her Buick represented an attitude that she had to get rid of. Ultimately she decided to leave Paris and "park" her attitude in California.

You may often have dreams so vivid and painful that you wake up shaking. One workshop participant dreamed that his Stradivarius violin was missing. He was so terrified that he woke up, got out of bed, and went to the closet to examine his violin case. He was so ecstatic to find his violin unharmed that he celebrated with a fine dinner in a restaurant. Another woman found her dream of an entirely redecorated apartment so vivid that when she woke up, she went to check the other rooms. She had not wanted to admit to herself how unhappy she was about the condition of her dwelling, and her dream encouraged her desire for change.

Connecting the dream to yourself

People have peculiar ways of disguising things they have trouble acknowledging about themselves and others. Regardless of how tempted you are, you must not analyze other people's dreams. You lack sufficient information to do this. If you stick to your own dreams and write about them in your journal, you'll begin developing a body-mind-spirit connection that may be missing in your own life.

Dreams don't exist in a vacuum. Events and emotions provoke them, and writing about the underlying connection between these events and your dreams encourages the healing process. It will also lead to improved connections with your intuition, and this strengthens the body-mind-spirit relationship upon which healing depends. Appreciating this fact is, for some survivors, a new way to live, one that's 180 degrees away from the perspective that does not value intuition or recognize the healing power that's within everyone.

Don't become discouraged if at first you don't have many dreams to record in your journal. Be patient and keep making the effort. It's also helpful to write about the feelings related to your efforts. You can learn a lot about yourself through your efforts to open to ideas and feelings you haven't considered before. Writing down your dreams helps you see your past, present, and future in new ways.

Just as you grow to understand that life works through you, so you'll come to see that your dreams work in a similar fashion. Your dreams are hieroglyphics written by you in your own personal language. Shouldn't you make the effort to read what you've written?

Resistance

Remember the powerful force of inertia you encountered when you first began writing in your journal? This might easily reappear when you begin to write about your dreams. It may take the form of reluctance to be involved with something that bores you, repulses you, makes you feel ridiculous, or seems completely without significance. Anything you're resisting can be a valuable subject for exploration in your journal.

You'll learn a great deal about healing if you let yourself write about this resistance. It's much more important to write about what you observe in yourself than to try to avoid or eliminate it. By giving yourself permission to feel your feelings, you invite yourself to make room for change. You can explore this in your journal now and return to it in the months ahead.

New directions

While some are willing to explore their resistance to writing about dreams, others suddenly believe they have the insight to understand their own dreams and everyone else's. This is another form of resistance. Making dreams into something harmless, something to explain away as if by magic, is resistance in another form.

Daytime consciousness is totally different from nocturnal consciousness. Nocturnal consciousness is alien to the waking experience of life; it's part of the "theater of the inner world." Appreciating this helps you understand that while attempts at interpretation may appear to be answers, they're not answers at all. They're reflections of personal wishes and ideas that involve not only you but your relations with other people. When it comes to interpreting the incredibly complex inner world of dreams, no one suddenly becomes an expert overnight. What's most important about beginning dream work is that you're making connections in your own life between what you're dreaming and what you're living. Getting your imagination to work is a key component of healing.

From *The Jungian-Senoi Dreamwork Manual*

If you're willing to explore your dreams and have the patience to be consistent in your efforts, you could try these techniques for getting in touch with dreams, offered by the *Jungian-Senoi Dreamwork Manual*.

The first is **key questions.** Make a list of the questions and issues that were raised in the dream, and explore these questions over several days in your journal. By picking up the thread of one issue, you may discover that it leads to many other issues you weren't even aware of.

The second is **dialogue.** Dreams are filled with many images and symbols. Choose the most compelling and write down the questions that come to you about it. Write whatever comes to mind; free-associate without trying to make sense of what comes up.

The third is **dream reentry.** As you sit quietly in a meditative state, eyes closed, identify the most meaningful aspect of the dream. By making the dream come alive again, you can sometimes connect with its insights.

The fourth is **outer-life dream-task visualization.** Several activities took place in your dream. Choose one and decide on a specific action connected with it that you'll perform next week. Observe the effects of this action.

In considering the use of any of these four techniques, you want to choose the one that's most comfortable and offers the least risk. You're just beginning to attend to dreams, and you need to develop some experience in working with them. Continue to write about dreams for as long as you find the activity helpful to your experience of living.

Participants' experiences

Ellen was absolutely certain that she never dreamed until the night she woke up screaming at the sight of herself on the balcony of her house, a blazing fire a few feet away. It gave off no heat, only brilliant flames. The dream was all she needed to begin paying closer attention to her nocturnal existence and writing about it.

Ida, a workshop participant who was blind, kept dreaming of cooking, especially when she ate food that was not as well prepared as the specialty dishes she used to make. It's not at all uncommon in dreams to perform certain activities you're not able to do in life. Dreaming of them helps to diminish your frustration.

Writing about dreams requires you to be available to your nocturnal mind. You don't suddenly become a "conscious" dreamer. It's only with practice and persistence that you'll be able to open a window on this dimension of experience. Practice and more practice in the effort to write about dreams will result in greater awareness of them.

The door is open

If you're interested in pursuing dream work beyond this initial introduction, look in the Resources section beginning on page 253 for books on the subject. Interest in dream work can develop over time. The greatest gift of journal writing is that you open the door to a new understanding of yourself. You want to encourage yourself, not discourage yourself. Follow where your intuition leads; don't force yourself on a journey you're not ready to take. You have many new directions you can explore. In the chapters to come, you'll encounter others.

Chapter 14
Now and Zen

Getting started

When you open a new window on the way you look at your life, you can gain some remarkable insights. If you're unfamiliar with eastern religion and philosophy, the journey you'll embark on in this chapter may open just such a new window for you. In the following pages, the advice of Zen Buddhist teacher Reverend Daigaku David Rumme will guide us as we examine a few ideas drawn from Zen teaching.

Physical, emotional, and spiritual well-being is your goal, and these few key Zen ideas will help you create the foundation for healing. This is a practical effort, not an intellectual exercise. If you wish to study Zen teachings in depth, an immense body of material is available. Here, you'll find some insights that will resonate in your own world and help you understand yourself and your efforts to live better.

Attitudes and impressions

When asked about the meaning of Zen Buddhism, workshop participants responded in many different ways. Some commented on its popularity in the 1960s and remembered attending lectures by famous writers and poets. Others identified Zen with the "flower children" and "hippies." And still others spoke of being invited to Buddhist temples, where they experienced a compelling spiritual atmosphere.

One woman who thought of Zen as a way of life wrote, "I remember that it encouraged people to take the time to smell the roses, to enjoy life more completely by taking in everything." A Japanese woman remembered her grandmother practicing certain rituals that included prayer, chanting, and the burning of incense. For her, Zen meant something very old-fashioned. Another participant thought Zen very remote and erudite, not something with practical application to everyday life.

At the beginning of this journey of exploration, write in your journal what you understand Zen to be. Later you can look back and compare this entry with what you'll come to see as you work with these ideas. Begin from this moment, *now*.

What is Zen?

The word "Zen" has special marketing appeal. Advertisements use the word to attract consumers; there's even a perfume called "Zen." It has an inspiring connotation for some people, like the woman who referred to the "Zen of good housekeeping" – her term for thinking positively about her house-work and the gratitude she felt toward her house for being easy to clean. In another example, a man who had stepped off the curb into the street and almost been killed by a passing taxi was asked to describe his experience. "It was very zen," he answered, using the term as a form of shorthand that he trusted his listeners would understand. Neither an unknown nor remote idea in the world today, Zen is very much a part of contemporary life.

The word "zen" is the Japanese pronunciation of a Chinese word that had its origin in India. The Chinese character for the word has two separate components. The character on the left means to indicate, to point. The character on the right means single, one.

Another way of saying this is found in the book *The Essence of Zen*. Author Sekkei Harada writes, "The Chinese character for Zen means 'to demonstrate simplicity.'"

At the core of Zen teaching and practice is the affirmation of the one-ness that underlies all that is. Zen also affirms that there is no separation between the action and the actor. In other words, if you're eating, just eat; if you're walking, just walk. It's doing, not *thinking* about doing. The present moment, the "Now," is gone the instant you begin to think about it; as you seek to define it, you're already living in the past. Zen practitioners learn to immerse themselves in this moment of experience by focusing on the movement of their breath. Their goal is to live in "everyday mind."

> This very moment
> Just think of this only
> The past cannot return
> The future cannot be known.
> –*Daigaku David Rumme*

You can't control the past or the future. Spending your life looking back at the past and regretting what's already happened results in pointless struggle and suffering. The past can't be changed; therefore, be present in the moment. Worrying about the future also keeps you from living in Now. Being here now is the focus of Zen practice.

This idea challenges you to consider the way you use your mental, emotional, and physical energy. Can you stop suffering over the past or dreading the future? Wouldn't living without suffering offer a different approach to life?

Zen teaches that instead of choosing to live with suffering, which is ego-centered, you need to structure your life to make it reality-centered. Reality isn't about the past or the future; reality is the acceptance of Now. The question, then, is what does it mean to live in the Now? How would you write about your life at this moment if you were explaining it to someone from another planet? What if you were telling it to someone who is dying?

Genesis: Separation
Twenty-six hundred years ago, Shakyamuni Buddha, a prince born into conditions of great wealth and privilege, became deeply distressed by the sight of illness and death in the world around him. He became obsessed

with the question of suffering in the world and struggled to learn how it might be overcome. Turning his back on his life of opulence and power, he left his palace to wander the world in search of an answer.

His quest led him first to monks who trained him in ascetic practices as a way to let go of the ego through physical deprivation. His self-denial and self-mortification became so extreme that he nearly starved to death. But this did not bring him the answer he was looking for.

Concluding that neither the self-indulgence of his early life nor the extreme deprivation of his ascetic practice had shown him how to surmount the suffering of the world, he sat down under a tree – the famous Bodhi tree – determined not to get up again until he had found the truth. He decided to sit quietly and meditate, his attention focused on observing the present moment. He did this for six years.

One morning, he looked up at the morning star. In that instant, he became one with the star and experienced a flash of illumination: "I and all things are one." He realized that if everything is an expression of one being, neither time, place, nor separation exists. This thought released him from all suffering, since it is in the sense of separation that suffering arises.

According to Shakyamuni Buddha, the mind of the individual is the source of the world's suffering. When we identify with and cling to the deluded processes of the human mind, we cling to a sense of separateness from others, from reality, from all that is, thereby creating and sustaining our own suffering.

For many, this is a difficult concept to grasp. One way to explore it is to start a list of personal "separations" in your life that make it difficult for you to experience any sense of wholeness. Begin by considering the state of your health, finances, relationships, and connections (or lack of connections) with the world. Next, consider what you have and what you *wish* you had. What do you lack that would make you truly happy? What separates you from the experience of being complete?

Identifying what you think is missing is the first step toward understanding the meaning of wholeness in your life. Over the next several days, make an inventory of all the things you lack. Then take a day to write about each of the items on your list, exploring as extensively as you can what it would mean to have everything that is lacking in your life. Because the conditions in which you live are constantly changing, you might remind yourself to create a new inventory each month. Updating this inventory on a regular basis each year is a valuable practice.

Staying started

Many people spend their lives being unhappy about what they don't have. They become defensive about the way they live because of what they feel they lack. Suddenly, they see themselves as sufferers instead of as recipients of the gift of life. Does this painful predicament sound familiar? Is it possible for you to begin to reconceive yourself from a different place? Explore this possibility in your journal.

Zen teaching

In Zen philosophy, everyone endures the four sufferings of birth, illness, old age, and death. Four more examples leap to mind: separation from those we love; having to live and work with people we cannot abide; never finding what we're searching for, no matter how long we search; and the inevitable problems that result from inhabiting a physical form.

Instead of enduring the frustration that arises from dwelling on a particular aspect of suffering, Zen encourages you to "become one with it," to let yourself experience your feelings not as ideas, but as the way you are. Rather than seeking to know or understand anything about illness or aging or any other source of unhappiness, just be in the moment of experience, and you'll find that you're at peace with yourself.

In Buddhism, there are 84,000 sutras (teachings) that encapsulate these basic ideas:

1. Everything is impermanent and constantly changing.
2. Because everything is changing, things have no self-nature.
3. Because everything is impermanent, there is no beginning or end; there is only Now.

Our failure to understand this deprives us of the freedom to live life fully. If you were able to realize the truth of this, you would experience liberation.

You would attain enlightenment (nirvana). Zen offers the guidance needed to accomplish this goal.

The practice of Zen opens the door to the treasure that is waiting for you without your even knowing it. To study the way of Zen is to study the self. To study the self is to forget the self. To forget the self is to realize liberation. No separation exists between the individual and flowers, mountains, rivers, trees, friends, enemies, anxiety, frustration, anger. All is one. It's the resistance to being one with everything that creates separation and suffering in life.

You create your own hell with your mind. When you understand this, you can experience nirvana, which is already within. "The way is neither knowing nor not knowing. Each of us, as we are, is the way."

The first step on the way

The first challenge is to awaken to the true nature of self. The annals of Zen are filled with paradoxical examples of how this is accomplished. This story, related in *The Essence of Zen*, illustrates what we must do in order to succeed.

> A monk once asked Joshu, 'I have just arrived at the monastery and don't know the proper way to go about practice. Please tell me what to do.' Joshu said, 'Have you eaten breakfast?' The monk replied, 'Yes, I've just finished eating.' Joshu said, 'Then wash your bowl.' On hearing this, the monk suddenly understood the point of practice. What did he understand? What did he understand to be the key to Zen practice? Reflecting on and examining the questions that arise from this kind of dialogue is the main point of practice.
>
> [Sekkei Harada, The Essence of Zen. *Daigaku David Rumme, translator. Kodansha International, Tokyo, New York, and London (1998)*]

It's not through doing something unique or special, but by bringing "everyday mind" into the experience of Now that you move into spiritual awakening. Many have been conditioned to think in terms of "miracles" in connection with spiritual awakening. They think that if there's no lightning and thunderclap, there's no chance of waking up with new understanding. Zen suggests a different perspective: The moment you appreciate the miracle, it's there.

In a prayer before worship found in the *Book of Common Prayer* there is specific reference to the "wanderings of mind," from which the petitioner asks to be delivered in order to receive what he prayed for. This fracturing of attention interferes with your efforts at prayer and therefore with the results for which you pray. With a clear focus on "everyday mind" and not "special mind," Zen directs one's attention to the practice of a different way of living.

Everyday mind, says Harada, "is daily life from the time you rise in the morning until the time you go to bed at night. But when 'everyday mind' is expressly pointed out in this way, you immediately reflect on the condition of your life and say, 'So that's what it is. My condition right now is 'everyday mind.'"

The words "everyday mind," he continues, express the condition of our lives free of our own ideas and opinions. "Washing one's face, brushing one's teeth, talking, taking meals, working – all these activities take place before thought."

The mind is capable of achieving enlightenment without our having to read philosophy, study religion, or make any other kind of academic preparation. Zen encourages us to become mindful in each moment.

Writing in your journal about what occupies your mind can make you aware of the frenzy of distractions that bombard you every hour of every day. Unless you become aware of this chaotic process, you take it for granted as natural to your mental state. Experiencing this as "the way it is for me" is a vital first step in becoming mindful of yourself.

For a specific period each day over the next week, write in your journal whatever comes to mind at that moment. Allow this to flow from your pen, making an effort to record the mind-as-it-is as accurately as possible. As strange as the effort to do this may seem, the result will help you to appreciate what is so complex and fractured about the workings of the mind. You need your own evidence in order to understand this, and your journal can help you accumulate it.

New directions

From your journal entries of the past week, it will be obvious why Zen concerns itself with the need to become aware of all of the distractions in life. As a survivor, you've often found yourself picking up scattered fragments of your life. For many, there will always be some missing pieces. Perhaps you'll never be able to recover all of yours. Consider looking at what remains from the perspective of simplifying your life. Start to focus attention on living in the present. Live in the "midst of the result" or what some philosophers have called "as if."

Participants have commented that this might be considered merely playing a trick on the mind. But the mind often plays tricks of its own. It pretends that it's in charge of almost everything you consider doing or responding to. Yet you have ample evidence that this kind of control is beyond the mind's capability. For example, the body perspires without the mind's direction; it also responds with many different kinds of reactions that have roots in past experience of danger and biochemical stimulation. The worry that you may feel over any problem or situation is the result of the mind's persistent effort to convince you that it's in control of an outcome

that in fact is beyond your ability to control. When someone tells you that you shouldn't feel the way you do about something, you appreciate directly how little the mind has to do with it. You feel the way you feel without any intervention of the mind.

Mindfulness

With the help of a teacher who understands the principles of Zen, you can develop a practice of *zazen*, an approach to experiencing yourself in the moment through seated meditation. "Becoming one" with anything is a very difficult task to accomplish, as Zen students through plish, as Zen students through

the ages have discovered. It's with the idea of actually achieving this condition that a *koan* (a Zen riddle) is given about a cow that lives inside a barn. The cow's owner leads the animal outside. The cow's head, feet, and body pass through the barn door, but the very last part of its tail won't come out. The problem is how to get the tail out of the barn?

Each individual is the cow. Your hesitancy to grasp enlightenment keeps you stuck in "the barn." With the assistance of a teacher and the practice of *zazen*, you'll be able to arrive at a different "definition" of yourself. Consider using your journal to develop this definition. Your journey into the Now of Zen offers a unique focus for the writing you pursue in your journal. Will you accept the invitation? If not now, perhaps at some time in the future? The choice is yours.

You set off in this new direction by writing about your understanding of Zen. Now it's time to write about how you've been living with your new ideas. Do the principles of Zen bring you further along the way to understanding the fundamental idea of simplicity and oneness? How do you begin to consider what you truly need? What cries out for healing within you? What separation and suffering can you leave behind in order to live with greater joy?

The very essence of simplicity is at the center of the poem offered earlier. As you read it again, can you appreciate the change in your understanding of what enables you to live better?

This very moment
Just think of this only
The past cannot return
The future cannot be known.

Perfect exactly as you are, you follow your journey … to what destination? You can explore this in your journal, noting "Now and Zen" results over the months and years ahead.

Chapter 15
"Not Yets"

Getting started

This chapter will explore the things you've put off dealing with. I call these areas "not yets." Well, the time for "not yet" is now. Your focus is on healing, which means that you may move into some areas that, initially, cause some agitation. This is good, say some seasoned journal writers – if you're not writing about the things that rile you, you're depriving yourself of the benefits of discovery!

When you explore both good feelings and feelings that are distressing, the experience helps you develop a new understanding of who you are and what you need to do to live better. In this journey, you'll continue this practice by encouraging yourself to confront and consider subjects that you might normally dodge while you're traveling the road of life.

Your immortality

One of the biggest "not yets" is thinking about your mortality. You have all the time in the world to do everything you'd like to do. You're going to live forever, right? I mean, you and I are going to live forever – everyone else is going to die sometime or other.

In your journal, you can begin the task of reconciling yourself to the truth of the human equation. Reading the names of friends, family, movie stars, or the rich and famous on the obituary page is comforting, in an odd way. You're here; they're not – and you have no intention of changing places with them.

Even though you may realize that you're not going to have all the time in the world to accomplish everything you'd like to do, the fact is that you live as if the opposite were true. It's important to understand this because there's always a significant reason for doing something that defies logic.

From many years of working with people recovering from addictive behavior, I know the crucial role that denial plays in our attempts to fend off change. Denial is a major factor that keeps most people from accepting their mortality. By not facing the idea that you're going to die, you're able to continue to float downstream, oblivious to any obstacle in your path.

And so it goes – until a medical diagnosis or some other life-threatening event brings an end to the ride. Then denial and inertia evaporate, and action begins.

"Not yets" registry

Consider all the promises you've made to yourself about "someday" completing a project. What kept you from finishing it? Ask yourself the question "If not now, when?" and make a list of these uncompleted tasks. Create a registry of the "not yets" in your life.

The list begins with what you've put off thinking about. Useful categories might include "Dreams," "Unfinished Business," "Fantasies," "Family Matters," "Things I'm Curious About," "Favorites and Unfavorites," and "Things Beyond My Control."

Open some photo albums and decide what places you might like to revisit and some of the people you'd like to see. Think about the promises you made to yourself; take this opportunity to consider them for your list. It will be the first step to appreciating your past as you anticipate the future.

Develop this inventory over a period of several days. Then select a few items to write about, exploring the way you feel about them in relation to your life today. You may find additional items to add to your inventory, perhaps some from the lists below.

Here are some "not yets" that workshop participants wrote about. "Graduate from school and marry." "Realize financial benefits, happiness, and success on the job." "Stay healthy and lose weight." "Meet the love of my life!" "See children and grandchildren grow up." On their lists, conditions creating the warmth and security of a supportive family life, both now and in the future, took precedence.

Professional success and recognition also stood high on many lists, which included outcomes desired for both the individuals writing and the people they were closest to. Sometimes financial gain was a consideration, but most of the time the focus was on happiness and success in achieving personal goals and aspirations. Other items included job security, publication, and recognition for accomplishments. Having a place of one's own, a retreat, was also linked with financial well-being.

Health and the ability to maintain it as the years advanced appeared on every list. For older people, the rising cost of medical care was the focus of a great deal of attention and anxiety. Key concerns included not being a burden on others, always being able to be responsible for oneself, and having the resources to meet all the unknowns that lay ahead. Exercise and maintaining a healthy weight were mentioned by many. Participants also frequently noted misgivings that the aging process might be overshadowed by Alzheimer's, heart attack, or stroke; the ineffectiveness of certain drugs used for chronic conditions over a long period; and recurrence of malignancy. And many older people were worried about the genetic implications of inherited diseases for their children and grandchildren.

Every list named places participants wanted to see for the first time as well as destinations they wanted to return to for the sake of happy memories. A short list of "not yets" in this category includes "Go to Oklahoma to attend church suppers." "Ride the Metro, visit the Louvre, eat *croque-monsieur* sandwiches, and drink wine in Paris." "Visit with old friends in Cologne." "Bathe in the waters at Hot Springs, Arkansas." "See an opal mine in Australia." "Ride the Trans-Siberian Railroad and see the Gobi Desert."

Participants also mentioned the following activities. "File my 1040 by April 15." "Write legacy letters to all my family members." "Take courses in perspective painting and portraiture." "Get more involved with volunteer work." "Purchase a laptop and learn to use it." "See a Democrat in the White House." "Join the Peace Corps."

Date your lists as you make them because six months or a year from now, you'll be listing different items. One way to appreciate yourself is to recognize the ways your lists change over time. You'll see this as you go.

Your journal constitutes a record of the path you've followed through life. It's there for you to read whenever you choose. Coming to a new understanding of yourself supports your self-esteem as few efforts can do. Your journal is a treasure-house of your personal evolution – one that is filled with healing discoveries.

Staying started

If the lists you've created don't have some fun and fantasy items on them, consider adding these now. What may seem impossible today may, over time, be exactly what you need to begin appreciating yourself. As poet Robert Browning wrote, "A man's reach should exceed his grasp, or what's a heaven for?" Fresh breezes need to blow through some of the stuffy ideas you may have about yourself.

From a practical perspective, another principal part of this journey is to identify some of the necessary things you've been putting off. Perhaps you've spent a long time avoiding such tasks as completing legal documents (updating wills, bequests, insurance beneficiaries, and property titles). Funeral and burial arrangements are also on the list of things that people don't generally want to deal with. Consider adding them to your "not yets" inventory with the intention of finally addressing them. Putting your affairs in order is a liberating activity that reduces anguish later when people are in pain or suffering from major physical or emotional trauma.

"What makes me feel good?"

The core of this writing journey is actually about addressing emotional well-being. Your inventory will help you consider "What makes me feel good?" To do this, you'll want to set priorities. Consider each category and rank the items on your list by order of importance. Which is number one? Number two? And so on.

After you create this order of relative importance, make a few journal entries about the significance of the first item on each list. What causes them to take precedence over the other items? Follow the same process for the second and third items on each list. Writing about priorities reminds you of the value you place on yourself and the way you've developed.

It's also useful to remember that you do what works. What elements of the first items can work in your life at this time? What about the second ones? And of the items at the bottom of each category, what about them isn't working in your life at this time?

You can understand a great deal of how you think about yourself and your future by exploring the categories you've created. Jane, a workshop participant, offered this in her journal.

> What's important to my happiness:
>
> Number one: Financial benefits are crucial to my survival. This includes government benefits and help from the family. I'd like to survive to old age and be able to sustain myself.
>
> Number two: my present and future medical care. Keeping track in my journal is important, and I've learned to do this recently. Exercising and losing weight are also important.
>
> Numbers three and four: meeting a boyfriend and having a supportive home life. Being in touch with friends. Travel to London, Paris, and Japan might be nice, but the expense is more than I can handle. And browsing the *Oxford English Dictionary* in twenty volumes would be exciting.

Over the years you create boundaries that are as confining as a prison cell of your own making. Because you take these limits for granted, you rarely have the opportunity to reconsider them. You may not say it, but how often do you think, "Oh, I could never do *that*"? Certainly, you don't respond with "Why not?" But now, in your journal, you can do this safely. Your response is for your eyes only.

As you consider priorities, you move more deeply into self-examination. This is followed by an effort at even greater discernment and analysis, which result in self-knowledge. You know many things about yourself that you rely upon without ever realizing how you know them. In your journal, take this opportunity to get in touch with your intuition. Stored in your imagination is the crystal ball that you use sometimes to your benefit, sometimes to your detriment. The possibilities here are many; you may now give yourself permission to make as many mistakes as you can possibly make. In your journal, you can allow yourself complete freedom to brainstorm with all the inspiration you can muster. You do this without predicting whether any of the results you record will actually happen; you're merely considering the possibilities.

Risk assessment

From your inventory, select an item to which you've given the number one. Write it down. Beneath it, write: What will happen if I do this? Then, in two columns, list as many of the potential benefits and negative possibilities as you can imagine. After you've finished, write: What will happen if I do *not* do this? Then, again in two columns, list as many of the potential benefits and disadvantages as you can imagine.

Here's an example of using this technique to explore the idea of "Writing legacy letters to my children and grandchildren."

What will happen if I write the legacy letters?

Positives	Negatives
1. I will accomplish something that I've been wanting to do for years.	1. Perhaps my children won't approve of the decisions I've made in my life and therefore will think less of me.
2. I'll be able to leave my children a way to know and understand me that's important for them now and in the future.	2. "What they don't know can't hurt them!"
3. When I think back about my own parents and grandparents, there are so many questions that I wish I had the answers to. It's as if I've been cheated of my own history.	3. The decisions I've made may influence them in a negative fashion.

Positives	Negatives
4. How I value my life is important to me; therefore, it's important that I share it with those who love and care about me.	4. They may be offended by some of the things I write about them.
	5. Putting things in writing often makes them much more definite. My own ambivalence about some things might even be distorted by the way I sound in the letter.

What will happen if I do *not* write the legacy letters?

Positives	Negatives
1. I'll have more time to do other things. Writing these letters isn't an easy task.	1. I won't complete a task I believe is important for me to do.
2. My children and grand-children will have nothing to complain about.	2. My family will never know who I really am and what's important to me.
3. Keeping my thoughts to myself is a good way to ensure that others will think better of me.	3. Whatever misconceptions they have of me will only be perpetuated.
4. I can look for another way to share my feelings with others.	4. I might not find a better way and they'll never know my feelings.

Over twenty years ago, I presented a workshop on creativity in Philadelphia and introduced this exercise as a way to help people focus on their goals. About five years later, I met a man who told me that he'd attended the workshop and had used this inventory method to reach a life-changing decision about becoming a writer. In fact, he was completing his second novel!

Throughout the week, use this approach with the first, second, and third entries on your lists. Be patient as you write the positives and negatives. Start with an easy one and the more difficult ones will follow.

You might want to ask yourself whether you define yourself by what you do (or by what you leave undone). It's especially helpful to remember the *koan* from "Now and Zen" about getting the cow out of the barn. It's how you *define* yourself that keeps you stuck inside.

New directions

Having considered the positives and negatives, ask yourself what steps you can take to realize some of these dreams and wishes. How do you plan to make them happen? They won't occur by magical means – though one participant told me that two days after she put an activity (something she thought would never happen) on her "not yets" list, she received a phone call inviting her to do that very thing. She said that it was as if she had opened the window of possibility by writing down the thought. Perhaps the same can happen for you.

Putting together an action plan

The ability to address some of the things on your list of "not yets" is part of the freedom you've achieved as a survivor. This may mean that you need more information than you have on hand. The Internet can help you search for answers that, only a few years ago, would have taken a great deal of time and considerable expense to uncover. Several search engines offer easy access to many of the answers you need. Obtaining this information may result in your being able to cross something off your list for now.

Unlike your use of the Web, asking others for information can seem a major obstacle. No one wants to be thought of as stupid or uninformed. ("I should know the answer to that!") There's also the fear of seeming vulnerable; it might be an invitation for someone to take advantage of you. Or perhaps you just don't want to be turned down. These fears confine you to the limits of the world you've created. When you see this, you can start opening some windows.

At a recent workshop, as participants contemplated possibilities on their lists, Jan told the group that she'd been brought up among Jews, and even though she wasn't Jewish, she couldn't bring herself to plan ahead for something like a "not yet." It would only invite disaster, she felt. Leo Rosten, in his book *Hooray for Yiddish*, writes about the expression *kayne horeh*. "All our forbears were afraid of offending the gods, and it was widely believed that jealous mortals cast an evil, lethal spell. To thwart the demons of the devil, phrases like [*kayne horeh*] were employed with whatever magical gesture (spitting, winking) was deemed effective." If your plans to realize any of your "not yets" make you feel anxious, please incorporate a few *kayne horehs* in your journal. (As Ida commented, "Listen, it couldn't hurt!")

Another participant said that just feeling free to plan a trip represented something quite new for her. In the past, she said, she was always asking herself, "At the end of my life, will I be happy with this decision?" Now she asks herself, "Will I be happy with this decision now?" Opening to this kind of change in thinking is very freeing.

How do you develop this perspective? By just doing it. Action itself is rejuvenating. It offers you new life.

Time, of course, plays a role in planning. You can use an actual calendar or a hypothetical one to plan for anything on your list of "not yets." It's your choice. Spend a few days writing in your journal about these possibilities. Your only commitment is to enjoy your life more and to celebrate this in your own world and your own way.

With such a point upon which to fix your compass for the journey, remember Leonardo da Vinci's last words, in which he asked God to forgive him for not painting all the paintings he could have painted. Your journal can help you live beyond yourself in ways that you may not have allowed yourself to imagine. The healing that comes of this is waiting for you.

Chapter 16

Legacy Letters, Part Two:
Creating the Letters

Getting started

Now that you've scaled the summits of some "not yets" in the last journey, the challenge of writing legacy letters (first introduced in Chapter 12) will seem less daunting. However, while many people feel a strong urge to write legacy letters to their children, grandchildren, or lifelong friends, others have no interest in this activity. It can wait until you're ready.

Shifting gears

Over the past months, you've written in your journal for your eyes only. You've learned to put your thoughts and emotions, your certainties and confusions, on the page with complete trust. But the legacy letters you compose, if you choose to send them, will be read by others. This introduces an entirely different element into the process.

Healing has been at the center of your journal writing. This also needs to be true when you write legacy letters. Your purpose needs to be clear in your mind. In your journal, ask yourself, "Can I create healing for myself by writing this legacy letter?" You may discover your answer only after several entries on this subject. In the meantime, approach these letters *as if* they will be a healing activity. Give yourself time to gather the evidence. Without any commitment to send these letters, you can write them with the same freedom you employ in your journal. You're writing these letters as a gift to yourself.

Using your crystal ball

Review the example in Chapter 15 that addressed the questions, "What will happen if I write my legacy letters?" and "What will happen if I do not write them?" Reread what you wrote in response. Then, review the journal entries you made in response to Chapter 12, "Legacy Letters, Part One." These thoughts, along with insights into your reasons for writing, offer the perspective you need. In reviewing some of your journal entries you may discover that you've already begun writing a legacy letter.

Be very selective about what you decide to include in your letters. Think of what you choose to reveal about yourself as a gift. Giving gifts is a custom that the ancestors of your ancestors engaged in, so look on the letters as an extension of this time-honored tradition. These letters are your legacy to family members and friends who may come to really know you only through what you write for them. Each letter creates a connection that will not exist unless you write it. It's an act of love.

It's much easier to write with someone specific in mind. Letters addressed "To the young" lack the context of family or friendship necessary to the healing process. Another consideration is that your unique voice needs to be heard. If you decide to quote from other writers, either through poetry or prose, personalize your choice by developing your own thoughts and ideas beyond the sentences you quote. Allow your own words and "music" to appear on the page in as much detail as possible. This document is a testament. It needs to bear the likeness of the one who is writing it – you. Your personal effort to connect, one to one, with the recipient is what makes it a love letter.

Write several entries in your journal about the intended recipients of your letters. Listing them by name will give them identities, which in turn will evoke a telling response within you. Also think about *when* you'd like them to read your letters. You may wish to write several letters to the same person, to be opened over time. The child you write to now will grow into a teenager, then an adult, and your letters can "grow up" with him. Indicate when each letter should be opened.

When you begin to think about who will receive each letter and when it will be read, many new ideas will come to you. You may wish to list them, so that you can develop them further in your daily journal entries. Here are a few. "The first time I saw you," "your parents' wedding," "the summer vacation I took with my parents," "seeing your mother off for college," "what it was like to live through the Cold War/growing up in the Sixties/

when the Berlin Wall came down/on New Year's Eve, 1999." Give yourself time to develop these entries with patience, and they'll be a source of personal pleasure and inspiration.

You can attach specific papers and family photographs to the letter. Recipients will appreciate the connections you're able to make with the past. While at first only your relatives may value your legacy letter, looking on it as a family heirloom, it may well grow in historical significance and become priceless as an antique. This has happened with many such documents.

Perhaps you want to write a legacy letter, but you don't know to whom. Think of someone who may not be alive now or someone with whom you missed an opportunity for connection. Consider someone you wish you had known better; they probably wanted to know you better, too.

You can also role-play. It's a valuable tool for understanding how others think. When you write a letter to yourself as if it were written by a loved one, it's possible to receive a gift that was never given, one that you can give yourself. The *parent* within us can use this opportunity to communicate with the *child* within us. (You're welcome to send your letter to my website, www.writeforlifeccp.com, for future publication in a book of legacy letters.)

Use your daily journal entries to create a list of people you might like to write to, and explore these entries as you write. Your journal offers intriguing possibilities for you to develop in the weeks and years ahead.

Staying started

To begin your letter, you need first to capture the attention of your reader so that he or she won't "file" it away unread. You know how often e-mails and junk mailings are discarded unopened. If you value the importance of making a connection with someone, you need to stimulate that person's attention. How will you do this? The personal touch is always a winner.

Setting the stage

A few ideas may help set the stage. Here's a brief list of introductory possibilities for the letter. Choose one or two, or invent your own.

1. The similarity or dissimilarity between you. (Age, generation, family, environment, etc.)

2. A humorous or touching event that revealed certain characteristics of the recipient.
3. Sincere appreciation for having this person in your life.
4. Words of comfort over the emotional pain your reader may feel when you're no longer alive.
5. If there has been anger, a misunderstanding, or a long silence between you and the recipient, an acknowledgment that what's important is living in the present.
6. A hope that, in time, a better understanding will develop.
7. A mutual problem or concern that the letter will address and resolve.
8. Your memories of the last time you saw the recipient.
9. Your curiosity about the differences between the time you write the letter and the time it is read.

Give your reader the reason that it's important for you to write this letter. Sharing your starting place will also help to create a personal touch.

For the body of the letter, choose journal entries you want to share and revise them so that your reader can understand your intention. Implicit in the letter is the value you place on your life. Your hope is that when others read your letter, they will also value what you say about yourself and about them. When you write from the heart, without preaching or posturing, you fulfill your intention of touching someone else.

The effort takes patience and the willingness to revise as much as you think necessary. Try setting the drafts aside for a few days or weeks. It's useful to write in your journal about other feelings that come up each day; it helps you gain some perspective. What may appear perfect today may change after you read it again next week. Be sure to save the drafts in a folder so you can review them later. Unless you feel some urgency, don't be in a hurry. Give yourself permission to take as long as you need.

New directions

Humor is a beneficial element in writing letters. Of course, there's a risk that what you think is funny won't amuse someone else. Nevertheless, your sense of humor is part of your personality, and what you write will lack authenticity if you don't reveal this aspect of yourself. But it's another good reason to let the draft of your letter rest for a bit. Then you can reread it to see whether what you thought was clever two days ago still seems funny.

The conclusion of the letter can sum up with a different twist what you've already written, or it can open a window on an entirely different subject for exploration. This technique creates a kind of suspense and is especially useful if you're writing a sequence of letters to the same recipient.

You letter should not simply ramble on and on, and then come to an end because it has reached the bottom of the page. Your intention in writing the letter needs to be as clear at the end as it was at the beginning. It's as if you have a mission, and you've accomplished it through your writing.

If you can end the letter on a memorable note, you'll find that you've lifted yourself up by your own creation. You'll also find that you've done some healing necessary to your well-being. This is a gift that only you could have given yourself.

The impulse to share wisdom and experience with those who come after us is a way to celebrate life. The two examples of legacy letters that follow may serve as starting places for your own ideas.

"Letter to Noah," by Jane Glassman Cohen

To Noah:

In the last few months, I've been looking at you with new eyes … trying to see who you really are. I'm humbled by what I see – a person with great strength of character, integrity, and a sincere openness and passion for life. I remember a conference we had with your teacher after last year's camping trip. She told us that one of your classmates was upset because no one wanted to share his tent with him – you volunteered. Another had forgotten his water – you were the one who offered to share. She said, "Your son is a noble person." The kind of nobility she was speaking of – compassion and generosity of spirit – is at the Center of the Jewish Heart, and is naturally and effortlessly at the Center of you. There are many qualities that are plentiful all around us, but nobility and compassion – these qualities are rare in the world. You are greatly needed, and I can only encourage you, as you are already doing so beautifully to continue choosing to be yourself ...

All parents want their children to be happy, healthy, and successful at school, with friends, in their career, and in their families. But I see people all the time who have success in all these areas and aren't happy at all – successful on the outside, but on the inside, they are empty.

My greatest prayer for you is that you grow up fulfilled on the inside, knowing who you are, knowing that there is a place for you in the world, an important reason for you to be exactly as you are, a path that is yours alone, and a contribution that only you can make if this world is to be a better place. The way to find your path and purpose is to choose again and again, with great courage, to be yourself – a simple, yet challenging task in a world filled with temptation and pressure to fit in, to be something you're not ...

I see you as a person who is true to himself. Each time you make the choice, you strengthen the anchor that holds you to your world. And as you grow and deepen into your own Truth, you will discover that you belong to something bigger than yourself, something wondrous, something Divine, that you have always been a part of ...

A few months ago, I had the good fortune of meeting a very wise woman. Though our paths seemed to cross by chance, I told her about your Bar Mitzvah and she said: "Don't forget the true meaning of the Bar Mitzvah. It is a celebration of your child." Today is not only a celebration of your coming of age – it is a celebration of you – the being that you are and the person you are becoming ...

Then she said: "The Bar Mitzvah is the time when the child is given back to God." I thought of you and I thought: "What a gift God is receiving today!" I love you.

[*From* Charting Your Course: A Lifelong Guide to Health and Compassion, *edited by Sally Coleman and David S. Anderson, University of Notre Dame Press (1998)]*

Reading this letter, you can appreciate what it meant to this mother to offer her son a look at what was in her heart on this special occasion. You have a similar opportunity to do this with those you love.

In the following letter from Anne Sexton to her daughter, the perspective is simple yet personal. You might choose this approach for your own letter.

"Dear Linda," by Anne Sexton

Dear Linda (Wed. – 2:45 P.M.),

I am in the middle of a flight to St. Louis to give a reading. I was reading a *New Yorker* story that made me think of my mother and all alone in the seat I whispered to her, "I know, Mother, I know." (Found a pen!) And I thought of you – someday flying somewhere all alone and me dead perhaps and you wishing to speak to me.

And I want to speak back. (Linda, maybe it won't be flying, maybe it will be at your *own* kitchen table drinking tea some afternoon when you are 40. *Anytime.*) – I want to say back.

1st I love you.

2. You never let me down.

3. I know. I was there once. I *too* was 40 and with a dead mother who I needed still …

This is my message to the 40-year-old Linda. No matter what happens you were always my bobolink, my special Linda Gray. Life is not easy. It is awfully lonely. *I* know that. Now you too know it – wherever you are, Linda, talking to me. But I've had a good life – I wrote unhappy – but I lived to the hilt. You too, Linda – Live to the HILT! To the top. I love you, 40-year-old Linda, and I love what you do, what you find, what you are! – Be your own woman. Belong to

those you love. Talk to my poems, and talk to your heart –
I'm in both: if you need me. I lied, Linda. I did love my
mother and she loved me. She never held me but I miss
her, so that I have to deny I ever loved her – or she me!
Silly Anne! So there!

XOXOXO Mom

[From Anne Sexton: A Self-Portrait in Letters, *Houghton
Mifflin, Boston (1977)]*

Both letters convey information about the writers and recipients in a
connection that is intimate and loving. Such letters are treasured.

Suggestions about legacy letters

Getting a letter started can be difficult. These suggestions may help.

1. Make it a priority in your journal writing. Put it on your daily
   calendar.
2. Don't choose to address the most difficult question or recipient first.
3. Don't think about it. Just begin by writing about themes – ideas to
   write about in the future. Make marginal notes.
4. Don't talk about your letter with others. It dissipates the energy and the
   will to do it.
5. Stay in the process. Don't get sidetracked by the results.
6. Remember, this is about who you are, not the person you tell yourself
   you are. Honesty is key.
7. Allow for ambivalence. Conflicting motivations are useful topics for
   exploration.
8. A legacy letter is written to help you frame thoughts and ideas. It's
   not a place where you have to worry about "looking good."
9. Allow the feelings to flow. If spiritual connections appear, write about
   them.
10. Look at old letters and photos.
11. Make a note of dreams that surface as you begin to write.
12. This is only a first draft, so stay out of your own way when you're
   writing it.

A few practical details

When you write your letters for others to read, you need to decide whether to use a typewriter or computer, or write by hand. For some, legibility is a concern. Nevertheless, if you take the time, you'll be able to write clearly enough that others can read what you've written. Intimacy should be apparent in whatever you write, and a letter written in your own hand is the most intimate kind of communication.

Your choice of writing paper can be another meaningful element. Your letters will reveal your mind and heart in a deeply personal way. You might choose a special kind of paper if this has meaning for you. Stationers and office-supply stores have a remarkable variety of papers in their inventories.

You may find it useful to create a schedule for writing your letters during the weeks ahead. It's a good idea to keep a separate page in your journal where you can list the names of your recipients and the dates you plan to write their letters.

To appreciate and share your legacy with others enhances your own growing self-esteem. Some of your letters may have a profound effect on their recipients. But what's most important is that you write them. They'll provide a new sense of continuity in your life, which you'll find is integral to healing. Your goal is to feel whole, not fractured, and these legacy letters can help you experience this. When you're ready, you'll write them.

Chapter 17
American Indian Spirituality

Getting started

The earth beneath your feet supports your steps on your healing journey. Millions have walked before you and others beside you. You're grateful for the help they've given you as they've ministered to your body, mind, and spirit, and your journal reflects this. Writing in your journal has helped you experience some connections that you no longer take for granted. You can expand them even further as you open your mind to new ways of looking at the world.

The view of the world you will now explore may be unfamiliar to you. You'll step back in time into the world of the ancients, not in Europe but in the New World. You'll see how the timeless ideas central to the beliefs of Native Americans contrast with the materialistic focus of contemporary popular culture. Until the coming of European colonists brought them under assault, the ideas of this ancient American civilization thrived for centuries. Over the past few decades, they have drawn increased attention from many mainstream Americans seeking a more spiritual way of living.

The American Indian way

Many people have become interested in Native American spirituality because of its ideas about the connections between body, mind, and spirit. Native American beliefs and practices range from reverence for the Earth to using herbs to heal. They all focus on improving one's relationship with the natural world. Today, many people are interested in these ideas because they support health and harmony in a world that seems fractured and distorted in countless ways.

According to the Indian Way, instead of owning or controlling the things of this world, human beings are merely caretakers. Our task is to tread lightly upon the earth, preserve what is living, and safeguard the resources we've been given. We are called upon to respect the sacred nature of the earth, trees, mountains, rivers, animals, and humankind. These things don't belong to us. We are their stewards; our lives depend upon how well we preserve the gifts of nature. We have responsibilities toward other life forms and toward the earth which we all inhabit.

While this idea was fundamental to Indian culture in the past, the concept of harmonious living has enormous resonance today. It's not abstract  ideas grounded in myth or superstition; it's a prescription for a better way to live here and now. Human negligence over the past few centuries has resulted in significant degradation of water, air, and soil, endangering plant and animal life alike, and the consequences loom larger by the day. We must accept the truth that not only our own lives are sacred. So is everything that exists. Our world and everything in it are gifts given by the Creator, which we must cherish and maintain for those who will come after us. We all travel together on the Good Red Road (the path of balance, right living, and reverence for life), and the manner in which we do so makes a difference to both the journey and the destination.

The continuing focus in the Write for Life workshops is on the nature of healing and the expression of every aspect of "dis-ease" through journal writing. According to the Indian Way, such a process of self-exploration is a medicine for the body, mind, and spirit, which are all intimately connected. Many medicines support the union of the spiritual and physical sides of our lives, including sacred herbs, prayer, dances, rituals and ceremonies, fasting, and the use of visualization. Journal writing is a medicine that helps you experience the connections between your own being and the world you live in. It opens you to exploration within and beyond yourself.

Look upon writing in your journal as your own sacred ceremony. During the next few days, think about the concept of interconnectedness and your own responsibility for the world around you. In your experience of body, mind, and spirit, how connected are you to family, friends, community, your work environment, and nature? If there is a "disconnect," what does it feel like? What would it take to enjoy life differently? What would it feel like to be in sync with the world?

Learning about the Indian approach to life can help you get in touch with attitudes that you take for granted. As you do this, ask yourself to revisit some of the answers you've come up with when you've looked at difficult relationship problems, noting any new realizations in your journal.

Staying started

In the book that accompanies her popular *Sacred Path Cards*, author Jamie Sams indicates that the idea of interrelatedness is basic to the Indian Way.

> The Uniworld is the universal Family of Creation. The Earth is our mother, the Sky is our father; our grandparents are Grandfather Sun and Grandmother Moon. Our Brothers and sisters are the Stone People, the Standing People, the Creature-beings, the Plant People, and other Two-leggeds. We are never alone. When our human family is separated or moves onto the Blue Road of Spirit through physical death, we have nothing to grieve if we remain connected to the universal Family of Creation. The Medicine Walk is one way of reclaiming those connections.
>
> [*Jamie Sams,* Sacred Path Cards: The Discovery of Self Through Native Teachings, *HarperSanFranciso (1990)*]

In this framework, everything is seen to enjoy a sacred space. Everything is a "person." Every mountain or rock is a Stone Person, every tree is a Standing Person, every plant is a Plant Person. In the sky, each cloud is a Cloud Person. Men, women, and children are "Two-leggeds" and animals are "Four-leggeds," and all are Persons, as are the natural elements.

Everything that exists has its own life cycle, or Medicine Wheel. And each has its own sacred space that merits respect.

Interconnectedness

The key to well-being and happiness is to recognize the interconnectedness of life, appreciating the sacred in each stone, flower, or bird. Each is unique, just as you are. Each has its own being, just as you have yours. Each inhabits the world you inhabit. Each is made of the same atoms you are made of and has arisen from the same mysterious place.

Sometimes it's easy to perceive the interconnectedness that runs through everything in our world. When you're happy, your awareness of the world is different from when you're fearful. The incredible beauty of a flower or a sunset, or your pleasure in the company of a loved one, can seem different with each experience, and your sense of connection may deepen or diminish according to your state of mind. Do you understand how holy *you* are as a witness to these countless manifestations of the sacred?

On your journey through the Uniworld, begin to look at nature with heightened awareness, guided by the direction and encouragement of the Indian Way. Consider the Medicine Walk that Sams describes.

> Imagine walking through your favorite forest, rolling hills, mesas, or green valley. See yourself surrounded by those creatures who are your Totems, or favorite animals. Notice which direction the Wind is blowing. Look to the Cloud People; do they take the form of faces or animals? Feel the warmth of the Earth Mother nurturing you in her gentle arms. Look at Grandfather Sun, see how his light plays upon the Earth Mother's breast. Taste the breeze and drink in the promise of rain. Respect and admire all that surrounds you. In this way, you are ready for the Language of Love to penetrate your senses in the silence of a quiet heart and mind.
>
> Each flower or rock can be your teacher. They wait to be acknowledged by you as you walk through the land you share. The Medicine they hold is freely and abundantly given, if you allow yourself to feel it. The Wind is the fore-runner of any lesson, for all spirit comes on the Winds. If

it comes from the South, it is offering a teaching on faith, trust, innocence, humility, or the child-within. If Wind blows from the West, it offers lessons on inner-knowing, seeking answers or goals through introspection. When Wind blows from the North, it beckons you to be grateful and to know the wisdom being offered as well as acknowledging the wisdom you hold personally. The East Wind brings breakthroughs, new ideas, and freedom through illumination. The East Wind will assist you in casting aside doubts or darkness by opening the Golden Door that leads to new levels of understanding.

Once we understand which type of lesson is coming our way on our Medicine Walk, we can then proceed by noticing which Allies call to us. When something catches our eye, it has called our attention and is speaking to us through the Language of Love. In caring for that messenger we establish a link that will allow the message to be received. In observing each Medicine Helper, whether it be Dragonfly or Ponderosa Pine, Petroglyph or Stone Person, we learn the lessons of nature. *[Jamie Sams, op. cit.]*

The lessons of nature

Perhaps you've visited natural wonders like the Grand Canyon, Yosemite National Park, Monument Valley, or Niagara Falls. What was it like being in those vast places, where you could experience the amazing power and diversity of nature? Use your journal to recapture your memories of natural places that were special to you. What sights, smells, feelings, and thoughts do you recall? What feelings do they give rise to today?

Even simple experiences can kindle your imagination. You might remember a special occasion when you received flowers. How did you feel, holding this token of affection?

Or write about a pet – either one that was dear to you while you were growing up, or the cat or dog or bird that shares your life at this moment. How does its presence affect your life? What have you learned from it?

What makes it special?

You can begin with something close to you or choose a past memory of an intimate experience of nature. You may not have visited such memories for a long time. Now you can reconnect with the sense of wonder you had as a child for the beauty of the natural world. A flower, a tree, a field, a stream, a hill – any image in which you place your attention can awaken your awareness. Over the course of several days, writing about these memories and experiences may evoke the same emotion as if you were reading a favorite poem from long ago. You can reconnect with something you value, something that is waiting within.

Next, step out of your imagination and visit a park or drive into the country. Bring your journal and find a spot where you can sit and write about what it feels like to be surrounded by the abundance of nature. When you return home, you can write about other natural settings that you've enjoyed over the years. Remember the colorful sights, the fabulous fragrances, the sounds that filled your ears, the objects you touched. The feast of connections awaits you.

New directions

Your journal helped you connect with more vital impressions of the Now. You may feel rejuvenated because you've been reminded of what it is to see – really see – the shape of a flower and smell its perfume.

After several days of writing, many workshop participants have commented with surprise on their heightened awareness of birds, animals, and flowers in their lives. If you open yourself to this awareness, you can observe the vitality that exists in all things. For example, Sara's son received a butterfly garden in the mail, complete with chrysalises. As she watched the insects hatch, she experienced a real sense of shared being, of connection. Janel watched her cat stalk and kill a hummingbird, and wondered whether this symbolized something deeper. Her father was ill; was this a sign? For others, everything in nature came alive – even the huge hill one participant observed from the bottom of a street took on new meaning.

Perceiving nature in new and different ways was a dominant theme of many journal entries. Everyone who wrote about nature mentioned vivid memories of profound emotional experiences. This led participants to consider how the spiritual dimension enters our lives and what it takes to experience a spiritual connection.

When the mundane and sacred connect through our emotions, revealing insights arise. Coincidence and surprise also assist the process. The spiritual is more apt to show up when we do something new. And sometimes, when we slow down and pay attention, it can produce amazing results.

In writing about the Indian Way, participants revealed that turning their attention to their families was especially useful. "The Good Red Road is traveled by many relatives who fill me with the experience of wholeness. When I feel isolated, it is I who have broken off my connection with the Uniworld, and then I must find the medicine that will restore me to the harmony and wholeness that truly exists." "My sacred space is of great value to me ... and to others. That I can heal myself with it, that I can show love for myself in it and with it, and that this love can therefore flow out to others and nourish them is a benefit." "I have an entirely new idea of medicine. Good medicine connects my body, mind, and spirit; bad medicine doesn't."

Sacred space

The emphasis on respect at the heart of the Indian Way merits special attention from all survivors. They have endured pain, hardship, isolation, or medical challenges. Such experiences often produce wounds in body, mind, and spirit. To undergo the trauma of illness, divorce, abandonment, or emotional and physical abuse often affects self-esteem. For the restoration of a sense of self-respect, there is no better medicine than to open in appreciation of other life forms and the world around us.

It may seem a simple effort, but when you make it, proof comes. The reverence you feel for nature and your participation in it as a partner in the scheme of things directly affect the way you feel about yourself. If you don't respect the sacred in the world around you, your feelings about yourself will exhibit the same neglect. Think of it as a golden rule. The Apache medicine woman Kachinas Kutenai writes, "An Indian commandment could be: 'Thou shalt honor the earth with all thy heart, and with all thy soul, and with all thy deeds.'" This is something to think about and act on when you feel out of sync with yourself and the world around you.

Chapter 20, "Meditation and Prayer," will explore other ways of opening to the universe. But for now, the Great Spirit Prayer from the repertoire of Kutenai's people offers a bridge to these ideas.

> O Great Spirit, whose voice in the wind I hear, and whose breath gives Life to all the world, Hear me.
> Small and weak I am; Your Strength and Wisdom I need.
> Make me to walk in beauty and in a Sacred Manner.
> Make my eyes ever behold the red and purple sunsets.
> Make my hands and heart respect all that You have made.
> Make my ears sharp to hear Your Voice or receive spiritual guidance, when I sincerely ask for a sign, a vision, a dream, or a prayer answered.
> Make me wise, so that I may understand the things You have already taught my people.
> Let me learn the lessons You have hidden in every rock, leaf and herb.
> I seek Your Strength, not to be greater than my brother or sister, but to fight my greatest enemy, myself.
> Make me always ready to live my life with Your eyes smiling upon me, when my deeds or thoughts are examined by me and You.

Make me always ready to treat my brothers, sisters, and Mother Nature's creations as I want to be treated: with love, justice, honor, dignity, integrity and respect.

When life fades like the facing sunset, let my eyes be clear, my hands and heart free of bloodshed, destruction, hatred, or disrespect for Mother Earth, so that my spirit may come to You without shame. Ho! [Amen]

[Kachinas Kutenai, American Indian Healing, Sacred Rainbow Circle, Emeryville, California, 1990]

To better understand the Indian Way and its significance for you, take the opportunity to experience the medicine of this prayer. Kutenai suggests that this prayer be recited every day. Write about what occurs for you when you do this.

Several participants reported a heightened sense of spiritual awareness following their daily recitation of the Great Spirit Prayer. The words made them particularly aware of their need for healing in many aspects of their lives. They also became far more conscious of the importance of prayer as central to their journey on the Good Red Road.

A basic tenet of the Indian Way holds that when anything is taken from the earth, some exchange should be made. Your journal writing can be an offering with which you acknowledge your debt to the Medicine Wheel.

Many have connected with their deepest wish as they wrote in their journals. Looking at the Indian Way from its unique perspective, you may discover the journal's wish for you: love and healing for yourself and others. Explore this as you write during the next several days.

As you unburden yourself of some of the baggage you've carried for decades, you'll find your journal reminding you of the essence of the sacred in your life. And by acknowledging your interconnectedness with others, you'll find yourself opening to the spiritual forces that are everywhere around you. On the Good Red Road, you'll experience yourself in a new way, as a traveler whose life is a gift.

Your journal practice promotes the healing of body, mind, and spirit. This is good medicine.

Chapter 18
Creativity

Getting started

When was the last time you took up a paintbrush and painted a picture? Or got your hands into some clay to fashion a figure or throw a pot? Or sketched with a pencil or piece of charcoal, or even doodled on a page? Perhaps not since grammar school. Maybe you've visited museums to see great art, but don't let it end there. Your appreciation for what others have created can excite and motivate your own creativity.

On this special journey of discovery, you're seeking that place in yourself where drawing and painting seem like the most natural activities in the world. In this place, you don't need to learn about art because self-expression means having fun. Here, you're not looking for approval from anyone, including yourself. You're opening to the experience of connecting with the creative wellspring that bubbles within you. This place has everything to do with expressing something that you may have neglected or forgotten. Once you reach it, you'll drink from that fountain of creativity that infused your childhood with wonder.

A place to be creative

You can paint, draw, or work with clay or wood anywhere. Most adult-education centers and senior centers offer painting classes. Community colleges may have hands-on art courses in the afternoons or evenings. In San Francisco, I often visit the Center for Creative Exploration; it's one of my favorite retreats in the city.

Those who can't find a studio can create at home. Every art-supply store sells watercolors, tempera paints, crayons, and Magic Markers. The sections of empty ice-cube trays make perfect compartments for holding different colors. Paintbrushes and drawing paper are all you need to begin the journey.

This July 18, 2002 entry from my journal captures my experience of setting out on this adventure into creativity.

When I think about what it is like to stand before the blank sheet pinned on the wall, with all of the colors of many rainbows beside me, I remember my first experience a year ago at the studio. I felt like a child standing at the window of a candy store looking in. There was so much to delight me in what I saw. In the painting studio it was about the images and configurations which were all waiting there in my imagination. They had been poised there, without my even knowing it, for what seemed eons, and I was excited with the immediate possibility of reaching inside my imagination to put them all on the page.

The colors themselves were like candy, and I "tasted" them on my brush as I applied them to the panel. They arranged themselves on my plate in forms I let flow from my hand. They were there, just waiting for me. And sometimes they represented exactly what I wished, and at other times not at all. That evening I painted a kitten lying on a quilt, but I was the only one who knew it. I have this as an experience of allowing something to emerge from within me that was recognizable only to myself.

The most important thing was that I was showing up in front of my paper for myself. I was taking the opportunity to connect with my idea, with nothing in the way to inhibit it. We had been warned about the critic who always intrudes, even when uninvited. So, I welcomed the critic and then sent him packing until some later time when I was *not* creating. "Not now!"

To create seems directly related to the healing process. As I bring something out of nothing from within, I seem to tap into the activity needed to restore the fibers of myself that have been destroyed or seriously damaged by cancer and its aftermath. The ticking away, molecule by molecule, of the life-restoring energies which go into restructuring a new mass different from the old me, before cancer, commences the moment I make the effort to begin.

How does the experience, the process, heal me? Bringing forward aspects of myself buried behind decades of explanations and excuses of why I can't paint or do anything that I've ever wanted to do creates a new energy, one that is rooted in discovery and innovation. I'm reminded of a conversation at Walter Reed Hospital with an old friend many years ago. He was dying of cancer. And he was busy drawing up plans to build a dream house he had always wanted to create. He was actually drawing it on paper. For him it was an opening out of his dead-end world into a universe of aspiration and hope.

Hope goes hand in hand with creativity. How do we open the door to hope? Taking up the paintbrush and touching the page with color unlocks the door. It is more than the experience; it is the connection with the *wish* to be more than we have been, and to visualize this with an eye that is accustomed only to experience what is. *That* is a new beginning for everyone who tries it.

Entering a painting studio is a magical experience. Paints wait on the table and paper is within easy grasp. The only obstacle to finding a new way into this world may be yourself.

"What do I do now?" asked one participant who stood trembling before a blank sheet of paper with a brush in her hand. She was face to face with the unknown. This is both exciting and baffling. This first brush stroke is what helps you to cross the threshold of risk, because once you've touched the paper you become a part of the mystery of creating something out of nothing. Dipping brush into pigment is an "open sesame" for the imagination, and through the simple effort of putting colors on the page, the body may experience a loosening up of tensions.

When you let yourself connect with your imagination, an energy flow begins. It's accompanied by many surprises, such as your delight in making a form you recognize or the colorful vitality that blossoms on the sheet before your eyes. You feel moved and at the same time liberated. "I felt as if I were embracing myself" was one person's comment. Another remembered an art teacher from her childhood and how much she'd learned about life from this woman. "I felt totally pleased with the mess I'd made and want to have the opportunity to reconnect with it again."

One participant called the creative dynamic "heavenly." She was able to leave the mundane behind and experience a different sense of herself. The thought of whether this feeling would continue called to mind the question, "What's the relationship between color and drabness in my daily life?" When vibrant colors suddenly make you notice dullness in the world around you, what do you do about it? Look at the colors of the clothes you've been wearing. Do they mirror this somberness?

Whether you're wielding your paintbrush or looking at your wardrobe with new eyes, you can be certain that sooner or later the critic inside your head will show up. "I'm doing this badly," you may think. "That is *not* the way to paint a leaf!" Or "These clothes have all got to go!" With the same effort you used to pick up the paintbrush, you can invite your critic to wait for you outside the studio door. (If it resists, let it know that it can always weigh in with its opinion after you've finished. That usually does the trick.)

Your impressions of the first time you wielded the paintbrush would make a good subject to explore in your journal. You can add some drawings to the page as another way to tap into your new source of excitement in everything you see around you. Ask yourself how you look at and see objects. Write about the questions that come up for you as you paint.

Staying started

The painting studio with its colors and brushes is just one introduction to the idea of creativity. For some people, life changes or the effects of illness may make it seem as if the world is closing in around them and they're imprisoned behind stone walls, prevented from fully enjoying life. For others, depression or geographical isolation may have a similar effect. As each day passes, they may feel more and more cut off from whatever creative activities they once enjoyed.

Find the doorway you can pass through to explore the idea of being creative, regardless of your circumstances. Einstein observed that imagination is far more important than knowledge. Remembering this can encourage you to step beyond what you know into the mystery of the unknown. This is the realm of creativity. It's not-knowing … open-ended … confusing … disorganized … without rules … pure possibility. It's a completely different place from the one inhabited by the mind that insists on having the answers.

When I think of creativity, psychotherapist Sheldon Kopp's definition of an adult – someone learning to live with uncertainty – immediately comes to mind. The child within you demands certainty, except (and this is the paradox) when it sets out to have fun and create. The adult has forgotten this exception and the paradox is lost on him. How can you rediscover it? If you're willing to not-know, you'll find your way.

For your creative process to find expression, you must jettison any old ideas you might have about needing to make a masterpiece or perform in concert. You're not showing at the Guggenheim or renting Carnegie Hall. You're just giving yourself permission to explore your imagination.

Revealing inventories

Where do you begin? A few inventories will help you find a starting place. Ask yourself, "What do I need in order to be more creative in my life?" In your journal, number the next page from 1 to 20 and see how many answers you find. This will give you the opportunity to see what's holding back your creative efforts. Your list will show what you believe you lack. It holds the key to dispelling inertia in your life. On the next page, make a second list to answer the question, "What are the obstacles to my creativity?" Your answers to these two questions will offer some insights into what your mind believes to be true.

Inventories like these are useful because they provide valuable material for follow-up entries in which you can connect the present with the past and find significance for the future. Once you've drafted an inventory, take the following week to write about each of the entries on your list. As you explore your entries, you'll learn more about yourself. Your inventory is the threshold to change, as you'll discover in the pages you write.

New directions

To further reveal how you see your creative potential, here's another inventory that should prove helpful. List ten answers to each of the following questions. "What are the benefits to my being creative at this time in my life?" and "What are the drawbacks to my being creative now?" Write about the reasons you've come up with. As you write, be as creative as possible.

Needs and obstacles

In the workshops, most participants compiled very similar lists of needs and obstacles. Some of the most common responses included lack of time, not having the right materials, having a busy life with no space for quiet and focus, lack of support for creativity, inertia over getting started, and fear of being judged. Two that were frequently cited might resonate for you: "It's too late for me to begin doing art" and "I don't feel inspired." Do these show up on your list?

One participant who went regularly to a painting studio thought it was absolutely fine for him to abandon his critical inhibitions – when it came to *painting*. He didn't know how to paint anyway, he said. But he couldn't give himself permission to write in his journal without judging. For everyone, confrontation with the obstacle presented by the perfectionist within becomes inevitable. "If I can't do it perfectly, I'm not going to do it at all!" With this attitude, it's impossible for anyone to be creative.

Perfectionism

Perfectionism is the major inhibition to creativity. Is it ever possible to leave this attitude behind? It thrives so naturally that you forget you're the one generating the values you use to judge yourself. To open the door to your creativity, you

have to make a conscious effort to give yourself permission to have fun. As with journal writing itself, you're giving yourself a gift, and instead of judging it, you need to say thank you.

When you look at your inventories, you'll find that much of what stands in the way of your being creative is not "facts" about yourself but only beliefs. When you value your survivorship, you can give yourself permission to suspend these inhibitions and become creative in all areas of your life. On another page in your journal, create an inventory of 1) the facts and 2) your beliefs about the place creativity occupies in your life. It's very helpful for you to explore these entries. By writing about each one, you'll gain further understanding into how your beliefs about yourself may have limited your efforts at self-expression.

After you've brought this information to light, make an inventory of ways you can bring opportunities for creativity into your life. The list may include such activities as clearing a space in the corner of a room for your projects, buying a small easel and some paints, finding a "how to" book to guide you, researching the subject on the Internet, talking with people who are already working in your chosen medium, writing in your journal about your project, and prominently posting an affirmation that declares support for yourself, such as "I *can* begin to _____ today, and I will applaud all my efforts."

And remember, thinking about it is *not* the same as actually beginning.

Taking the first step

The blank page is an unconditional opportunity you rarely offer yourself. On it, you can break all the rules. It represents freedom to the nth power, beckoning you out of hiding and into brilliant and life-restoring sunlight.

It's a matter of making the first effort, getting the first brush stroke on the blank sheet of paper. You don't have to know what will happen or where your art will take you. Creativity is not knowing where you're going, but giving yourself permission to get there. Once you make this initial effort, you'll be amazed at what comes next. Let the texture and the material speak to you and help you find your way.

For individuals who may be in the throes of an ongoing trauma, getting unstuck from the disaster that has overtaken their lives is the first step toward coping with day-to-day living. Journal writing, your first effort at creativity, gets you emotionally unstuck because it helps reveal the quicksand of thoughts whose origins are buried in pain and suffering. When your consciousness is caught in quicksand, you're prevented from living in the moment. Open up the body-mind-spirit connection that's fundamental to creativity. It's the key to healing.

On the blank sheet of paper you come face to face with yourself. This includes coming face to face with your problems. For some, this is difficult and painful; for others, it provides an "aha!" If you're having difficulties, it can help to frame some of these problems on a journal page and then capture them afterward – along with alternatives and solutions – on the canvas. Let a sketch appear on your journal page; let a journal entry appear in your picture. A project awaits you there; you have only to begin. Link the journal entry with something you're creating with colors. Break all your rules and risk all there is to risk. You're painting only for yourself, expressing yourself in a new way that will open you to new understanding.

Use the metaphor of the blank page in every area of your life. Reach out and take hold of those projects you shelved or buried under excuses. Perhaps you've found new subjects you can address. Now is the time to explore those possibilities with your uncensored imagination.

Stretching

Yoga, like creativity, is about stretching. Are you up for it? In the past, instead of venturing out yourself, you've admired others' "talent," "competence," "flair," or "virtuosity," and you've created hurdles for yourself that make it impossible to initiate the creative process. Now, instead of using labels and being the critic, begin risking. Taking a chance. Saying yes instead of no. What do you really have to lose?

When you risk, you always gain in some way. You meet a force or idea that challenges what you take for granted. You discover that boundaries give way before you. Pressing yourself to go beyond old conclusions keeps you moving on your journey. When you don't risk, you settle for less. You yield to inertia – and inertia is the force that stands in your way.

Stretch. Stretch around yourself. Your willingness to stretch opens the pores of your being to healing and renewal. Your journey is about exploring yourself as completely as possible, and now is the time to do it. This means being willing to reach out with your spirit. Embrace yourself with gentleness and care, and you'll experience something mysterious.

The artist paints on stretched canvas. Today, you're offered the opportunity to reach out – to stretch into your own canvas. And when you reach out, what happens?

Whether it's recovery from illness or achieving something you've always wanted, what is it that you're risking? This is exactly what you've been given the gift of life for. Vision often dims as you age, but the opportunity to see is always yours.

You can be creative at any time. What inhibits you? Are you one who sees the drabness of the world instead of the exuberance of color? When was the last time you wore purple? Several years ago, just for fun, I started a purple shirt collection, and I'll tell you what – I've had fun with it!

Breakthrough

A workshop participant named Jan commented that she had always had high expectations of old age. Her goal was to be free and not care about criticism from others. Eventually she realized that the only person who can give Jan this freedom is Jan! When you discover this, it's a breakthrough.

Similarly, the creative process is about making breakthroughs. When you think you're finished with a project, you're just at the first level. There's more beyond. The creative process is about entering the wilderness … embarking on a great adventure … finding out what you don't know. It's discovering a new country in which "I don't know!" is a good answer.

> [From my journal]
> I went to my painting class yesterday to celebrate the 4th of July. It was a good session. I made the discovery that I am "suspicious" of the warm colors. I feel strange using them … almost as if they do not belong on my palette. Yet, the painting I am working on is all done in warm colors, including black and white (and gray also). They are making me stretch. It is part of my discovery process.
>
> The creative process provides everyone with access to the spiritual dimension of life. The energy we tap into here is essential for healing and health. It may take us by surprise when we suddenly discover that it has been waiting for us all the time. We are the ones who have been reluctant to tap into it. We dare not wait to be inspired by Muses, or the Divine, for we will spend our lives waiting and waiting and waiting for that to happen. We need to take the first step.
>
> "Creativity is God energy flowing through us, shaped by us, like light flowing through a crystal prism," says Julia Cameron in *The Artist's Way*. "Creativity is a spiritual issue. Any progress is made by leaps of faith, some small, some large."

When you begin to trust that the Great Creator has shared some of the gifts of creation with you, you give yourself permission to share this creativity with yourself. Use the journal you turn to each day – use every word you write – as a springboard into your creativity.

Chapter 19
Work and Play

Getting started

Both work and play offer opportunities for self-discovery. In this chapter, we'll explore ways they can lead to healing.

Can you think of anything that has consumed more time in your life than work? When you were in school, you had homework, chores, and busywork; then there were your after-school and summer-vacation jobs. After that, you found yourself in the midst of your life's work. You may have had jobs with and without pay, perhaps more than one career, and duties and responsibilities at home as well as at the office. Some of it was tedious; some of it was such a joy that you hardly even thought of it as work. Nonetheless, it all consumed a great deal of attention and energy.

To begin your journey through the years that work has consumed in your life, let's examine your own definition of work.

What is work?

Write in your journal, "At this time in my life, work means _____." Now, compare this with what was written by some retirees in San Francisco.

> **Mary:** "I need to get rid of lots of things in my room and make myself more comfortable. Work is straightening things up. Hard for me to do."
> **Rita:** "Having to do chores (make the bed; clean the bathroom, doing the laundry). Keeping order in a very small space is work."
> **Marion:** "Getting rid of clutter; washing clothes, ironing; accompanying groups who like to sing."
> **Cary:** "Work is the half-hour before I go to bed at night – putting lotion on my skin, brushing my teeth, curling my hair. Throughout my life, cooking was work for me – a dinner party was forty-eight hours of cold sweat. And what if guests came too early?"

Next, these participants wrote a definition of what they had regarded as "work" twenty-five years earlier. Before you read what they wrote, finish this sentence in your journal. "Twenty-five years ago, 'work' was _____."

Cary: "I had a job in my husband's office. Never a mistake. It was sheer fun. I loved doing anything that did not require responsibility. No reports."

Marion: "Each day, I got in the car; drove five miles; sat at a desk supervising others; ordering texts, etc."

Rita: "I was a secretary at the Hotel Frontenac in Montreal. Then, I was hired by someone from L.A. who liked my work, and I left Canada to come to the States."

Gerda: "I spent my time working for doctors. I was on my toes to stay alert for problems that might arise in the office."

Ida offered two longer definitions.

Ida: [Now] "Work is whatever causes me to feel less free and more constrained by someone who is monitoring my performance. I guess the word performance is the key. When I have to do something in a certain way that has been determined by others, it has the impact of 'work.' Anything is work for me if I'm not in charge."

[50 years ago] "If I was earning meaningful support from the activity, I called it work – even though I loved doing it. I often spent a great deal of time completing tasks or initiating tasks that I thought either (a) needed to be done or (b) were worth doing. I have resigned many jobs just because I thought someone else could do them. Some creative element or aspect was essential for me to stick with it."

Reading these different definitions, observe how they contrast with what you wrote. How did you feel when you read them? How do you spend your time now?

Our attitudes toward work have been significantly influenced by our observations of the work our parents and family members did as we were growing up. Explore in your journal your impressions of the attitudes your parents had about their jobs. You may discover a new way to look at your own work and career choices.

What you value

Think back to the first job you had for which you received payment. Write about the value you placed on your job. Next, think about the most recent job you've had and the value you placed on it. These two entries will provide a framework for the work you've done over the course of your life. Develop a chronological list of the intervening activities. This list, an inventory of your jobs, will provide a basis on which to examine the much larger question of how you value yourself in the work you've done.

Think about the work you've done in terms of self-fulfillment. How great an element was creativity? Risk-taking? Adventure? What role did advancement, personal growth, status, or recognition play on the job? Were responsibility and independence significant factors in your career choices? Was financial security an important motivation? As you write about what you've valued most in making work decisions, you may come to see yourself from a new perspective.

As you make these entries, include your attitudes toward authority and control, competition and accomplishment, and teamwork and loyalty. Did your priorities change when you changed jobs? It's useful to write about this because of its influence on your body-mind-spirit connection. You connect with your work on all levels, and writing about what you've valued helps you become clearer about the choices you've made and those that may be available to you now.

It's not uncommon for people to feel undervalued in their work. Have you undervalued yourself? You might write about this possibility. Many people stay in dead-end jobs and wonder why their abilities don't lead to advancement. This can be a profound source of disappointment and regret – not to mention ill health and depression. Reflect on your underused abilities, then identify some opportunities (perhaps educational opportunities) that will enhance these strengths. Using your journal to explore your feelings about the work you've done and the work you wish you had done may open a door you've shut against yourself.

Some workshop participants have been startled to discover that despite their disappointment with their work, they never thought about making a change. By writing about what might happen if they expected something other than disappointment, they found that they were freer to imagine a different outcome. Just as your expectations may limit you, so, too, can they free you. In the last chapter, "Creativity," you explored the healing effects of connecting with your imagination. Apply this technique to your expectations of what you wish to choose as your work (1) at this time, (2) three to five years from now, and (3) ten years from now. Perhaps you can sketch a vastly different picture of your life, one that begins at this very moment.

Staying started

When you're without work, you're miserable; when you're employed, sometimes you experience even greater misery. Sometimes it's because of the nature of the work you do; sometime it's the people who supervise you or the company itself. And sometimes, it's regret over choices you wish you'd made, but hadn't. Or, to put it in the words of Marlon Brando in the film *On the Waterfront*, "I coulda been a contender!" Instead of dismissing any regrets you may hold, give them names, identify the circumstances and the people involved in your decision, and write about them as extensively as you can. Consider the choices that you didn't make from the perspective of that earlier time in your life; then, write from the perspective of today.

The choices you made

After writing about the choices you didn't make, create a list of the choices you did make, and attach to each one your related accomplishments. Creating this inventory of accomplishments you're pleased with will show you how well you've done in your work life. Looking for approval from others often results in little satisfaction. Approving of yourself is what's important here.

Healing begins when you accept responsibility for your choices instead of blaming them on others. Your appreciation of yourself as a survivor is one of the most significant aspects of work. Being grateful for what you *have* found and appreciating yourself for having found it is a crucial point to reach. It's one that many people have missed, and their experience isn't the same without it. Here are the words of a fortunate man who found his way.

> At 17, I announced to my brother that I wanted to be a writer, and his response – "What will you live on?" – affected the choices I made. These same choices have helped me to survive and to grow beyond the place in which I made the announcement. No, I did not become a famous writer. And I *did* use my talent and energy to write – along with my other talents. Writing has been my bliss, even though I did not devote my entire professional life to it. If not the happiness of a writer, I have enjoyed great happiness writing – and I feel gratitude that my journey has taken me to this high hill from which I can look back over many wilderness places to see how far I have come.

You may also write about difficulties like dismissals, resignations, and other work-related events that are still "unfinished business" for you. Carrying heavy baggage like this over the decades deprives you of energy you could be using more effectively now. To acknowledge this is the first step toward accepting the responsibility to consider them from the perspective of today. Denial is a powerful topic to write about.

As you embrace the choices you've made, explore this reevaluation of yourself for a new understanding of your relationship with work throughout your life.

New directions

Now, let's shift the focus to play, a different use of your time. For some people, the time spent working each day isn't that distinct from their play activity. Others need to create a definite separation between the two. As Mark Twain said in *Tom Sawyer*, "Work consists of whatever a body is *obliged* to do. Play consists of whatever a body is not obliged to do." Do you agree? Certainly, as a child, you had a very clear idea of what you were obliged to do. And playtime meant spontaneous fun.

Consider this excerpt from Charles Dickens' *Great Expectations*. Pip, a penniless boy, has just arrived at Miss Havisham's mansion.

> "I am tired," said Miss Havisham. "I want diversion, and I have done with men and women. Play."
>
> I think it will be conceded by my most disputatious reader, that she could hardly have directed an unfortunate boy to do anything in the wide world more difficult to be done under the circumstances.
>
> "I sometimes have sick fancies," she went on, "and I have a sick fancy that I want to see some play. There, there!" with an impatient movement of the fingers of her right hand; "play, play, play!"

Being ordered to "Play!" by an authority figure contradicts the necessary spontaneity at the heart of play, and Pip is unable to do as he has been commanded. Have you ever experienced this dilemma? What can you do that's spontaneous and offers delight and fun? Is play something you can plan, or must it happen accidentally? Just as you observed in Chapter 14, in the *koan* about the cow in the barn, it's all in the way you look at the question.

The world of play

Some of our most basic social responses are learned through childhood play, such as getting along with other children, competing and being fair, expressing ourselves without parental interference, and feeling what it's like to be in charge. We explored our talents and felt the special joy of winning.

Some workshop participants have noted how important the concept of fair play is to children *and* grown-ups. For youngsters, encounters with fair play are their first confrontation with rules outside the home. Kids have different attitudes toward breaking rules, cheating, taking control, and trying to get away with something. In your journal, explore some of your childhood memories of these issues.

Getting in touch with yourself as a child at play will provide some useful insights into how you have fun. In today's journal entry, describe the games you remember playing as a child and the children you played with. When you wanted to have fun, what did you do? Name the games you played with others and those you played alone. Have you forgotten these details of your childhood? If so, this writing may be a different kind of entry into self-discovery.

Childhood games

Participants have written about many different toys, games, and pastimes, including dolls, toy soldiers, coloring books, paper dolls, model airplanes, jacks, tug-of-war, hide-and-seek, spinning tops, quoits, roller coasters, merry-go-rounds, seesaws, sliding boards, pickup sticks, checkers, board games, chess, tiddlywinks, hobbyhorses, marbles, puppets, slingshots, BB guns, roller-skating, ice-skating, card games, stickball, Little League, matchbox cars, Lincoln logs, Legos, erector sets, pedal-cars, bicycles, and tricycles. Then there were party games and competitive activities such as footraces and gymnastics. Memories of play inspired many insights.

Adult games

When you allow yourself to connect with the idea of having fun, it can reveal some of the inhibitions you may have developed over the years. Such inhibitions limit the kinds of activities you let yourself consider appropriate. Does it seem as if you don't have fun very often? If you start to look for the reasons, you may be amazed at the narrow range of choices you've given yourself. Take the time to list some of the choices you've made over the past eighteen months. After completing this inventory, add a few lines to each item about the impact it had upon your body, mind, and spirit. What do you do for mental fun? Physical fun? Spiritual fun?

It's possible that the diversions you choose exercise only one aspect of yourself, while others are neglected. Watching television (the recreation cited most by workshop participants) is often responsible for feelings of isolation. When TV is your only choice, you can feel permanently stuck as merely a passive spectator of life.

In Chapter 9, "Self-Caring," you explored some activities that enhance the health of your body, mind, and spirit. Review those journal entries now and add specific *play* activities that will provide some of the fun that's been missing from your life. Some activities to consider might include music lessons, finding a new hobby, photography, collecting something that delights you, playing chess, reading the books you never had time to read, learning bridge, joining an exercise program, hiking, practicing yoga, taking a class at a community college – and what about journal writing? This is *your* list. Your choices need to be there.

Retirement

Work and play assume entirely different meanings when you're retired. The change is significant, and many people understand that the rules of life they once followed have changed. Your physical capabilities may have

diminished, but that doesn't mean that you've lost any creative vigor and enthusiasm for life. Changing the rules means that you're now free to make as many mistakes as you need to in order to try new choices and explore the things that will enhance your enjoyment of life.

Many of your old rules affect the way you now play. In his poem "Portrait of the Artist as a Premature-ly Old Man," Ogden Nash reminds us, "No, you never get any fun/Out of things you haven't done." If you're willing to discover new ways in which to have fun, you'll find them. But you may need to encourage yourself to do this.

Consider in your journal what it would take to encourage yourself to remain playful. List at least three activities that would bring you fun for the body, fun for the mind, and fun for the spirit. Then write about each one, asking yourself how you might enjoy it. In retirement, you no longer find it necessary to be an expert, and at this stage of the journey, setting per-fectionism aside is one of the greatest gifts you can make yourself.

Discoveries

After some workshop participants developed these entries, they shared a discovery: The greatest aspect of play was simply to enjoy a game for its own sake. Taking pleasure in the activity far outweighed the satisfaction of winning or having a high score at the end of the game. The fun was in the participation, in putting energy into being a player.

As you write about the roles of both play and work in your life, the discoveries you'll make are part of the process of connecting with your intuition, which happens through your journal work. Play is crucial to health and well-being. Survivors often neglect this aspect of recovery, yet it's of the greatest importance to living better; you must plan on building it into your daily program. Now, in your journal, consider how to do this.

The Sioux Indians have a very wise saying. "The first thing people say after their death is 'Why was I so serious?'" You can ask yourself this same question right now.

Make a commitment to yourself to spend some time each day in simple play. "Am I having fun today?" is a good question to answer in your journal every day. The child inside is waiting to be invited into the game, and you can see this in the delight with which you write about all the different things you enjoy.

Chapter 20
Meditation and Prayer

Getting started

Walk in a garden at sunrise or watch the sunset from the beach, paint a picture or write a poem, play with a puppy or embrace a dear friend. Without any preparation, you experience another level of consciousness. Your feelings shift. You're flooded with a sense of well-being. You go on from there, sometimes recognizing what has happened, sometimes not. The experience of this flow of energy is always waiting for you. Many live in hope of these moments and treasure them when they come.

You can invite these moments into your life. The time-honored processes of meditation and prayer offer one approach. Journal entries you've already made offer directions you can pursue. (See your entries for Chapter 9, "Self-Caring"; Chapter 14, "Now and Zen"; and Chapter 17, "American Indian Spirituality.") Another way to evoke this special state of being is to relive in memory the peak experiences that embodied it. What was it like when you felt united with another person by a bond of sheer joy? When your senses thrilled to an exquisite chord of music? When your blood sang with exhilaration as you ran or biked or swam or danced with all your being? When your heart filled with gratitude because your prayer was answered?

The list you compile will offer you a key to self-understanding as well as a surprising new way forward. You can choose at any time to invite this energy into your life.

Meditation

Many workshop participants have discovered that daily meditation is an activity that improves health as well as increasing energy. The purpose of meditation is to quiet the mind, relax the body, and bring peace to the spirit. Contemporary health-care workers are discovering what teachers and practitioners of meditation have long known, that meditation improves one's health by decreasing the body's reactions to stress and thereby strengthening the immune system.

Many different forms of meditation are practiced today. Perhaps one of the best-known is yoga, a practice that arose in India thousands of years ago. The word "yoga" itself refers to union: Yoga "yokes" the mind, body, and spirit. Through physical postures, breathing exercises, and concentration, the practice of yoga can bring about a sense of inner peace and harmony. (Be aware that in yoga it's essential to have the guidance of an experienced teacher; it's not an activity to attempt on one's own. By investigating the different varieties of yoga, you can discover which approach may suit you best and find the teacher who's right for you.)

There are many other kinds of meditation, including such simple practices as breath-counting, visualization, chanting, and the use of very brief prayers known as mantras. Like journal writing, both meditation and yoga help bring a different focus to your mind and peel away the extraneous thoughts that interfere with your enjoyment of life. Some people meditate before they write in their journals. They say it helps them get into meaningful subjects more quickly and use their writing time more efficiently.

Here's a Write for Life workshop activity that connects your awareness with the body and its sensations. Turn off the television and unplug the phone. Close the curtains if light disturbs you. Sit in a straight-backed chair with your feet on the floor and your hands resting lightly on your thighs. Shut your eyes. When your mind seeks to distract you with the noise of all its thoughts and ideas, just acknowledge them and invite them to wait until you've finished the exercise.

Then turn your attention to the experience of your body. Tune into your sensations, starting with your feet. Are they tired? Sore? Try tensing them as tightly as possible, then relax them. Do the same with your legs, thighs, trunk, back, chest, arms, shoulders, neck, and head. By the time you've gone through your whole body, you may find that you're feeling far more relaxed and calm than when you sat down. When you've finished, thank yourself for allowing this experience and slowly return your attention to your surroundings.

Processes like this one can be powerful tools. The mind is a wily and persistent source of distortion and distraction. Learning to turn your attention away from it and focus instead on your physical state is a very effective approach to meditation. And meditation is the portal through which you can receive energy from the spiritual part of you. When you're grounded in your physical sensations, you can discover far more awareness of your body, your mind, and your spirit. From this state of awareness, you can experience that flow of energy that fills you with an indescribable sense of well-being.

Once you begin to look on meditation as you do walking, eating, bathing, and any other natural activity – as a way to keep yourself healthy and ready to live your life more completely – you can begin to appreciate its role in unblocking your life.

When you feel anxious or fearful, you have an awareness of the world that's different from when you're peaceful and happy. As you begin to make your body the focus of a daily meditation, you can use your journal each day to record your emotions and the insights that come to you. Explore this over the next week. Use the centering exercise suggested above and then write about what happens while you're doing it and how you feel afterward. Do you find yourself reacting any differently to events of the day? In what way? Be willing to identify some of the obstacles that intrude upon you as you open yourself to this effort. And whatever comes to you in your search – write about it.

Staying started (1)

The body is a sensing threshold, across which different impressions are received. Writing about the body itself – not about its aches or pains, but simply about its sensations when you ask yourself to become aware of them – can be almost startling. "It's almost as if I never think of my body in that way," wrote one workshop participant. Another noted, "It was like remembering something D.H. Lawrence wrote that I read years ago. The deep connection between the body and the spirit. Wow."

How do *you* feel about meditation? Be sure to record your answer in your journal.

A visual approach

Henri J.M. Nouwen, a cleric and author whose writings probed deeply into the heart of the spiritual experience, offers an alternative approach to meditation. In *The Return of the Prodigal Son: A Story of Homecoming*, Nouwen uses a Rembrandt painting from the Hermitage in St. Petersburg as a stepping-off place for exploring relationships. Focusing on the three figures in the picture helps him discover the thoughts and emotions evoked by what he sees and connect them with his own life and experience.

He begins by writing about his associations as a younger son. In the chapters that follow, he turns his attention to the elder son and then to the old man who has laid his hands in blessing upon the prodigal kneeling before him. The book offers a fold-out illustration of the Rembrandt painting, which helps you enter your own experience of the picture and enables you to relate it to your own thoughts, feelings, and experience, opening the way to reflection and exploration of your own spiritual nature.

In another book, *Behold the Beauty of the Lord*, Nouwen writes about four Russian icons that have had special meaning for him during his life. "I have chosen icons because they are created for the sole purpose of offering access, through the gate of the visible, to the mystery of the invisible," he says. "Ikons are painted to lead us into the inner room of prayer and bring us close to the heart of God." Then, as he studies the icons and impressions arise, he relates them to various facets of his life.

In exploring their relationship with the spiritual, many people use art as a focus. You can also put your attention on such natural objects as a seashell, a stone, or a flower in a vase. You can use visualization as a way of deepening your impressions and see whether this supports your meditation. Try it with your eyes open and then another time with your eyes shut. Were the experiences different for you? Write in your journal what you've discovered.

After a prolonged period of great distress, Cary determined to meditate for the first time. One day, she decided to sit in a chair and just do it. Here's what she said.

> There was no reason that I could pinpoint which would cause such despair. I was physically well, was provided for, had friends, hobbies. Still, I was beside myself with anxiety.
>
> I had some vague notion of meditation. I sat down, placing my open hands on my knees and tried to eliminate all thought. It was too difficult. So I switched to creating just one image and concentrating on it. It was a mountain road along a cliff. I dwelled on it for twenty minutes.
>
> It worked. Calm descended on my life and has stayed with me.

That single experience eliminated her anxiety, apparently once and for all. Many people have experienced results that were similar in nature, if not so dramatic. Daily meditation has changed and enriched their lives, they say. During the course of the week, encourage yourself to meditate and write about what happens.

Staying started (2)

Many participants wrote extensively in their journals about the obstacles they encountered when attempting to meditate. Some of them just couldn't get past the countless mental distractions that scattered their attention in every direction. Others wrote about how boring they found meditation and said that they often fell asleep. These reactions are common to everyone who begins the practice of meditation. The mind feels threatened when it's not busy, so it resists. That's why giving it an activity to focus on, such as breath-counting, visualization, or repeating an affirmation or mantra, is so effective. It provides a directed channel for mental energy.

When you feel your mind becoming restless and starting to generate distracting thoughts, stay relaxed. Don't meet resistance with resistance. Your mind will respond better to comforting directions than it would to frantic ones. Resting your hands on your thighs, firmly but calmly invite the distractions to "wait for me outside the door for ten minutes." Each time new thoughts bubble up in your mind, calmly repeat this direction and then return your focus to the chosen object of your meditation.

Repeating the syllable "Om" very slowly ("Oooooohhhhhhmmmmm") is another technique that participants have found effective. Others have used special meditation tapes designed to soothe the mind and focus attention.

A great deal of scientific research has been done on the effects of meditation on the body and the mind. Meditation has been shown to decrease pulse and respiration rates as well as blood-pressure levels. Improved blood flow to the heart has also been recorded. This is significant for people suffering from angina and arrhythmia. And the National Institutes of Health recommend meditation to lower blood-cholesterol levels, saying:

> Although changes taking place through the endocrine system are still not well understood, some research results are startling. For example, the deep relaxation of meditation may enhance the immune function of the body, with research showing increased defense against tumors, viruses, colds, flu, and other infectious diseases. From meditative relaxation, diabetics can experiences a lessening of the emotional reactions that often precede attacks. Asthmatics experience improved flow in constricted air passages. Chronic pain patients reduce their reliance on painkillers and lessen the level of pain.

Richard Peterson, author of *Creative Meditation*, says that research has shown meditation to have these psychological benefits:

- Decreased neurotic tendencies
- Improved study efficiency and exam performance
- Increased problem-solving

- Improved creativity in the visual arts
- Decreased drug and alcohol abuse
- Increased psychic sensitivity

With patience and persistence, you'll find that the practice of meditation will become a source of ongoing improvement in your quality of life. Your journal can be your faithful companion along the way, as you discover what happens as you meditate.

Beyond meditation

A newspaper photograph of U.S. Marines huddled in prayer over a fallen comrade in Iraq is a poignant reminder of the impact of crisis and death. At such a time, our experience of life suddenly becomes intense, and this spike in consciousness penetrates any shell. No ritual has been initiated, yet you open to a connection beyond your ordinary waking consciousness. Your vulnerability has carried you across the threshold into an experience of spirit.

Those huddled marines had survived a combat mission. You may have survived the loss of dear ones or physical or emotional assaults that left you reeling. Perhaps it was a crisis of conscience. People often remark that cancer was the wake-up call alerting them to what was missing from their lives. In times of crisis, you become vividly aware that for all the wisdom you may possess, you're still searching for answers to life-and-death questions. Instinctively, many turn to prayer for support.

When there's no crisis breaking, can you open yourself to the spiritual in your journal writing? Ask yourself, "How does prayer (or meditation) work in my life?" Are there any obstacles to prayer that you can identify? Write about these ideas from several perspectives, including this moment, ten years ago, and twenty-five years ago. Writing about what you do in times of stress and crisis often brings into sharp perspective many key developments in your life that you may have taken for granted. It may also help you recognize changes you might wish to make in the future.

Exploring the obstacles and the ways you can open yourself to the spiritual in journal writing is a rich source of insight. Sara wrote, "I ask myself to describe this moment. I think doing that would help my writing tap into a deeper, more spiritual level, allowing connections to form from the here-and-now, spreading out in any and all directions. I also am reminded of the American Indian idea of asking permission of things. It makes me think of the value of personification – that we've lost something by deriding the cultures that do it – maybe a humility or sense of the connectedness of all things. I think about prayer as gratitude, about sunrises and leaves and pebbles. Spirituality is in everything, even in the act of writing."

Participants have also written about the difficulty of bringing any kind of spiritual practice into their daily schedules. "I have so many other things to do, I'll have to put that off until I get the time," wrote one, answering herself with "Well, Sugar, you ain't gonna get any more time than you got right now. You are finite, and that means able to die at any moment, so if you're not making yourself available for a connection, there just ain't gonna be one!"

Another wrote, "Making myself available to God is one of the ways I have found that opens me as well to others. Opening one door, I discover that I open all the others. Closing that door isolates me from everyone. So now I can think of asking to be open more and more."

Mac, another workshop participant, admitted that he doesn't have an easy time writing, but attending the ballet was a spiritual experience for him. He mentioned how difficult he finds church ritual, yet he is moved by the artwork, architecture, and Gregorian chant. For Mac, the relationship between the aesthetic and the spiritual is a subject rich with opportunity for exploration in his journal.

Favorite material

Several participants wrote of using certain prayers daily that they found particularly supportive. The first two are from the *Book of Common Prayer*.

In the Morning

This is another day, O Lord. I know not what it will bring forth, but make me ready, Lord, for whatever it may be. If I am to stand up, help me to stand bravely. If I am to sit still, help me to sit quietly. If I am to lie low, help me to do it patiently. And if I am to do nothing, let me do it gallantly.

Make these words more than words, and give me the spirit of Jesus. Amen.

Prayer attributed to St. Francis

Lord, make me the instrument of your peace. Where there is hatred, let me sow love; where there is injury, pardon; where there is discord, union; where there is doubt, faith; where there is despair, hope; where there is darkness, light; where there is sadness, joy. Grant that I may not so much seek to be consoled as to console; to be understood as to understand; to be loved as to love. For it is in giving that we receive; it is in pardoning that we are pardoned; and it is in dying that we are born to eternal life. Amen.

The Serenity Prayer, by Reinhold Niebuhr

God, grant me the serenity to accept the things I cannot change, the courage to change the things I can, and the wisdom to know the difference. Amen.

Positive Prayer

In Chapter 17, "American Indian Spirituality," we considered some practices that look to nature for a heightened understanding of prayer. In her book *American Indian Healing*, Kachinas Kutenai has an entire section devoted to "Positive Prayer" that made a significant impression on workshop participants.

It is necessary to be specific in prayers. It is also important to know that the Creator doesn't cut off communication with humans. Humans are the ones who do that: They stop praying after they pray devoutly for something which is not miraculously given to them to their liking.

When offering a prayer, always *thank in advance* instead of saying "Please." You must make a prayer. The creator doesn't respond to begging, and Apaches do not beg.

The strongest kind of prayer comes from the standpoint of childlike innocence and blind faith in the Creator's miraculous powers. Sometimes we become too upset to pray effectively. Then we must have the wisdom to reach out to others and ask them to pray. When a person is truly upset, it is wise to call upon the prayer force of someone who prays daily. Those who pray frequently do not feel the guilt that others may feel from having prayed too little to be heard.

The depth of meaning is lost when praying with memorized words. It is wise to keep the channels of prayer open, for we never know when we might need a strong prayer force. Prayer force can only be made stronger by repeated use.

Always phrase a prayer as though it has already been answered. Be specific.

Say your prayers for a minimum of 21 days. Then feel free to stop. The Creator is not deaf. You have been heard. The Creator speaks through the silence. You must listen and be aware to receive your answer. A sign that your prayer is answered may come in a dream, or a visit from your totem – perhaps a bird at your window, or a butterfly that lights on your shoulder.

Twice every day, dare to visualize your prayers answered.

These ideas from the American Indian tradition offer some valuable insights. Remember, there's no right or wrong way to pray. But if there are obstacles to prayer, you're creating them. For workshop participants, the obstacle often was their feelings about the religious traditions in which they had been raised – not always the religion itself, but what they *thought* about the practices they were obliged to perform as children.

When they wrote about this subject, participants realized that fear, anger, and guilt had a lot to do with their inability to open to the possibility of prayer. For many, there's a great deal of healing to be done in this area. Your journal can help you. Take several days to write about this. Your memories of the pain as well as the joy you knew as a child, adolescent, and adult will tell you a lot about why you've turned toward or away from prayer in order to survive. Insights into healing are waiting in these entries.

New directions

The wilderness

Some people feel perpetually under siege. To them, life is a wilderness teeming with danger, where they struggle against forces beyond their control. They often fear that to take any action will make their circumstances even worse. Confusion can often lead to despair. At these times human beings need something to hold onto. They grope for comfort and support.

Writing about this in your journal can illuminate your exploration of meditation and prayer, and it can strengthen you for your next encounter with such challenges. Wilderness experiences always present you with the need to find your way into and through them. Sometimes you must ask for help from others. Sometimes you must rely only on yourself. Your journal can offer unexpected support as you discover that what you need is within you.

Other forms of support also come from within yourself. Meditation develops crucial body-mind-spirit linkages that make it possible for you to have a more whole – and holy – experience of life. When you feel fractured, everything seems fractured; when you feel whole, your reality mirrors this greater unity. The Talmud refers to this. "I do not see the world the way it is; I see the world the way I am." Just as years of patient exercise and training are necessary to develop the muscles of an athlete, so regular meditation works to develop the inner strength that carries you to a richer experience of life. And when a wilderness experience descends, your meditation practice can hold your world together and bring you signs that you are not alone.

You seek many answers during your lifetime. Meditation assists you in discovering and understanding truth, for the more whole you are, the more powerful your ability to perceive truth will be. Meditation hones the intuition, making it increasingly receptive to impressions coming from all sides, all the time. As you develop the linkage between body, mind, and spirit, your intuition also develops.

Prayer, when you are ready, opens you to the dimension of spirit as you affirm your willingness to make yourself an active channel for spirit in life. You'll discover that awareness of spirit becomes far more possible when you open yourself through prayer. As with meditation, prayer opens you to the wisdom within you, and in the process you receive healing from the spirit beyond yourself. Prayer is one of the most significant ways you have of opening up. Write about your own experience of this now in your journal, from the perspective of both the heights and the depths of the journey, for it will support you in the future when you turn to it in need.

On different days of the week, write several prayers that reflect your present state of mind. There is power in words you speak from your heart, a special affirming force that will strengthen your ability to find your way. Writing these prayers in your journal makes it a special kind of repository. Using them at the end of your meditation connects you with your deepest hopes and dreams.

Many participants have developed prayers in their journals that have increased in meaning and value for them over the years. Because a prayer is a representation of your own sacred space, it is therefore of great value to you. You can heal yourself with it. You can show love for yourself in it. And this love can flow out to others and nourish them. These things are among the greatest truths you can discover as you make prayer part of your journey in life.

Chapter 21
The Experience of Joy

Getting started

What will sustain and support your emotional center? In your journal, you've already investigated what you need to nourish the body. You've explored from many different perspectives what can heal your body, mind, and spirit. Now you embark on another adventure, one in which you develop and sustain emotional well-being.

When you write in your journal, many things you've taken for granted can seem new once you look at them from the perspective of Now. In today's entry, write your definition of happiness. Doing this will make you more aware of what it takes to make you happy. What you write may surprise you.

From time to time, you may feel that you're missing out on the experience of joy – that somehow, your time for happiness has passed you by. Even when you feel good, you may not identify that feeling as happiness. Let's explore this.

Definitions of happiness

Here are a few definitions that participants wrote when asked to define happiness.

> **Cary:** "It must include excitement, discovery, newness; without these elements, I would only apply the word 'contentment.'"
> **Anne:** "Good health, good friends, going to concerts, enjoying nature, getting rid of pests (human)."
> **Rita:** "Happiness is when a person has no worries, has all the necessities of life and does not envy the riches of others, and feels blessed by all life offers. And the ability to enjoy and love their own surroundings. It means companionship, good friends, good health."

Snow: "I feel lifted up – I might soar! I see freely, without apprehension. And sometimes, [I see] a new possibility to enjoy a person that, before, had been blocked."

Ida: "Having absolutely nothing to do. Or having nothing that I have to do."

Marion: "To be able to read! My eyes no longer allow me to read for more than thirty minutes at a time. Being able to do something that helps others! I can no longer read to others at the health center, and I feel bereft. Thank God I can still play for group singing!"

It's interesting to consider what happiness meant to you when you were a child, a young adult, before marriage, after divorce, or before health alarms that called your future into question. Think back to these times and write about them. Along with these definitions, include the things you desired or the results you wanted at that time.

Happiness in focus

Use your definition of happiness today. Start a new page in your journal. Create four columns headed BODY, EMOTIONS, MIND, and SPIRIT. In each column, list the activities that make you happy. Some might well show up in more than one column. Your page may look like this.

BODY	EMOTIONS	MIND	SPIRIT
healthy, exciting meals	caring relationships	books	caring relationships
realistic diet	journal writing	music	meditation
dining out			
exercise			

The inventory developed on your journey through "Self-Caring" (Chapter 9) may be useful now as you think about the idea of happiness. If some of your entries surprise you, write about these surprises as part of today's journal entry. Record whatever makes you happy. "What about overeating, getting drunk, beating a ticket, cheating on taxes?" asked someone. My answer: The journey is as real as you are honest with yourself. If you have other thoughts, explore them in greater detail during the week.

Staying started

Consider the emotional support that sustains you. Turn your attention to your relationships with the most significant people in your life – from your earliest years to the present. In writing about these relationships, as you consider the past, think about what can make a difference in the present and the future. After exploring your relationships, consider some of the activities that arose from them that give you pleasure and delight.

Relationships

Make a list of people in your life who have been there for you (or who haven't) among your parents, siblings, grandparents, extended family, mentors, teachers, friends, lovers, clergy, employers, co-workers. (Some workshop participants included pets, and some included fellow hobbyists.) This list will evoke an amazing procession of people who have meant something to you in your life. Writing about your memories of each person is an activity that may fill a great many journal entries in the months ahead.

For now, organize these lists by time periods or by the significance of each person to your emotional development. People who have shared time with you have had a profound influence upon your body, mind, and spirit. Begin with the family into which you were born. Then create other lists, including people you've worked with, people from the different neighborhoods and cities you've lived in, and people with whom you've had noteworthy personal relationships. After creating the lists, select two individuals to write about. In the future, you can continue writing about the other people on your lists.

People in your life have been sources of both joy and sadness. Putting their names on your list may evoke nostalgia, perhaps even some regret if you've lost contact with them. Some of these relationships left you fulfilled and secure; others drained your energy. Acknowledge your feelings. Be grateful for having known the people who came into your life. In your journal, you can reconnect with them and continue to savor your relationships with them. In writing about them, you may discover that many moments of joy occurred without your even realizing it.

The past and its significance

Past relationships have a profound effect on how you express yourself. Think back over your relationships with parents, siblings, friends, and other close associates. What did you enjoy most about being with these people? What least? What kind of emotional support did they give you or you give them? What characteristics of theirs did you appreciate?

In his *Meditations*, Marcus Aurelius paid homage to the most influential people in his life as he considered the gifts he was fortunate to receive from them during his lifetime.

> From my grandfather Verus, a good disposition and control of my temper.
>
> From my father's fame and memory, modesty and manliness.
>
> From my mother, respect for religion, and a love of liberality; and the habit not only of checking evil actions, but also of repressing evil thoughts. From her, also, a simple way of living and avoidance of luxury.
>
> From my great-grandfather, that I did not attend the public schools, but employed good teachers at home, and learned that for things of this nature it is wise to spend freely.
>
> From my tutor, to be a partisan neither of the Greens nor of the Blues in the chariot-races, nor of the Parmularii or the Scutarii in the gladiatorial contests. He taught me also to endure toil, to have few wants, to be industrious, to mind my own business, and to despise slander.

In Marcus Aurelius' tributes are some ideas that may help you to create your own appreciation of the people who have played prominent roles in your life. Here are some examples from my journal.

When I think of my grandfather, I remember a man whose high principles and piety did not get in the way of his unconditional love for me. I think he is the only person in my life from whom I experienced unconditional love, and it is a rock in the center of my experience that I can cling to when I lose hope.

He gave me his attention when I needed it, and he risked doing things someone his age should not have attempted. We walked into the park once and got lost; we spent hours finding our way home. He was, at the time, only five or six years older than I am right now, and I did not realize his courage. He never indicated that he was even worried how we would find our way home.

One of the dearest memories I have of him was during the radio speech FDR made to the nation on Sunday afternoon, December 7, 1941. The tears that flowed from his eyes were the first tears I had ever seen a man shed. Until then, I had only been threatened with "crying towels" by my father when I cried. This offer only prompted even more tears from me. My grandfather was the single most important influence on the first 10 years of my life, and I am so grateful he was there for me.

For the next week, think about the people who have been part of your life, including those separated from you by death. Explore the things these relationships have taught you. What's missing? What do you need? Consider the future. What are you responsible for? What actions do you need to take to nurture your relationships? What role would acceptance and reconciliation play in each instance? If you are to live in happiness, what can you do to bring it about?

As you write, memories of experiences both delightful and painful will surface. You'll remember the gifts as well as any lingering grievances, unfinished business, or anger. What memories have surprised you and brought you joy?

In writing about these surprises, one participant shared his memory of a former colleague, who had sent him a letter from which a page was missing. In it, the colleague announced that he had felt obliged to inform the IRS about the man's failure to properly file income taxes while he was overseas, and that –. The letter broke off there. Now, he could laugh about it; then, it was different story. But writing about this incident touched a place in him that he thought he had lost contact with.

The idea of emotional sustenance is a very rich area for exploration. In addition to your relationships, it needs to include material from other aspects of your life, For example, are you nourished by:

- The places you've traveled to or lived in?
- The books you liked so much that you planned to read them again?
- The music you've heard at concerts and festivals?
- The theater?
- The people who accompanied you to these events?

Your life has encompassed many wonderful events. It offers a banquet of adventures you can savor in your journal. The best thing to remember when you feel starved for excitement is that you can change your diet just by writing about the rich experiences you've already enjoyed.

You can explore additional ways to extend your emotional well-being. Create a list that includes books, music, art, writing, collecting, dreaming, travel, shopping, sex, sleep, celebrations … Include everything that gives you joy. Then consider what you're doing to bring these experiences into your life now.

New directions

When you consider the relationships that have figured in your life, successful and unsuccessful ones alike, think about the role you played in each of them. Was there any "unfinished business"? If so, what kind of effort can you make to complete it?

As you think about happiness, either in your relationships or in any of the other activities you enjoy, what does it feel like to think of yourself as an active agent, rather than a passive one? How "powerful" are you in terms of creating an experience? Have you discovered anything about yourself as you wrote about these past experiences? What did you learn about the obstacles to your happiness? What could support your efforts to change a relationship that concerns you? How can you find happiness right now in your life? Explore these questions as you look back over the past.

Consider these three statements.

"When no one pays attention to me, I feel _____."
"When others pay attention to me, I feel _____."
"What am I doing to enjoy life, both alone and in the company of others?"

When you begin to see yourself actively creating opportunities for finding happiness, you observe a significant shift. Are you negligent or even miserly and ungenerous with yourself when it comes to taking responsibility for your own happiness?

What if you suddenly discovered that your task in life is to find happiness? How would you assess your efforts? Understanding yourself as the source of value in your life, do you think of yourself as responsible for your happiness? Explore this idea as you look back over the years and consider the opportunities you regret not taking.

You can start by clarifying what happiness means to you. The next step would be to decide what you need to do. Writing about what you can do for yourself is a valuable antidote to boredom and isolation.

Too many people are content to sing the blues. Does being sad actually give you satisfaction? If so, be sure to include it in your definition, so that you'll know when you're in the midst of the "performance." Perhaps George Bernard Shaw was on the right track when he wrote in *Man and Superman*, "A lifetime of happiness! No man alive could bear it: It would be hell on earth." Explore this idea in your journal entry today.

To know when you feel happiness is a vital factor in your well-being. If you're waiting for the spontaneous arrival of happiness, you'll find that such an approach is a major reason that you may feel starved and unsatisfied.

To begin living better, consider what you need to do or change to accomplish this and encourage yourself to do it. Marcus Aurelius wrote, "To live happily is an inward power of the soul." Your awareness that you already

have this power may be all the invitation you need.

What are you grateful for? Toward whom do you feel grateful? Grateful people are happy people. By creating a gratitude inventory, you can achieve a deeper appreciation of your own happiness or insight into its absence. This effort, which you can make each day, brings new discoveries.

Your search

Many workshop participants have introduced visualization techniques into their lives in order to actively bring about joy, instead of passively expecting it to appear. They've also created a linkage between the idea of celebrating their lives and the use of language to invoke excitement and vitality. "I am excited about …" is often a way into excitement.

When you prod your memory to reveal occasions that gave you joy, you get to feel that joy a second time. Professor Joseph Campbell called this "finding your bliss." As you'll discover, the search for bliss is *not* a myth.

One of the mysteries you'll encounter on the quest for joy is the realization that by giving joy to others, you receive something as well. People who volunteer at hospitals and for social-service organizations know this. In your journal, develop a plan to find joy in your life. It will provide you with encouragement and help you move forward.

Now that you've taken the opportunity to explore the terrain, return to the definition of happiness you drafted as we began this chapter and consider how you might revise it. How can you make it more relevant to your life at this moment? When you consider your physical, mental, emotional, and spiritual well-being, think of how happiness can resonate in each of these dimensions.

Those who have heard my definition of happiness have encouraged me to share it.

> Happiness is, for me, the opportunity to share with others, and to help others solve problems in their lives. It is in serving something higher in life than "I want" or "I don't want."
>
> Happiness is seeing the success I am able to have with the things I work at and also to see the successes of others.
>
> Happiness is the good feeling I get when I can be useful; the discovery of a connection in my life with something I did not know was there; the contact with old friends and the development of new relationships; observing the success of my children; exploring a new area of interest; finding "treasure" – whether a book, a friend, or a restaurant ...
>
> It is also being appreciated and thought "worthwhile."
>
> It is feeling that my body is a temple and not a prison.
>
> It is being in the presence of aesthetic beauty – art, music, etc.; preparing a new dish in the kitchen; being with people who are willing to explore the unknown; waking up refreshed after a nap or a night's sleep; being stimulated about the possibilities that are waiting for me; sensual appreciation; experiencing one of my "not yets"; the comfort of a relationship; being in Yosemite; eating a fine meal in a great restaurant.
>
> Happiness is completing a project I have been working on; appreciating what I can do – am able to do – instead of what I cannot do. The act of writing itself provides me with joy.
>
> In the fewest words, happiness for me is exceeding expectations, experiencing no boundaries, tasting my own freedom, and perhaps most important, self-acceptance.

The journey you've embarked upon opens an infinite array of joys that you can experience in your life – and in your journal entries. Paying attention to your inner life is just as important as the search for happiness that you carry on outside yourself. Museum visits, symphony concerts, ball-games, church attendance, family celebrations – all these and more are waiting for you. But you're waiting for *yourself* to discover the bliss within you. Your journal helps you do this. When you write, you open yourself to this discovery. Start today!

Chapter 22

Last Rights:
Embracing Life and Death

Getting started

Many participants prefer not to write about the subject of death. Thus far in our work together, you've avoided the subject. Think about giving yourself permission to start considering it. Remember, you'll commence this journey only when you feel ready for it. It will wait for you until then.

A paradox

Have you ever asked yourself how you feel about dying? Write your response to this question in your journal. Your answer might surprise you.

While you may have shunned the thought of dying, you also may have been drawn to discover what poets and playwrights have said on the subject. That would have been easier, since the poems and plays you read were about other people. You were merely a spectator.

Workshop participants have reacted to the idea of writing about their own deaths with such comments as these: "There are so many other things to write about, why write about that?" "I'm afraid it will only depress me." "Since I won't be around at the time, it's a pointless effort." "I'll leave that to the gerontologists!"

Physician Daniel R. Tobin, in his book *Peaceful Dying*, encourages people to confront their fear of dying by reflecting on the natural condition of impermanence. He believes that the effort to look at one's own death can be "one of the greatest catalysts for growth."

This suggestion may startle you. Can you connect it with other experiences in your life? Or do you find the suggestion too troubling? Think of it this way. When you confront something that once caused you pain or distress, it no longer has the same power over you. To write about your own death will benefit you, just as writing about other "no-nos" on your list has benefited you. You'll be empowered.

Your expertise

In interviews with people who are approaching the end of their lives, I've found that their greatest concern is fear of the unknown. I believe this is true for most people. Facing the final unknown is our greatest challenge, even for those who have been great risk-takers during their lives.

Everyone takes risks, and over the past months you've written about them from your experience as a survivor. Your journal is a record of your struggles and how you've grown into the person you are. You've survived and become stronger for it.

In Chapter 15, you looked into your crystal ball to come up with benefits and drawback to items on your "Not Yet" list. Create a similar appraisal of "Writing About My Death" and "Not Writing About My Death." When you appreciate the benefit of doing something you've avoided, you uncover a powerful motivation for undertaking the task.

On each of these journeys, you've experienced the healing effect that writing can have on the body, mind, and spirit. Now do the same on this journey, "Last Rights," with the understanding that you're confronting ideas that philosophers and theologians have debated for generations. Note the concerns, confusions, and apprehensions that leap out at you when you feel vulnerable.

In your journal over the next few days, write as many of your questions about dying as you can think of. Don't censor any of your thoughts or feelings. Write about connections you've had with loved ones who have died or are close to death. Your willingness to express your thoughts and feelings about your relationships with them can offer some insights into the way you live.

Staying started (1)

Writing about death reveals many issues that at first you may want to avoid. They may not be the kind of responses you want to see because they reveal your uncertainty and fearfulness. But noting these concerns is a necessary first step to understanding areas of confusion and distress. For most participants, writing about death is a new experience, and it feels strange.

- "It's something I've never given myself permission to write about before."
- "Because I did it from the point of view of my questions and my concerns, it lost the science-fiction aspect that I had always connected with it."
- "Thinking about my questions and writing them down was a first for me; I had always taken them for granted."
- "Writing about family and friends who have died was much easier to do than to write about the questions about death. Though I did get around to them, finally."
- "I thought it would depress me, but it didn't. It became an opportunity to put some of my thoughts together that have been floating around in my head for years."
- "Would I write about dying if I hadn't been encouraged to? No, I wouldn't. But now that I have, it seems as if it was something no longer taboo. I learned some things about myself that I took for granted."
- "The world didn't fall apart. My universe didn't collapse. My journal now contains some different kinds of entries. That's a good thing."
- "It wasn't easy, but I am wondering whether now that I've begun, it might get easier. I'll have to discover this as I go on writing."

Marian wrote, "I don't fear it. The idea of it seems so consistent with my observations about nature, about cultures, about relationships, even about food and flowers. There's a life span – a birth or creation, a maturity, a classic period, and an ending, a deterioration. It's an aesthetic view. I remember saying at Janette's memorial service that she lived her life as an art form. My life hasn't been an artistic performance, God knows, but there's a discernible pattern to it. Yet maybe there's something lurking around that I'm not facing. I find it hard to even begin thinking about what it might be."

Questions about death

When workshop participants were asked to write about dying, they cited a broad range of concerns. Here are some of them.

- "I've seen several people die. They were in great pain. Will I have to go through the same ordeal?"

- "I haven't done much with my life, and I wish I'd done more. What can I do now, under these circumstances?"
- "What will happen to me after all that I've done in my life? Some of the things weren't very pretty. My religion tells me I'm gonna have a lot to answer for."
- "I'm alone now. My family has all passed on. I feel abandoned."
- "I've suffered a great deal in my life. Will the next one be better?"
- "My affairs are in such a mess. Will there be time to leave them in order?"
- "Will I be able to accomplish all the things I want to before I die?"
- "Alzheimer's really worries me. I worry that I'll have it and live in a devastating condition for years without even knowing it. What can I do about this?"
- "Do I need to make funeral arrangements? If I make a will, what happens if I change my mind?"
- "Was all this worth it?"
- "Will I appreciate my death, just as I have appreciated my life?"
- "My dearest wish is to rejoin my husband. How can I be easier in myself about this?"
- "Does it make any difference what I think?"
- "What is there about the idea of an afterlife that concerns me most?"
- "Will death be an end or a beginning?"

Some participants didn't frame their responses in the form of questions, but everyone reported worry, concern, and stress. Some spoke of the deaths of friends and the comfort they found in seeing a soothing kind of "completion" to their friends' earthly sojourn. They also raised questions about religion and wondered whether others who had already passed on would be with them and whether their accomplishments would be recognized.

At this point, the famous admonition of Socrates recounted in Plato's *Apology* comes powerfully to mind.

> To fear death, gentlemen, is nothing other than to think oneself wise when one is not; for it is to think one knows what one does not know. No man knows whether death

may not even turn out to be the greatest of blessings for a human being; and yet people fear it as if they knew for certain that it is the greatest of evils.

The great happiness reported by people who have survived near-death experiences adds some support to this alternative possibility.

Weighing in

Respond to Socrates' exhortation in your journal by considering the image of a balance scale. In one pan, place your worries and concerns about dying, and in the other … What *do* you put in the other pan? Choose five experiences of profound joy – perhaps a journey, an encounter with nature, music heard and never forgotten, a public ceremony, a private event, a moment shared with another person, or an experience of a special place. Write about these joyous occasions; then expand the list to ten items.

Choose one item, close your eyes, and for the next ten minutes visualize. What did you do to prepare for the event? Imagine what you saw, how you felt. Recall as many details as possible. Feel the depth of joy and gratitude, and experience the difference it made in your life. Live through it again.

Open your eyes and write about this in your journal. You may discover as you write that even more details of the event occur to you. Over the following weeks, repeat this visualization exercise with each of the joys that appear on your list. The more you write about these experiences, the more balance will appear on the scale. You'll discover that having the answers to many of your questions is not as important as having the scale in balance. Balance is crucial to experiencing the fullness and richness of your life.

Staying Started (2)

Your legacy

"For the first time in my life, I felt important. I never had before!" wrote Martha in her journal about a joyful incident that occurred while she was growing up during the Great Depression.

Ideally, you'll be in a balanced place in yourself when you take on the tasks of making a will, planning health care, recording personal wishes, and making funeral arrangements. In order to experience this balance, give yourself the opportunity to live through the joys in your life. You'll find it a powerful incentive to completing the task before you – a welcome alternative to feeling overwhelmed by fear and apprehension.

One of your rights as a citizen is to leave legacies to anyone you choose. Writing a will is one of these rights, and you do well to exercise it for your own benefit as well as for those who must put your affairs in order after you're gone. Consider for a moment how you'd feel if you were deprived of this right.

One of the reasons people are reluctant to write a will is that they can't decide who should receive a legacy. Whether your family is small or large or no longer exists, there are usually many contenders for whatever you might leave in your will. You don't want to offend anyone, do you? You want to leave behind a good memory of yourself, not one that creates animosity. Leaving no will avoids this, right? Wrong!

Many people don't realize that when there's no will, the state decides who receives the estate. Court dockets are filled with conflicts over disposition. You can prevent this legal nightmare by creating a written will that's properly witnessed under law. (Different states have different requirements, and you need to find out what is necessary in your state.)

Your journal is a useful place to get in touch with your feelings about the family members, friends, and institutions you may be thinking of naming as legatees in your will. You can explore thoughts that carry you back over the years, provide useful details about the present, and anticipate possibilities far ahead in the future. To allow your intuition and imagination to connect with what you value in yourself and with the recipients of your legacy is a rewarding activity.

Several participants found that they experienced some guilt when they considered family members or friends who'd be disappointed not to be named in their wills. Writing about these feelings over time will help you to live better; denying them limits you.

Just as a plan can be revised, so can a will. It's not cast in stone. Your will reflects your wishes. Using an attorney is a good idea, but it's not a requirement. The advantage of hiring an attorney who's familiar with wills and probate is that you can be sure the document will be properly executed and the terms carried out according to your wishes.

You can find many answers to the questions on your list in books and articles about wills and living trusts. This information can give you the confidence you lack and end any fear and confusion you may feel about the mechanics of creating these essential documents.

Health-care directives

You should also consider the kind of health care you'd like to have at home or in the hospital when you need it. It's best to plan for this while you're in good health and have choices. Whether you're young or old, you have the right to choose someone to make these life-and-death decisions for you. Your journal is the perfect place to consider your relationships with family, friends, and professionals who might assume this responsibility. Writing about this subject helps you focus on an aspect of healing directly related to your care and well-being. You can create some peace of mind for yourself by making this decision now.

In addition to choosing someone to make decisions in the event of your incapacity, you also need to consider the kind of life-support treatment you want to receive. How do you feel about medical devices, pain medication, and major surgery that could be used to maintain your life? Writing about this can help you to develop a health-care directive that will provide doctors with explicit information about when to use resuscitation, major surgery, blood transfusions, and other procedures. Your wishes need to be recorded for those who may someday struggle with decisions to be made on your behalf.

Many physicians and hospitals require patients to have a health-care directive on file. In a time filled with concerns about patients' rights, exercising this choice enables you to provide the kind of direction that gives you greater ease and comfort while giving others the benefit of understanding your values and concerns. (Make a point of talking to your physician to make sure that your medical team and the hospital will follow your directive.) You can obtain information about creating health-care directives by calling the Robert Wood Johnson Foundation at 888-594-7437 or by visiting www.agingwithdignity.org.

Funeral arrangements

Funeral arrangements are another subject to consider. These decisions don't have to be made by loved ones during a time of crisis if you take responsibility for this matter. Get information from such professionals as counselors and clergy. You may be quite startled by what you learn. If you write about this, it will help you change the context of some of your questions. Depending on the information you obtain, you can consider alternatives that may not have occurred to you before.

Making funeral arrangements can allay your concern about being a burden to others, and taking this responsibility will teach you a lot about dying. Explore these ideas in your journal while you consider what's right for you. The significance of your values and opinions doesn't end when it comes to making arrangements that are necessary for the end of your life.

As you consider the form of the memorial service and the place of interment, you'll develop answers to questions you may have about the religion you've practiced (or not practiced) during your lifetime. Religions have staked out their claim to a traditional role in burial arrangements, but you need to realize that your own spiritual well-being comes first.

Workshop participants raised many questions of deep spiritual significance, and you may explore your own perspectives here as you've done in other chapters while you continue your journey in your journal.

Putting it all together

From your journal entries you can develop a record of decisions about your will, health-care directives, and funeral arrangements. These documents can be left with relatives, friends, attorneys, or in safe-deposit boxes (as long as you leave instructions to others where to find them). The envelope headed "To be opened in the event of my death" is something you can prepare at any time in life. You can develop the information for this envelope over time, and you can create a schedule for writing about your wishes – and revising them as well – over the next weeks and months. You no longer need to avoid this activity. Attending to your issues and concerns is part of the healing process. Beginning with today's entry, you can work on this over the weeks to come.

New directions

In 1969, Elizabeth Kübler-Ross wrote in her book *On Death and Dying* about five stages she identified in her patients who were confronting death: denial and isolation, anger, bargaining, depression, and acceptance. In 1999, Dr. Daniel Tobin noted six reactions that a person facing an end-of-life diagnosis experiences: shock, grasping, grief, letting go, healing, and serenity.

For many, how they feel about their own death is unexplored territory. When people are undergoing chemotherapy, radiation, or other major medical treatments, these experiences are often accompanied by feelings of guilt or shame as well as an intense sense of vulnerability that arises in the face of the unknown. Many hospitals have established support groups to help patients deal with these issues.

Your journal can also help you. Accepting your mortality, accepting dying, is a big step. By turning your attention to what you know about yourself, you make it possible to heal the body, mind, and spirit you've been actively shaping throughout your life. Getting to know yourself better through writing helps you to appreciate your journey and how far you have come. You may not know anything about your death, but you certainly know a great deal about your life. You prove this to yourself with every journal entry you make. Something remarkable happens in the process, which you can experience only as you write. In this segment of the journey, you'll find this out for yourself.

It's time to turn your attention to this subject. No one else can do it for you. And as a survivor, you need to do this. It's your right, and in claiming it, you open yourself to healing.

Telling stories

Over the weeks and months of journeying through the pages of *Write for Life*, you've written about many pieces of your story from many different angles. A great deal of the story is there for you, and you can add to it by writing about another subject you may have avoided: the deaths of loved ones, friends, those you have mourned. As they began expanding their own stories, workshop participants shared some personal experiences that came up for them as they wrote.

Ellen, a nurse, told this story about a dying woman who lay in a coma in the hospital's intensive care unit. Seeing a note on the woman's chart that she was Lutheran, Ellen whispered to the patient to hang on – she'd get a priest for her. After several hours of telephone calls, Ellen finally reached a priest who was able to come to the hospital. The priest administered last rites, and the line on the patient's monitor immediately went flat. With that final fulfillment, she released her connection to life.

For another participant, an early childhood memory suddenly surfaced as he wrote about facing death. He'd been enrolled in kindergarten in September, and in January, many of his friends went on to first grade. They "graduated," while he was left behind. Sixty-five years later, many of the good friends he'd known during his life had again "graduated" before he had. Remembering this childhood experience of passage resonated within him in a new way; he realized that he'd just have to wait his turn. It was coming, and he was okay with it.

In Thornton Wilder's *Our Town*, Emily Gibbs reveals how she views life from her place in the cemetery. To everyone still alive, she says, wake up! Experience joy while you still have time.

We're moved by her words, just as we're moved by Margaret Edson's Pulitzer Prize-winning play, *Wit*, in which college Professor Vivian Bearing has been diagnosed with cancer.

The professor is a scholar whose specialty is poet John Donne, and early in the play, Vivian recites the magnificent opening lines of Donne's famous sonnet, "Death be not proud, though some have called thee/ Mighty and dreadfull, for, thou art not soe." The scene is a flashback to an encounter she had as a student with her own doctoral advisor many years before. Criticizing Vivian's use of a semicolon in her paper, she changed it to a comma.

"Nothing but a breath – a comma – separates life from life everlasting. .... Life, death. Soul, God. Past, present. Not insuperable barriers, not semicolons, just a comma." Vivian calls this statement a metaphysical conceit – wit, in other words. But the professor responds: "It is not wit, Miss Bearing. It is truth."

The play dramatizes the devastating effects of medical intervention as the dying Vivian Bearing reassesses her life, examining feelings she took for granted and changing her way of looking at the choices she made in her life.

Everyone is as vulnerable as she is, and everyone has struggled with the same issues, problems, and choices. Along with Vivian, you come to the realization, no longer limited to the text of a poem, that death is separated from life "only by a comma." As you've already discovered, your journey through the wilderness invites you, too, to think and to live with this revelation.

Wit also examines the idea of dying with dignity. When it comes to last rights, you need to address the issue of how you wish to die. Investigate hospice programs to learn about some of the aspects of dying that you may never have considered. You have lived with dignity; you should be able to die with dignity.

You've been dealing with matters of major significance. Over time, you've considered troubling issues from the safety and privacy of your journal. Writing about them has given you the courage to make decisions you may have avoided in the past. By accepting responsibility for healing yourself, you can order your affairs by setting up a plan, with dates and documents. From it will come answers to many of your questions about dying.

Dr. Tobin, in *Peaceful Dying*, wrote about the healing stage of the process, in which it's possible to see the lessons life has taught and to accept your life exactly as it is, without judging. He goes on to say that with forgiveness comes appreciation of your life's meaning and purpose as revealed by your experiences as well as a sense of having learned a great deal through them. "Once you forgive yourself and realize that you have benefited from life, you are able to enter ever more deeply into compassion and self-love. You are also able to extend such feelings to others. When healing occurs at this level, it transcends all bitterness, regret, and self-condemnation."

Remember the paradox that began this chapter? You may have wondered when you first read it how confronting your own death could possibly promote growth. As you look back over the latest pages of your journal, you may find that this paradox has begun to yield to understanding.

Chapter 23
Pilgrimage

Getting started

Virgil's advice to Dante as he began his journey was "Do not be afraid!" This is excellent advice for you as well as you continue to explore your own life. In each journey you've taken, you've written about life experiences, and with each journal entry you've discovered forgotten memories of events or people no longer in your life. A complex tapestry of recollection has emerged from your efforts. As you use your journal to connect body, mind, and spirit, you continue to live *better*. But where do you go from here?

Being a pilgrim

It's remarkable how often the idea of "pilgrimage" appears in the media. From travel writers to spiritual seekers, countless people seem to have the idea of making a pilgrimage on their minds. What fascinates readers about people undertaking physical and/or spiritual journeys is that we get to learn from travelers what they have come to understand about the meaning of life.

On your pilgrimage, you've passed through time and space in your body, mind, and spirit. While the terrain of your life is unique, often it may have felt like a strange country. Many kinds of experiences – education, career, marriage, divorce, loss of dear ones, health crises, and the process of aging – have taken you into new territory. Since your first breath, you've been "on the road," whether or not you understood where your destination lay. Along the way, you've experienced opportunities you hadn't dreamed possible. Look at the lists you've compiled throughout your journal and you'll see how much you've lived.

The milestones of your journey

From your pilgrim's vantage, make a list of milestones, the key events that have made a difference to your past and present. To create a context for these milestones, you can put this "Book of Myself" into chapters with such headings as Family, Friends, Relationships, Education, Work, and Health. Add others if they seem appropriate. As you develop your lists over the next several days, other milestones may surface. Writing in your journal about one event may bring into focus another that you forgot. Over the weeks and months ahead, take the opportunity to explore each milestone from the broader perspective of your journey into the present.

Staying started

Cancer and other major assaults on the health of the mind and body are part of your journey. In Chapter 11, "Travel," you wrote about basing your preparations for a journey on what you'll take with you – your wardrobe, travel reservations, letters to friends who have offered hospitality, and the financial arrangements that make your journey possible. Every journey involves some risk, and you've written about events you never anticipated and how you dealt with them. A life-threatening diagnosis initiates a different kind of journey, one that you begin with what may seem no preparation at all. But you've been making ready for it all your life without knowing it. You may even be on your way at this very moment.

Preparation for the life journey: Education

Consider some of the preparations you've made in the past. Your education gave you knowledge. Create a list of the schools you attended, and in an additional column list the teachers who influenced you for better or worse, and what they did to provide you with the tools you needed for life. In previous journal entries, you wrote about family members who were your first teachers. Include them on this list if you feel they belong here.

Next, make a list of the significant books that inspired you and gave you pleasure. You'll use other journal entries in the future to write about their unique contribution to your life.

Employment, career, and travel

In your journey through work and play (Chapter 19), you created a list of the jobs you held and the projects you undertook. Explore in new entries the jobs you enjoyed or detested as well as the ones that consumed your energy and offered the least return. What did you learn from these activities that prepared you for your journey?

Then, list the places you visited, lived, and continue to think of when you remember the joys and sorrows of your life. Whether these places were fifty miles away or 500, you learned something about yourself wherever you went. In each instance, was it a wasted trip, did it meet your goals, or did it reveal something very different from what you expected?

Each list you're developing helps you gain some deeper perspective into yourself. In the weeks ahead, explore your inventories in depth. In what way have they developed your understanding of yourself and the past? Are you experiencing your life in a way that is new, different, exciting? And now that you've been using your journal for a while, what insights have you received about the place that writing holds in your life?

Here's an excerpt from Nicholas Crome's *A Journal of My Travels in Ireland*. It reveals what many who have kept journals discover.

> Things I had thought I'd need, but which proved to me nothing but a burden until I got rid of them were: all my camping gear – in good weather, you can sleep out without gear, while in rotten weather the hostels were so much better a choice; spare tire, spare tube, patch kit, tire tools, pump, etc. I didn't have a single tire problem in 700 miles. If I'd had, getting it fixed locally would have been smarter than providing 700 mile pounds of transport for repair gear; the portable radio. I listened to it only about 3 minutes during the whole trip. I was too busy seeing and doing things, and writing in my journal when I had any leisure. My most enjoyable luxury was my bike computer – it always let me know how I was doing, how far I'd come, how much further I had to go that day, etc. It was a constant source of interesting figures for me to entertain myself with by mental calculations. Pound for pound (it weighed less than two ounces), it provided more interesting diversion than anything else I carried.

There were frequently times when it would have been so much easier to relax or nap or read than to write this journal. I'm so glad now that I was conscientious, because it has proved the most valuable artifact I brought back from the trip. Precious as are the hundreds of photographs I took, I'd be much less affected by losing them than by losing this record. No sooner do I look at it than the most vivid scenes and recollections rise to new life in my imagination; it is the magic touchstone that brings back to me all the signs and sounds and smells and texture of this wonder month on the road.

Similarly, the entries you've been making over the past months capture your travels on the road of life.

Søren Kierkegaard said that life has to be lived forward, but understanding is achieved through looking at it backward. Journal writing makes it possible to appreciate the truth of this statement. In writing about the events of your life and the feelings they brought up, you've lived through in a new way everything that has prepared you for today. Connections with what you overlooked or missed before have brought you into a creative and *healing* relationship with your intuition.

The present: Five crises that got you here

Each experience you've lived through has in its own way prepared you for today. You've confronted obstacles and crises, and made key decisions that changed the way you were living. Consider these developments more closely by identifying five events that resulted in your changing direction in some way. You may think of other turning points, but select five for this task. To get some idea of the direction your life has taken, put them into chronological order.

Write about one event each day. Begin with the circumstances surrounding the event, then address questions that perplexed you, fears you had to overcome, and risks you took. Encourage yourself to reenter each experience and explore what you may have forgotten or suppressed. Live through them now as if they were happening again. This time, however, you're looking back at the obstacles instead of facing them.

Examining key decisions you've made in the past gives you the opportunity to change how you feel about yourself in the present. Unfortunately, many people are so attached to suffering over the past that they can't imagine life without it. They identify with their suffering, as if it's who they are. Because of this, they carry around a tremendous amount of old baggage without even realizing it. Are you one of these people? Do you live behind the invisible walls of the past, where you are both prisoner and jailer? Healing cannot occur there.

To explore these five crises you've survived opens the way for you. While you can't change the past, the impact of finally understanding past actions can change the way you look at yourself now. I know this from my own experience. For six years after an accident that almost killed me, I never took a breath without thinking that it had ruined my life. I took for granted that this was true, until I began to explore the event in my journals. By writing about my experience for several months, I gradually came to understand that my life had been changed, *not* ruined. On the day I understood that, I stopped living in the past.

New directions

Baggage requirements

The need to overcome suffering is a major challenge on the journey. This, along with other obstacles you've surmounted, has left you with certain strengths. Develop a list of these strengths, so that as you face the future you can begin to rely on them more. List them in your journal, starting with courage. The rest of your strengths will follow. Acknowledging your courage is like discovering a vein of inner gold waiting to be mined.

Your inventory of these strengths is helpful for whatever lies ahead. After all, as long as you live, you'll encounter change. Yes, change can represent risk, but not many people understand that lack of change is just as risky.

Look at your list of strengths as you would a road map for a journey you're planning. What do you know about this journey? How important is it to your life at this moment? What might you sacrifice by undertaking the journey? As a survivor, you may have more than a passing acquaintance with sacrifice. You're not a newcomer to this territory.

Your wish

You know what brings you joy, and you've grown to understand that you're responsible for creating it in your life. Answer this question honestly: "What do I wish?" Travel through life with this question, and always expect to make your desires real. By using your journal to help connect the mile-stones of your life, you can move into the future with an appreciation for yourself that will be different from the attitude you journeyed with in the past. If you begin to live your wish, you find the way to "follow your bliss." By bringing yourself across this threshold to live your wish, you'll step into Emily Gibbs' perspective and awaken to living better each day, instead of taking your life for granted. It will challenge your life.

Create a list of wishes over the next several days or weeks, and take responsibility for realizing them. They are your passport into your future, an atlas in which you'll discover yourself, an invitation, and a prescription in your own handwriting to live better. As you make this list of "Significant

Wishes," note in your journal the story behind each wish. Be especially mindful of your feelings about how each significant wish will affect your life. This will help you make discoveries about yourself in the future. When you've completed these entries, write about how the experience of writing them affected you. As you go forward with planning, keep a weekly or monthly progress report.

Over these past months of journal writing, you've been healing yourself with your stories. Your list of significant wishes is a way to celebrate the journey you've made and your journey into the future. It will remind you of how grateful you can be to have come so far as well as your anticipation of what lies ahead.

It's the journey, what happens when you show up, that truly matters. None of us knows our destination when we start out. Each of us has to accept the task of being a pilgrim. Many have forgotten this, in the same way that they've forgotten that the *process* of writing, like the process of doing anything, is far more important than the result.

When you learn to accept this, you'll discover the tremendous progress you've made on your journey. Acknowledging this milestone will inspire you to go further on your healing pilgrimage than you ever imagined possible.

Chapter 24
Lifelong Journaling

Getting more perspective on your life is truly an accomplishment. Deeper perspective provides a sense of fulfillment vital to healing. This chapter offers a plan for journal writing over the months and years ahead as well as for connecting the ideas and experiences arising from your journals. Its purpose is to create a process that will make it easy for you to go on sampling the banquet of possibilities and enjoying them to the fullest.

So far, you've been actively writing in your journal. You can use these entries as a springboard into painting, sculpture, photography, crafts, dance – the possibilities are endless. Once you walk through the doorway of your journal, you find that the way forward into healing lies within yourself.

Chapter 1: Square One

Earlier, you chose not to attempt some of the journeys suggested in *Write for Life*. List them now and set a date on your calendar to begin. Just as you've done with locations you've visited in your life, you may also like to return to certain topics to explore them further than you did on your first visit.

Chapter 2: Getting Started

After you've been writing for several months, you'll find it very interesting to look at the "noise" that began your journal entries. You usually take distractions for granted. As you look at your early entries, you can discover a great deal about yourself from the issues and concerns you noted, which you can look at now with different eyes.

Chapter 2 suggested four questions for journal writing: "What surprised me the most today?" "What moved me the most today?" "What do I most want to remember about today?" "Is there any 'unfinished business' in the past that I can connect with the questions I'm writing about?" Did these questions open the way for further entries? Are you including as many daily "surprises" in your entries as you did when you began?

Another suggestion was about drafting affirmations. When was the last time you updated them? Have you given yourself permission to draw and doodle on the page? Have you allowed your imagination to explore other scenarios? What have you discovered about yourself that you like more now than when you started your journal?

Chapter 3: Staying Started

Months ago, you wrote your own definition of inertia. Consider whether this definition needs to be changed or developed in some way. Just as your definition may have evolved, so your needs may also have evolved. "What I need from my writing now is _____." This may have changed from your initial response.

The same is also true of the obstacles you initially identified. Have new obstacles presented themselves? Have old ones dissolved? This assessment will give you a new perspective on your personal progress.

The practice of journal writing has enabled many people to become more open to different perspectives and solutions, rather than needing always to have the answers from the start. This is a different way to deal with issues. Is this true for you? Consider some specific examples and write about them.

Periodically update the list of "no-nos" you drafted as you worked through this chapter. Can you now remove some items from this list? Are there others to add? Do this with the idea of taking a new look at some old baggage. As you continue writing, the contours of the world change; unless you acknowledge this, you go on believing its shape is the same. When you appreciate the changes that have occurred, it strengthens your motivation to continue the process.

In the beginning, you may have found the idea of joining a journal-writing support group without any merit. Do you still feel that way? Does the idea of inviting a few other people to form a journal-writing group now seem like an interesting possibility? Consider the help you could receive when others are writing with you. Whom would you invite to participate in this activity?

Chapter 4: Survivors and Surviving

The list of crises you've survived in the course of your life is amazing. In journal entries, you've considered some of them, gone around others, and completely avoided several of the most significant. Perhaps you've become more ready to explore some of these. While you're not the only survivor in this world, in your own way, you're unique. It's *your* story. The need to heal is yours, and your opportunity to do this through journal writing has expanded far beyond your initial expectations. The understanding that has unfolded through your entries has made it possible for you to live more richly and meet life in new ways, with deeper consciousness of what has gone before. Developing your list can be the beginning of many journal entries that lead to further detailed exploration in the future.

Chapter 5: Journal Excerpts

Daily writing has reinforced the practice you started months or years ago. You've had the benefit of what you've recorded about yourself. This chapter on journals written by others offers you encouragement to explore yourself even more fully. When you understand that others have survived the traumas in their lives through writing about them, you may discover that some of the areas you've been reluctant to look at are indeed just waiting to be set down on paper. That you're not alone, that others have been over the same territory, may be for you as it has been for many – a revelation.

During the next months or years, your writing agenda may include some areas that have never appeared on your list of "no-nos." Your journal has a direct relationship with feelings and emotions that you may have neglected or hidden behind denial. Waiting for you is deep-down material that you've known intimately during your life. You've survived, and your journal offers the opportunity to tell the story of your success. The fulfillment and happiness you're hoping for may depend on your willingness to identify and explore such areas through your journal entries.

Chapter 6: Scientific Research and Writing Techniques

The exploration of other journal-writing approaches is an interesting ongoing activity, since writing journals is a life's work that you can enjoy from many different perspectives. Amazon.com offers a constantly growing list of titles for your review and consideration. And a monthly visit to the neighborhood bookstore is an exciting adventure for every journal writer. The titles listed after this chapter under "Resources" (page 253) may also suggest possibilities for follow-up reading.

Chapter 7: Healing the Survivor

Change is difficult to observe in yourself. One way to examine your attitude toward healing is by reviewing the growing body of material in your journal. Here are a few helpful questions: As you've taken a more active role in maintaining your health, have you changed any of your ideas about your needs? How? In what ways have you changed your attitude toward the significant people in your life? How has your perspective on the significance of survivorship shifted?

Your journal has provided a laboratory for exploring the healing connection between body, mind, and spirit. You can reread entries to see whether you've neglected any of these crucial dimensions. If you wish to continue to make progress in helping yourself and receiving help from others, these areas of your life should receive equal attention. You must work at all levels if you are to improve the quality of your life.

Through writing, you've discovered that the more you write, the more you wish to write. Exposing a new obstacle to the writing process is like opening another sealed door in the castle. You welcome the opportunity to explore it when it arises; any distress you may be experiencing is an opportunity to stretch beyond your present comfort zone. To remind yourself of this on a regular basis is more good medicine.

Chapter 8: Expectations

No matter what you expected when you first began your journal, you can't fail to be surprised by what actually appears on the pages. You may have encountered slow spells when you've given in to inertia. But then you've picked up the pen again and gone on. The pages covered with your handwriting demonstrate a persistence few would have imagined. Many who put aside their journals years ago have returned to them in Write for Life workshops, finding support for an activity they feared had dried up. As one participant said, "It made a new life for me!"

Feelings about ourselves and others are key to the energy that moves the process. All the facts in the world can pile up around you, but coursing far beneath the surface of events, your feelings may find outlet only in your journal. When you're distressed and can't put your finger on the reason, allow your feelings to bubble up on the page and you'll make the missing connection.

You may want to see the events of your life and your relationships in ways that are logical and rational, but feelings are not subject to this same demand for order. They are themselves, and they appear on the pages (when you allow them) in the jumble and diversity of their natural state. If you haven't discovered this yet, it's time to let it happen. Many participants have said that expressing their feelings – even discovering that they really *have* them – is a boon they never expected when they began the journal. And there are more unexpected rewards. Through opening the door to your feelings, you've connected with the richness of intuition. While you may not have expected this when you started, you can see the evidence when you read through your entries.

What about the actual expectations you started with? If you never made a list, now is the time. If you already have a list, update it now by finishing this sentence: "What I want from my writing is_____." Make the list as complete as possible; it will motivate you to continue what you've begun. To move into new areas and discover new ways of expressing yourself is the ongoing process of journal writing.

Chapter 9: Self-Caring

Reexamine your initial responses to the question, "How can I be more loving and accepting toward myself today in body, mind, spirit, and emotions?" You've learned a great deal about yourself throughout these journeys, and the material you've uncovered will enable you to expand your original inventories. Every three or four months, you can reconsider your needs in these areas and actually take steps to meet them. You can use this review to explore how well you're looking after yourself throughout the year.

Chapter 10: Food and Nourishment

You've already explored the list of obstacles that stand in the way of your writing. Have you also considered your attitude toward food and nutrition over the past months? Have there been any changes? What are they? Are you paying more or less attention to the food you eat and when and where you eat it? You can review the seven questions that begin Chapter 10 and reconsider several others as well.

The link between self-caring and the food you eat is significant. Exploring this in relation to body, mind, and spirit may offer valuable insights as you look at ways to improve the quality of your life. The kind of attention you developed in journal writing can help you choose the nourishment that's right for you.

Chapter 11: Travel

You've been writing about the places you've visited. Has this helped you to consider new destinations? New travel companions? Perhaps you traveled with a spouse or dear friend who is no longer with you. How does this influence your ideas about travel now? How have the places you've visited changed over the years? Have you found everything you've been looking for? Are there still things to be curious about? Have you decided that your questing days are over? Exploring these questions may offer some big surprises, and you can write about them as they present themselves.

For older people who are interested in travel, ElderHostel tours offer opportunities that meet special needs. You can go to the website www. elderhostel.org for more information. Also, tours are listed in publications that appear several times a year. Even a cursory look at some may whet your appetite for exploration. You can discover many other travel opportunities on the Internet.

Chapter 12: Legacy Letters, Part One – Laying the Foundation

When you first encountered the idea of a legacy letter, you asked yourself "How do I wish to remember myself?" You may have written your answer months or years ago. Now you can answer it from the point of view of today. Once you do so, return to look at your original answer.

Journal writing has helped you to see yourself differently. Where you're standing today may be a long way from your first response. That first entry is an opportunity to acknowledge both what was then and what is now. The contrast helps move you into the future. No longer stuck in an imaginary idea of yourself, you're face-to-face with an evolving self. Change is very difficult to appreciate unless you have a benchmark. Your first entry is your marker.

Perhaps you can develop the rest of the framework you set down at that time. You have the advantage of the time and space travel your journal has provided over the months. You also have a deeper appreciation of your values and the effect on them of the aging process. What once may have been quite simple is now far more complex, and what might have seemed terribly complex is now quite simple.

You recorded many questions that you wished your parents, grand-parents, and other relatives were around to answer. Review these lists and consider additional ones that may have emerged over time. Then begin to respond to these questions as if your children, grandchildren, nephews, and nieces had asked them of you. What you wanted to ask your elders is what others would like to know about you.

Chapter 13: Dreams

As you've continued to write, your dream life has continued to address issues that have emerged in your entries. In Chapter 13, you found useful suggestions about how to gain access to these sources of information about your inner self. Have you used these techniques on a regular basis? If you've neglected to use your dreams to improve your connection with your intuition, you can direct your attention to this fruitful area for healing as you move forward in your journal.

The body-mind-spirit relationship benefits when you make conscious the connections that support healing. You can turn to your intuition daily. Are you connected? Are you listening? Are you using this information to make decisions that are more self-caring? Survivors understand that there is a healing power within and that dreams are an excellent way to find access to this power.

Even if you haven't done so before, you can begin today to develop this dialogue. Your feelings are a useful way into this connection. Remembering to be sensitive to what your dreams reveal is an ongoing activity. Workshop participants often keep dream notebooks to make this area of their lives a priority. Would using a dream notebook help you be more consistent about recording your dreams? If it will keep the door open to your dreams, do it.

Chapter 14: Now and Zen

Because circumstances are constantly changing, much can be learned by making a monthly inventory of what you think of as missing or incomplete in your life. It's possible that your ideas about wholeness have undergone transformation over these months. Going back to review what you've written about may open a new way into what the Zen teachings offer.

These teachings are available in an enormous body of literature. Have you begun to explore this rich source of healing and inspiration? Ideas that extend understanding of life and healing nourish us on many levels. Have you made any attempts to explore the ways this material might nourish you? A good first step is to visit a library or bookstore and explore what's on the shelves. Once you're there, perhaps other titles will attract you. You can take your interest and curiosity anywhere, and what is "missing" or "incomplete" within will respond.

The ideas of wholeness and mindfulness have taken on attributes that act as beacons. The chapter on travel mentioned compass points. We have internal compass points that help to guide us; perhaps some of yours are reflected in your journal entries from the past months. Explore them in greater detail in the months to come.

Chapter 15: "Not Yets"

As you look back over the inventories you created, you see the dates on which you wrote them. Since then, you've completed some of the items on your lists; others no longer have the same significance. What's valuable is that you have that record. You can plan to develop a new "not yets" list every six months. Perhaps some of the items on the previous list will find a place on the new one; certainly there will be items that have just appeared on the horizon. First develop the new list, then compare it with the previous one and observe what has changed. Recognizing the changes you've undergone helps you appreciate yourself more; when you can savor a new understanding of yourself, you enhance your self-esteem. The treasure house of your personal evolution is waiting within the pages of your journal.

Just as your lists change and develop, so do your priorities. These priorities reveal a great deal about the complex phenomenon of aging. In your journal you're writing your own book about what happens as you move through different stages of life. You may wish to analyze what you discover about yourself over time, or you may just want to use your journal as a record of what is happening. Consider taking a brainstorming approach to your "not yets" list and the priorities you've set on a regular basis, perhaps every six months or every year. There may be many items on your "not yets" list for which you've never done any pro-and-con risk assessments. You can do this for any entry at any time.

It may be time to plan what may have seemed out of the question earlier. When you value yourself and are willing to make a commitment to pursue your aspirations, you start to take responsibility for celebrating your life in the world you live in. This is what happens through journal writing. Each year, you can look at the idea of planning in new ways and discover new things about yourself in the process. Your "not yets" list is the springboard for this activity.

Chapter 16: Legacy Letters, Part Two — Creating the Letters

The list of people to whom to write your legacy letters expands and contracts over the years; some are no longer alive, while with others your relationship has changed. Still others have assumed such significance in your life that you truly want to leave them a legacy letter. The memories that your *Write for Life* journeys have recaptured may also offer new material for inclusion in these letters. As you review your initial list, you may see that some of your priorities have changed. Some of the children on your first list may have grown up, and you can write to them now in a different way. Perhaps grandchildren have been born. Updating your list is a yearly activity you can prepare for in your journal.

Your decisions about whether to send these letters will change over time. As your self-esteem evolves, so does your wish to reveal yourself to others. Suddenly the possibility of writing and sending a legacy letter may become a source of pleasure and inspiration.

Chapter 17: American Indian Spirituality

One of the most significant aspects of journal writing is your discovery of insights into unfinished business and the mysteries that confound you. Both the Zen and Indian approaches to the world we live in help us get in touch with such unresolved issues, which offer an interesting menu of areas to write about and return to each year.

Taking your journal outdoors to write in nature may become a practice that can inspire you with old memories and new connections integral to your own healing. The change of the seasons, a holiday at the seashore or in the mountains, a visit to the zoo – all are major opportunities for connection with nature. "Wake up and smell the roses" is an invitation you must remind yourself to accept. Your journals are fragrant with memories that have wafted across your years on the Good Red Road.

In your journal you unburden yourself of baggage you've carried over the decades. To remind yourself of the sacred and spiritual dimensions of nature promotes healing of body, mind, and spirit. You can experience this after a day in the country, so plan one on a regular basis. It's good medicine. And bring your journal along.

Chapter 18: Creativity

You drafted several inventories pertaining to creativity. Your first inventory addressed the question "What do I need in order to be more creative in my life?" Now you can develop your list further with insights you've acquired over the past weeks and months of journaling. This question becomes ever more central as you continue to write.

Your second inventory asked, "What are the obstacles to my creativity?" You'll have a far deeper understanding of these as you continue to write in your journal. Just as you change, so do your obstacles. It's useful to update your assessment of obstacles at six-month intervals.

Your journal stays alive with you as it reflects the changes in your life. While it's difficult to measure certain attitudes, keeping these inventories in your journal over the years helps you appreciate the thresholds of change you've crossed on your way to living better.

Chapter 19: Work and Play

Looking at your previously recorded assumptions about work in the context of your ever-evolving values, you can compare them with what has actually happened. Is there anything you'd like to change right now? What about in the next three to five years? In the next ten years? Your journal has helped you to become your own good friend. Good friends tell each other truths they need to hear. Performance reviews are usually made on a yearly basis. You can do this for yourself to great benefit if you'll take the time.

You also wrote about specific crises that now may appear entirely different from when you first wrote about them. How you see yourself and the roles you've played through life has a direct impact on your self-esteem. And what may have seemed like a disaster at the time it occurred or even last year may now appear quite different.

As for play, you developed several lists of activities that offer fun for the body, mind, and spirit. If you neglected to do this, it's time. If you did it several months or years ago, it's time to write new lists and get started with the activities you've listed. If the old list includes some things you can't do, identify activities that you *can* do. Having fun is vital food for the body, mind, and spirit.

Many people forget to create and update a plan to enjoy life more. Journals often reflect the need for new expression and you can respond to this need first by recognizing it and next by doing something about it today, next month, and next year.

Chapter 20: Meditation and Prayer

For some, journal writing has provided the impetus to seek out spiritual practices. Communing on the page has opened the door to the need for other types of communion. Writing in your journal makes you vulnerable in ways you hadn't realized, and this vulnerability opens you to the desire for greater participation and wholeness in your life. The resistance to the spiritual that you experienced during formative years may have diminished as you continued your journal writing. As you become more aware of yourself, your awareness of the spiritual dimension of life evolves.

In addition to transcendental practices and spending time in nature, you can also nourish your spirit by attending concerts or visiting art galleries or museums. Continue to search until you find what's right for you. Whatever practices you've adopted, the need for exploration of the spiritual is ongoing. What serves you best may change over time. Staying open to your needs is life-sustaining, and your journal can help you do this.

Chapter 21: The Experience of Joy

Your journeys have taken you through many experiences of joy, sadness, and places in between. When you think of happiness in the abstract, it may often seem elusive or absent from your life altogether. However, when you thought back over your actual experiences, you were able to identify periods, events, and moments when you were happy. Having recorded your definition of happiness you can explore it further on a regular basis. With your changing abilities and your deepened connection with intuition, you're able to redefine the experience and use this updated measure as you write about events taking place in your life today. Happiness is always a Now experience. Your *unwillingness* to make it Now is often the obstacle. You may often find yourself writing about the past. However, you're living in the Now, and it offers infinite opportunities for the experience of joy.

You made a list of activities that offer joy for the mind, body, spirit, and emotions. Over time you can write about each of these entries, adding others as they suggest themselves, using the definition you created most recently. There's a crucial link here: You create your own happiness, and in this process, you create yourself in new ways. Stepping into the present with greater availability for joy prepares you to step into a better future.

Each day can offer an opportunity to explore what sustains you, what gives you joy. You can also ask yourself what's missing and what you can do to change this. You've written about what you wanted your relationships with others to be like in six months or a year. You can reconsider what has happened since then and look at the action you've taken to bring about what you wished for. The answer to the question of what you can do to bring about your own happiness is constantly changing. It's a rich area for ongoing attention in your journal.

The role of acceptance and reconciliation in your life has also been responsible for changing many ideas about happiness. Your journal offers daily opportunities to live through anger and come out the other side into living better. There may be some loose ends in your life. When you identify them and begin to explore approaches to resolving them, over time you increase the daily quotient of happiness in your life.

You created a list of activities that would enhance your emotional well-being. Writing about them is one thing; doing something is quite another. When was the last time you looked at your list? You could do that today. Next, look at your plan for engaging in these experiences in the next months or years. Your journal is a reminder of all of the ways you can begin to live more fully. It's a companion on the voyage; it helps you on your way. And the help it gives you is something you can feel deeply grateful for.

Chapter 22: Last Rights

This chapter offers many practical suggestions for considering some of the questions that may have appeared on your "no-nos" list, along with ways to exercise your rights while you live and have command of all your faculties. To make a detailed review of these suggestions and take action on them is of the greatest priority.

It is time-consuming to update wills, living trusts, health-care directives, and funeral arrangements. Nevertheless, these matters need your attention. While journal entries help you prepare, they do not take the place of action. Getting your thoughts in order is a first step, and the rest, which includes obtaining needed legal advice, awaits you.

You may have had a change of heart about writing a legacy letter or letters over the past months. If so, you can explore those chapters – Legacy Letters, Part One and Legacy Letters, Part Two – in your journal.

Chapter 23: Pilgrimage

You created a list of key events you've experienced. As you continued through the chapters of *Write for Life*, you may have discovered milestones you overlooked when you first made your list. Add them now, and explore the ones already on your list from the deeper perspective of all your journeys.

You also made an inventory of the places you've visited, lived, and continued to think of when you remember the joys and sorrows of your life. You can return to this list to find ideas for entries that will occupy you for years to come. Whatever priorities you assigned them originally, you may wish to change the order to meet your changing perspective.

The Now you're standing in is different from when you were writing each entry. You can explore the changes in the way you look back on your experiences. Your appreciation for yourself may also be different, and you can explore this in your journal as well.

You face an exciting opportunity as you prepare for your pilgrimage into the future. Part of your preparation is to connect with your deepest wishes, so return to the entries you made for each significant wish. You'll need to determine what steps are necessary to realize the wishes with the highest priority. Perhaps you've already set a date to begin to do this. You can change your priorities. It's also possible that a new significant wish may have entered the arena of your possibilities.

Just as you reapply for an expiring passport, your own passport into the future needs periodic revalidation. Always remain open to doing this. The greater appreciation you have for yourself in the midst of your pilgrimage, the more open you'll be to moving in new directions.

****

The life catalog you've opened should be regarded as a valuable research tool in creating new and exciting activities as you continue your journey through life. Are you using it for this purpose, or are you caught in a loop of simply taking things for granted? Your consideration of your priorities and values helps you to make important decisions about your future. Your use of your journal to explore these priorities and values has a direct impact on your expectations for the future.

When you take the opportunity to engage with your past, present, and future, you discover what having fun really means. The exciting adventure of self-discovery is an invitation you open each time you sit down to write. It can always be new, and surprises are always waiting. The bond you develop with the explorer who is writing develops over the years into a source of support and affection, and you become a friend to yourself at a time when you need this the most.

In a very important way, your journal helps you to make connections that enable you to change your ideas about what may seem fragmentary and diverse aspects of life. It's natural to feel a profound need for continuity, and you'll experience a growing sense of wholeness day by day as you fill these pages.

"Getting it together" is a term some have used to describe the effect that journal writing has on them. In doing this, you forge the body-mind-spirit linkage that is essential to healing. As you embrace the individual you have been, you encourage the individual you can become. In this process, you evolve beyond yourself. As you grow with your journal, you discover more joy and satisfaction in life than you ever could have anticipated.

Text Credits

The author and Cleveland Clinic Press thank the following individuals and organizations for granting permission to quote from copyrighted materials.

Chapter 14, Now and Zen
PenHouse Ltd. (*The Essence of Zen*, by Sekkei Harada; Daigaku David Rumme, translator. Kodansha International; Tokyo, New York, and London, 1998)

Chapter 16, Legacy Letters, Part Two
University of Notre Dame Press ("Letter to Noah," from *Charting Your Course, A Lifelong Guide to Health and Compassion*, edited by Sally Coleman and David S. Anderson. Notre Dame, 1998)

Houghton Mifflin ("Dear Linda," from *Anne Sexton: A Self-Portrait in Letters*, edited by Linda Gray Sexton and Lois Ames. Boston, 1977)

Chapter 17, American Indian Spirituality
Kachinas Kutenai (*American Indian Healing*, Sacred Rainbow Circle, Emeryville, California, 1990)

HarperSanFrancisco (Jamie Sams, *Sacred Path Cards: The Discovery of Self Through Native Teachings*, San Francisco, 1990)

Chapter 20, Meditation and Prayer
Kachinas Kutenai (*American Indian Healing*, Sacred Rainbow Circle, Emeryville, California, 1990)

Chapter 23, Pilgrimage
Nicholas Crome (*A Journal of My Travels in Ireland*. Published privately.)

Special thanks go to Thomas Mallon, author of *A Book of One's Own: People and Their Diaries*, for generously taking the time to share his knowledge of the use of copyrighted material.

Resources

Kathleen Adams, *The Way of the Journal*. Sidran Press, Baltimore (1998)

Mitch Albom, *The Five People You Meet in Heaven*. Random House, New York (2003)

Mitch Albom, *Tuesdays with Morrie*. Doubleday, New York (1997)

Nancy Slonim Aronia, *Writing from the Heart*, Hyperion, New York (1998)

Jane Austen, *Jane Austen's Letters*. The Folio Society, London (2003)

Mike Avery, *The Secret Language of Dreams*. Eckankar, Minneapolis (1992)

Virginia M. Axline, *Play Therapy*. Ballantine Books, New York (1947, 1969)

Francis Bacon, *Bacon's Essays & Colors of Good and Evil*. Macmillan, London (1891)

Adam and Ali Blatner, *The Art of Play: An Adult Guide to Reclaiming Imagination and Spontaneity*. San Marcos Treatment Center, P.O. Box 768, San Marcos, Texas (1985)

Jean Shinoda Bolen, *Close to the Bone: Life-Threatening Illness and the Search for Meaning*. Scribner, New York (1996)

The Book of Common Prayer. Oxford University Press, New York (1979)

Robert Bosnak, *A Little Course in Dreams*. Shambhala, Boston (1998)

Edmund J. Bourne, *The Anxiety & Phobia Workbook*. New Harbinger, Oakland (1995)

Simon Brett, *The Faber Book of Diaries*. Faber and Faber, London (1987)

Adelaide Bry with Marjorie Bair, *Visualization: Directing the Movies of Your Mind*. Perennial Library, New York (1979)

David D. Burns, *Feeling Good*. HarperCollins, New York (1980, 1999)

David D. Burns, *The Feeling Good Handbook*. Penguin Books, New York (1989)

Julia Cameron, *The Artist's Way*. Tarcher/Putnam, New York (1992)

Julia Cameron, *The Artist's Way Creativity Journal*. Chronicle Books, San Francisco (2000)

Jack Canfield and Mark Victor Hansen, *Chicken Soup for the Soul*. Health Communications Inc., Deerfield Beach, Florida (1993)

Lord Chesterfield, *Letters to His Son: On the Fine Art of Becoming a Gentleman*. Dingwell-Rock Ltd., New York (1925)

Sally Coleman and David S. Anderson, editors, *Charting Your Course: A Lifelong Guide to Health and Compassion*. University of Notre Dame Press, Notre Dame (1998)

Mary Frances Connors, *Sweet Blood and Fury*. Far Western Graphics, Sunnyvale, California (2000)

Phil Cousineau, *The Art of Pilgrimage*. Conari Press, York Beach, Maine (1998)

Cyndi Dale, *New Chakra Healing*. Llewellyn Publications, St. Paul (1998)

Lois Daniel, *How to Write Your Own Life Story*. Chicago Review Press, Chicago (1997)

Louise DeSalvo, *Writing as a Way of Healing*. Beacon Press, Boston (1999)

Kat Duff, *The Alchemy of Illness*. Harmony Books/Crown Publishers, New York (1993)

Margaret Edson, *Wit: A Play*. Farrar, Strauss & Giroux, New York (1999)

John E. Fortunato, *Aids, the Spiritual Dilemma*. Harper & Row, New York (1987)

John Fox, *Poetic Medicine*. Tarcher/Putnam, New York (1997)

Terri Gibbs, editor, *A Father's Legacy: Your Life Story in Your Own Words*. Thomas Nelson Inc., Nashville (1999)

André Gide, *The Journals of André Gide*. 1889-1949. Knopf, New York (1947)

Natalie Goldberg, *Wild Mind*. Bantam Books, New York (1990)

Natalie Goldberg, *Writing Down the Bones*. Shambhala, Boston (1986)

Caren Goldman, *Healing Words for the Body, Mind and Spirit*. Marlowe & Co./Avalon Publishing Group, New York (2001)

Daniel Goleman and Joel Gurin, editors, *Mind-Body Medicine: How to Use Your Mind for Better Health*. Consumer Reports Books, Yonkers (1993)

Earl A. Grollman, editor, *Concerning Death: A Practical Guide for the Living*. Beacon Press, Boston (1974)

G.I. Gurdjieff, *Meetings with Remarkable Men*. Dutton, New York (1969)

Kay Leigh Hagan, *Internal Affairs: A Journalkeeping Workbook for Self-Intimacy*. Harper & Row, San Francisco (1990, 1988)

Sekkei Harada (Daigaku David Rumme, translator), *The Essence of Zen*. Kodansha International, Tokyo, New York, and London (1998)

Hannah Hinchman, *A Life in Hand: Creating the Illuminated Journal*. Gibbs Smith/ Peregrine Smith Books, Salt Lake City (1991)

Edith Holden, *The Country Diary of an Edwardian Lady*. Webb & Bower, Exeter (1977)

Roger Hudson, editor, *The Folio Book of Days*. The Folio Society, Glasgow (2002)

Arthur Crew Inman, *The Inman Diary*. Harvard University Press, Cambridge (1985)

Beth Jacobs, *Writing for Emotional Balance*. New Harbinger, Oakland (2004)

Natania Jansz and Miranda Davies, *Women Travel*. Prentiss Hall, New York (1990)

Elizabeth A. Johnson, *As Someone Dies*. Hay House, Santa Monica (1985)

Jon Kabat-Zinn, *Wherever You Go There You Are*. Hyperion, New York (1994)

Alfred Kantor, *The Book of Alfred Kantor*. McGraw-Hill, New York (1971)

J. Kantor, C. Krohn, and J. Shulevitz, editors, *The Slate Diaries*. Public Affairs, New York (2000)

Dharma Singh Khalsa and Cameron Stauth, *Meditation as Medicine*. Pocket Books/Simon & Schuster, New York (2001)

Sheppard B. Kominars and Kathryn D. Kominars, *Accepting Ourselves and Others*. Hazelden, Center City, Minnesota (1996)

Sheldon Kopp, *An End to Innocence*. Bantam, New York (1987)

Sheldon Kopp, *If You Meet the Buddha on the Road, Kill Him!* Bantam, New York (1976)

Sheldon Kopp, *Rock Paper Scissors*. Compcare, Minneapolis (1989)

Elisabeth Kübler-Ross, *Living with Death and Dying*. Macmillan, New York (1981)

Elisabeth Kübler-Ross, *On Death and Dying*. Macmillan, New York (1969)

Milan Kundera, *The Book of Laughter and Forgetting*. Penguin, New York (1981)

Harold S. Kushner, *When Bad Things Happen to Good People*. Avon, New York (1981)

D.H. Lawrence, *D. H. Lawrence and Italy*. Penguin Books, New York (1985)

Kachinas Kutenai, *American Indian Healing*. Sacred Rainbow Circle, Emeryville (1990)

Kevin Leman and Randy Carlson, *Unlocking the Secrets of Your Childhood*. Thomas Nelson Inc., Nashville (1989)

Stephen J. Lepore and Joshua M. Smyth, editors, *The Writing Cure: How Expressive Writing Promotes Health and Emotional Well-Being*. American Psychological Association., Washington, D.C. (2002)

Harriet G. Lerner, *The Dance of Anger*. Harper & Row, New York (1985)

Lawrence LeShan, *How to Meditate*. Bantam Books, New York (1974)

Stephen Levine, *Healing into Life and Death*. Anchor Press/Doubleday, Garden City, New York (1987)

Stephen Levine, *Who Dies? An Investigation of Conscious Living and Conscious Dying*. Anchor Press/Doubleday, Garden City, New York (1982)

Michelle Lovric, *Love Letters – An Anthology of Passion*. Shooting Star Press, New York (1994)

Shirley MacLaine, *The Camino: A Journey of the Spirit*. Simon & Schuster, New York (2000)

Patty McConnell, *A Workbook for Healing*. Harper & Row, San Francisco (1986)

Frank McCourt, *Angela's Ashes*. Scribner, New York (1996)

Frank McCourt, *'Tis*. Scribner, New York (1999)

John H. McMurphy, *Living Deliberately: Experiments in Practical Spirituality*. Amaranth Publishing, Dallas (1993)

Thomas Mallon, *A Book of One's Own: People and Their Diaries*. Ticknor & Fields, New York (1984)

Katherine Mansfield, *The Journal of Katherine Mansfield*. Knopf, New York (1927)

Marcus Aurelius, *Wisdom of the Emperor Marcus Aurelius*. Nathan Haskell Dole, Boston (1903)

Carl and David Marshall, *The Book of Myself*. Hyperion, New York (1994, 1997)

David McCullough, *Truman*. Simon & Schuster, New York (1992)

Deena Metzger, *Writing for Your Life: A Guide and Companion to the Inner Worlds*, HarperSanFrancisco, San Francisco (1992)

Gustavus Hindman Miller, *The Dictionary of Dreams*. Prentiss Hall, New York (1984, 1986)

Mary Jane Moffat and Charlotte Painter, editors, *Revelations: Diaries of Women*. Vintage Books, New York (1975)

Margaret E. Monroe and Rhea Joyce Rubin, *The Challenge of Aging: A Bibliography*. Libraries Unlimited, Littleton, Colorado (1983)

Thomas Moore, *Care of the Soul*. HarperCollins, New York (1998)

Jerrold Mundis, *Break Writer's Block*. St. Martin's Press, New York (1991)

Jacob Needleman, *Time and the Soul*. Doubleday, New York (1998)

Jacob Needleman, *A Little Book on Love*. Doubleday, New York (1996)

Sherwin B. Neiland, *How We Die*. Knopf, New York (1993)

Nigel Nicolson, *Portrait of a Marriage*. Weidenfeld & Nicholson, Ltd., London (1973)

Henri J. M. Nouwen, *Behold the Beauty of the Lord*, Ave Maria Press, Notre Dame (1987)

Henri J. M. Nouwen, *The Return of the Prodigal Son: a Story of Homecoming*. Doubleday, New York (1992)

Henri J. M. Nouwen, *The Wounded Healer*. Bantam, New York (1979)

P.D. Ouspenski, *In Search of the Miraculous*. Harcourt, Brace & World, New York (1949)

Carol S. Pearson, *The Hero Within: Six Archetypes We Live By*. Harper & Row, San Francisco (1998)

M. Scott Peck, *The Road Less Traveled*. Simon & Schuster, New York (1978)

J.M. Pennebaker, editor, *Emotion, Disclosure, and Health*. American Psychological Association, Washington, D.C. (1995)

J.M. Pennebaker, *Opening Up: The Healing Power of Expressing Emotions*. Guilford Press, New York (1997)

J.M. Pennebaker, *Writing to Heal: A Guided Journal for Recovering from Trauma and Emotional Upheaval*. New Harbinger, Oakland (2004)

Michael Picucci, *The Journey Toward Complete Recovery*. North Atlantic Books, Berkeley (1998)

Samuel Pepys, *The Diary of Samuel Pepys, 1659-1663*. G. Bell & Sons, London (1924)

Richard Peterson, *Creative Meditation: Inner Peace Is Practically Yours*. A.R.E. Publications, Virginia Beach (1990)

Ira Progoff, *At a Journal Workshop*. Tarcher Inc., Los Angeles (1975, 1992)

Tristine Rainer, *The New Diary*. Tarcher Inc., Los Angeles (1978)

Rachel Naomi Remen, *Kitchen Table Wisdom: Stories That Heal*. Riverhead Books/Penguin/Putnam, New York (1996)

Richard Reoch, *To Die Well: A Holistic Approach for the Dying and Their Caregivers*. Harper Perennial, New York (1996)

Kenneth Ring, *Heading Toward Omega*. William Morrow, New York (1984)

Sogyal Rinpoche, *The Tibetan Book of the Dead*. HarperCollins, San Francisco & New York (1994)

Bill Roorbach, *Writing Life Stories*. Story Press/F&W Publications, Cincinnati (1998)

John W. Rowe and Robert L. Kahn, *Successful Aging*. Pantheon Press, New York (1998)

Jamie Sams, *Sacred Path Cards*. HarperSanFrancisco, San Francisco (1991)

Mark Salzman, *True Notebooks*. Alfred A. Knopf, New York (2003)

Andrea Sankar, *Dying at Home: A Family Guide for Caregivers*. Bantam Books, New York (1991)

May Sarton, *The Fur Person*. Norton & Co., New York (1983)

May Sarton, *Journal of a Solitude*. Norton & Co., New York (1973)

Pat Schneider, *Writing Alone and with Others*. Oxford University Press, Oxford (2003

Ilene Segalove and Paul Bob Velick, *List Your Self: Listmaking as the Way to Self-Discovery*. Andrews & McMeel, Kansas City, Missouri (1996)

C. Norman Shealy, consultant editor, *The Directory of Complementary Therapies*. Chartwell Books Inc., Edison, New Jersey (2002)

Gail Sheehy, *Passages: Predictable Crises of Adult Life*. Dutton, New York (1976)

O. Carl Simonton and Stephanie Matthew-Simonton, and James L. Creighton, *Getting Well Again*. Bantam Books, New York (1978)

Richard Solly and Roseann Lloyd, *Journey Notes: Writing for Recovery and Spiritual Growth*. Harper & Row, San Francisco (1989)

Susan Sontag, *Illness as Metaphor*. Farrar, Strauss & Giroux, New York (1977, 1978)

Linda Spence, *Legacy: A Step-by-Step Guide to Writing Personal History*. Swallow Press/Ohio University Press, Athens, Ohio (1997)

Richard A. Sternbach, *Mastering Pain*. Putnam, New York (1987)

Hal and Sidra Stone, *Embracing Your Inner Critic*. Harper/Collins, New York (1993)

Richard Stone, *The Healing Art of Storytelling*. Hyperion New York (1996)

Irene and Alan Taylor, *The Assassin's Cloak: An Anthology of the World's Greatest Diarists*. Edinburgh, Scotland, Canongate Books (2000)

Frank P. Thomas, *How to Write the Story of Your Life*. Writer's Digest Books, Cincinnati (1984)

Daniel R. Tobin, with Karen Lindsey, *Peaceful Dying*. Perseus Books, Cambridge, Massachusetts (1999)

Eckhart Tolle, *The Power of Now*. New World Library, Novato (1999)

Carlos Valenzuela, *Belleza: How to Feel and Be Beautiful*. Carlos Valenzuela Inc., San Francisco (1989)

Marilyn Webb, *A Good Death: The New American Search to Reshape the End of Life*. Bantam Books, New York (1997)

Simone Weil, *Waiting for God*. Putnam, New York (1951)

Michele Weldon, *Writing to Save Your Life*. Hazelden, Center City, Minnesota (2001)

Jennifer Westwood, *Sacred Journeys: An Illustrated Guide to Pilgrimages Around the World*. Henry Holt & Co., New York (1997)

Evelyn E. and James D. Whitehead, *Christian Life Patterns*. Image Books, a division of Doubleday & Co., Garden City, New York

Elie Wiesel, *Legends of Our Time*. Holt, Rinehart & Winston, New York (1968)

S.K. Williams, *Jungian-Senoi Dreamwork Manual*. Journey Press, Berkeley (1980)

Irvin D. Yalom, *Momma and the Meaning of Life*. Basic Books, New York (1999)

William Zinnsser, editor, *Inventing the Truth: The Art and Craft of Memoir*. Houghton Mifflin, New York (1998)

Index

traumatic experiences, writing about, 61-62
    See also scientific research/writing techniques
travel
    companions, 110-112
    as cure, 114
    ElderHostel tours, 242
    expectations, 112-113
    fictional travelers, 107
    getting lost, 113
    getting started, 107-108
    journey's end, 115-116
    journeys you've taken, 108
    new directions, 113-116
    preparations, 109-110
    quest/mission, 114-115
    staying started, 108-113
    See also pilgrimage
Truman (McCullough), 6
Truman, Harry, 6
trust, 36-37
Twain, Mark, 70
twelve-step programs, 67, 73, 82

U
Ulysses (Joyce), 114
"unfinished business"
    as journal subject, 21, 98, 189, 211-212, 237
    and healing, 33
V
value
    of life, 47, 78, 158
    of prayers, 206
    of self, 31, 46, 94
    of stories, 81
values
    and funeral arrangements, 224
    and health-care directives, 223
    in legacy letters, 158
    and memories, 170
    and perfectionism, 181
    and prayers, 206
    and work, 187
victims vs. survivors, 43-44
visualization, 204, 214, 221
vitamins, 76-77
vulnerability, 41, 247-248

Cleveland Clinic Press

Cleveland Clinic Press publishes nonfiction trade books for the medical, health, nutrition, cookbook, and children's markets. It is the mission of the Press to increase the health literacy of the American public and to dispel myths and misinformation about medicine, health care, and treatment. Our authors include leading authorities from Cleveland Clinic as well as a diverse list of experts drawn from medical and health-care institutions whose research and treatment breakthroughs have helped countless people.

Each Cleveland Clinic Guide provides the health-care consumer with practical and authoritative information. Every book is reviewed for accuracy and timeliness by the experts of Cleveland Clinic.

www.clevelandclinicpress.org

Cleveland Clinic

Cleveland Clinic, located in Cleveland, Ohio, is a not-for-profit multi-specialty academic medical center that integrates clinical and hospital care with research and education. Cleveland Clinic was founded in 1921 by four renowned physicians with a vision of providing outstanding patient care based upon the principles of cooperation, compassion, and innovation. *U.S. News & World Report* consistently names Cleveland Clinic as one of the nation's best hospitals in its annual "America's Best Hospitals" survey. Approximately 1,500 full-time salaried physicians at Cleveland Clinic and Cleveland Clinic Florida represent more than 120 medical specialties and subspecialties. In 2006, patients came for treatment from every state and 100 countries.